JOSEPH CONRAD: A COMMEMORATION

JOSEPH CONRAD

A Commemoration

Papers from the 1974 International Conference on Conrad

Edited by

NORMAN SHERRY

Professor of English Literature
University of Lancaster

BARNES & NOBLE
BOOKS
10 East 53d St., New York 10022
(a division of Harper & Row Publishers, Inc.)

First published 1976 by
THE MACMILLAN PRESS LTD
London and Basingstoke

Published in the U.S.A. 1977 by
HARPER & ROW PUBLISHERS, INC.
BARNES & NOBLE IMPORT DIVISION

Printed in Great Britain

Library of Congress Cataloging in Publication Data

International Confederation on Conrad, Canterbury, Eng.,
    1974.
    Joseph Conrad: a commemoration.

    Includes index
        1. Conrad, Joseph, 1857–1924 – Congresses.
    I. Sherry, Norman.
    PR6005.04Z489   1974   823'.9'12   76–24069
    ISBN 0–06–496233–4

Contents

TO JOSEPH CONRAD'S SONS,
BORYS AND JOHN

Action in its essence, the creative art of a writer of fiction may be compared to rescue work carried out in darkness against cross gusts of wind swaying the action of a great multitude. It is rescue work, this snatching of vanishing phases of turbulence, disguised in fair words, out of the native obscurity into a light where the struggling forms may be seen, seized upon, endowed with the only possible form of permanence in this world of relative values – the permanence of memory. And the multitude feels it obscurely too; since the demand of the individual to the artist is, in effect, the cry 'Take me out of myself!' meaning really, out of my perishable activity into the light of imperishable consciousness.

Joseph Conrad: 'Henry James, An Appreciation' (1905); reprinted in *Notes on Life and Letters* (1921).

International Conference on Conrad, 1974, commemorating the fiftieth anniversary of Joseph Conrad's death

Organising Committee

Professor Norman Sherry (Chairman)
Professor R. A. Foakes
Mrs Juliet McLauchlan
Miss Margaret Rishworth
Dr C. T. Watts
Professor M. M. Mahood
Dr Eloise Knapp Hay (U.S.A.)
Professor P. Mroczkowski (Poland)

Chairmen of Sessions

Professor Ian Watt
A. van Marle
Professor Bruce Harkness
Professor M. M. Mahood
Professor R. A. Foakes
Professor Thomas Moser
Professor Norman Sherry
Professor Donald C. Yelton
Professor P. Mroczkowski
Professor Alan W. Friedman
Professor Marion C. Michel
J. C. Maxwell
Jean Deurbergue

Notes on Contributors

NORMAN SHERRY is Professor of English Literature and head of that department at the University of Lancaster. In addition to books on the Brontës and on Jane Austen, he is author of *Conrad's Eastern World*, *Conrad's Western World*, *Conrad and his World* and *Conrad: the Critical Heritage*, editor of five major Conrad novels, and U.K. general editor of the forthcoming variorum edition of the complete works.

ALBERT J. GUERARD is Albert L. Guerard Professor of Literature at Stanford University, a chair named in honour of his father. He is a novelist and critic, his critical works including the major study *Conrad the Novelist*, *Thomas Hardy* and *André Gide*. His latest book, *Dickens, Dostoevsky, Faulkner*, was published in 1976.

TONY TANNER is a Fellow of King's College, Cambridge, and a University lecturer. He has recently returned from the Center for Advanced Study in the Behavioral Sciences at Stanford University. He has written *Conrad's 'Lord Jim'*, *Saul Bellow*, *The Reign of Wonder* and *City of Words*.

IAN WATT is Professor of English at Stanford University. He is author of *The Rise of the Novel: Studies in Defoe, Richardson and Fielding* and is now working on a two-volume critical study of Conrad as well as *Four Western Myths: Faust, Don Quixote, Don Juan, and Robinson Crusoe*, based on lectures given at the University of Toronto in 1974.

ELOISE KNAPP HAY is author of *The Political Novels of Joseph Conrad*, and has contributed articles to many journals. She now teaches at the University of California in Santa Barbara.

EDWARD W. SAID is Professor of English and Comparative Literature at Columbia University and has been a Fellow at the Center for Advanced Study in the Behavioral Sciences at Stanford. He is author of *Joseph Conrad and the Fiction of Autobiography and Method* and *Beginnings: Intention and Method*.

ZDZISŁAW NAJDER is editor of *Twórczość*, Warsaw. He has taught both philosophy and English and Polish literature in America as well as Poland. His publications in English include *Conrad's Polish Background* and *Values and Evaluations*. He is working on a biography of Conrad.

EDWARD CRANKSHAW is best known as an authority on the Soviet Union and has also written three books on the Habsburg monarchy. The first of his many books, however, was *Joseph Conrad* (1936; second edition 1976); and his other works on literature include *Tolstoy: the Making of a Novelist.*

ANDRZEJ BUSZA teaches English at the University of British Columbia Vancouver. He is author of *Conrad's Polish Literary Background* and of two volumes of poetry, and has translated a number of Polish poets into English.

AVROM FLEISHMAN is Professor of English at the Johns Hopkins University. His books include *Conrad's Politics* and studies of Jane Austen, Virginia Woolf and the English historical novel. He is now working on English autobiography and a collection of essays on Victorian and modern fiction is in preparation.

MURIEL CLARA BRADBROOK has been a Fellow of Girton College, Cambridge, since 1932 and Mistress since 1968. She has been Professor of English Literature since 1966. Her many books include *Joseph Conrad* and studies of Elizabethan literature, Ibsen and Malcolm Lowry.

KENNETH W. DAVIS is Professor of English at Texas Tech University. He has published many articles and is now editing with Donald W. Rude *The Nigger of the 'Narcissus'.*

DAVID LEON HIGDON is an Associate Professor at Texas Tech University and joint general editor of *Conradiana*. He is editing *Almayer's Folly* and *Under Western Eyes.*

DONALD W. RUDE is also an Associate Professor at Texas Tech University and joint general editor of *Conradiana*. He is now editing, with Kenneth W. Davis, *The Nigger of the 'Narcissus'.*

FREDERICK R. KARL is Professor of English at the City College of New York and director of its graduate programmes in English. He is author of *A Reader's Guide to Joseph Conrad* and *The Adversary Literature: The English Novel in the Eighteenth Century*. He is currently editing the Collected Letters of Joseph Conrad.

THOMAS C. MOSER is Professor of English at Stanford University. He has published *Joseph Conrad: Achievement and Decline*, a critical edition of *Lord Jim*, and *Wuthering Heights: Text, Sources, Criticism.* He is now working on a study of Ford Madox Ford.

IVO VIDAN is Professor of English and American Literature in the University of Zagreb. He has published three books on literature in Croatian and a number of articles in English on Conrad (the latest being 'Heart of Darkness in French Literature'), and on James and Crane.

BARBARA KOCÓWNA is an Assistant Professor in the National Library, Warsaw, and teaches Polish literature at the University of Warsaw. Her books include *Reminiscences and Studies on Conrad* and '*Lord Jim*' *by Conrad: an Analysis*.

UGO MURSIA is a publisher in Milan, President of the Joseph Conrad Society of Italy and national editor for Italy of *Conradiana*. He edited the first European edition of *The Sisters* and the Italian translation of Conrad's fiction. He had written numerous studies of Conrad and has an important collection of Conradiana.

ADAM GILLON is Professor of English and Comparative Literature at the State University of New York at New Paltz and President of the Joseph Conrad Society of America. His books include *The Eternal Solitary: A Study of Joseph Conrad* and *Joseph Conrad: Commemorative Essays*. He received the 1967 Alfred Jurzykowski Foundation Award for his translation of Polish literature.

Editor's Introduction

Józef Teodor Konrad Korzeniowski was born in Russian-occupied Poland in December 1857. He died in England in August 1924. During his lifetime he had been, at the age of five, a political exile with his patriot father, an orphan at the age of eleven, an exile from his country at sixteen, an emigrant to England speaking only a few words of English at twenty, an ordinary seaman in the days of sail, a master in the British mercantile marine, a traveller to the Far East, Africa and South America, a naturalised Englishman and a renowned novelist in English. Poland's loss was, in a sense, Britain's gain. Joseph Conrad chose England as his country and English as his medium, and England was in the process to acquire one of her greatest novelists, one whose experience was international and ranged from the society of the Polish aristocracy to that of seamen before the mast, whose life spanned the last years of the nineteenth century and the earliest years of this century, who knew Carlist gun-running in the Mediterranean, the quiet existence of British villages, the lost lives of traders in the jungles of Borneo and the literary life of London as well as the life of its docks.

The magic of Conrad's work is attested by two diverse persons. W. H. Chesson, at one time reader for T. Fisher Unwin, recalled how, in reading Conrad's first novel (1895), 'its note of haunted loneliness called [him] into isolation' from 'the clamorous heart of London'. And W. N. P. Barbellion, shortly to die at the age of twenty-eight, recorded in his *Diary of Disappointed Man*, in November 1917: 'It is a great relief to be down in the country. Zeppelins terrify me. Have just had a delightful experience in reading Conrad's new book, *Victory* – a welcome relief from all the tension of the past two months.' Though at the other end of the scale, Virginia Woolf wrote: 'I would not like to find *The Rescue* signed Virginia Woolf.' She suspected that the fault lay in Conrad's never seeing anyone 'who knows good writing from bad, and then being a foreigner, talking broken English, married to a lump of a wife, he withdraws more and more into what he once did well, only piles it on higher and higher, until what can one call it but stiff melodrama' (entry for 23 June 1920, *A Writer's Diary*, The Hogarth Press, 1972, p. 27).

Conrad's literary reputation was hard-won, and suffered a decline after his death. There is no denying that it has since formed the material for a critical industry, but this in itself signifies the esteem in which his work is now held. An international conference to com- memorate the fiftieth year of his death needed, even in the age of literary conferences, no apology.

The proposal for such a conference was put at the International Conference on Conrad held in London in 1971, and the idea was developed at the International Colloquy on Conrad in Poland in 1972. The obvious site for such a conference was Canterbury. Conrad was, after all, buried in the cemetery of St Thomas's Roman Catholic Church in Canterbury. And, since his death, the University of Kent has been established at Canterbury and was willing to provide hospi- tality. The subsidence of a building on the campus the day before delegates assembled on 15 July 1974, which cut off heating at Ruther- ford College, would have satisfied the novelist's ironic sense of fate.

The organising committee's aims were to make the conference truly international and truly representative of the range of Conrad's genius as well as to provide some fresh insight into his life and work. In all, one hundred delegates attended, thirteen countries were represented and literary, critical, historical, biographical, source and textual studies were dealt with in the papers and seminars. A television film of *Almayer's Folly* came from Italy, and a tour of Conrad's homes in the area was organised by Conrad's elder son, Borys, who produced a pamphlet on the houses. Mr Borys Conrad and Mr John Conrad answered questions about their father at an informal session, an exhibition of Conradiana, including photographs, manuscripts and texts, was set up in the University Library and an exhibition of books on Conrad in the University Bookshop. The Arts Council of Great Britain provided financial assistance and the British Council funded Polish delegates.

The essays in this volume show the range of Conrad studies repre- sented at the conference, though it cannot give any indication of the content and quality of the discussions which the papers inspired.

It is appropriate that Albert J. Guerard's essay should come first, since in dealing with this expatriate writer he is attempting to define the distinctive voice of an author who claimed 'a subtle and unforeseen accord' with the English language, a voice which he apprehends as 'a grave interior one . . . regardless of the narrative point of view and whether or not a fictional personage is speaking or writing'. It is a rhythm and irony which comes through even the words of the American capitalist Holroyd in *Nostromo*. It is determined by characteristic movements of mind unconsciously aimed at controlling and composing experience.

Language and narration are approached from a different angle in Tony Tanner's article, where, in specific relation to the story 'Falk', narration (telling) is seen as 'a crucial component of living, at least living with "a sense of corporate existence"', and where 'the narrator has to speak the unspeakable, and in so doing . . . encounters the insoluble problematics of utterance.'

Although the sources of Conrad's work have received much attention since J. D. Gordan's seminal study of this author, *Joseph Conrad: The Making of a Novelist* (1940), there is still room for speculation as to the influence on his work of specific writers and of specific literary and philosophical movements. A group of papers here concern themselves with these influences. According to his friend, Ford Madox Ford, Conrad thought of himself as an impressionist, but he wished also to snare the invisible into a shape. Ian Watt takes these two attitudes and with *Heart of Darkness* specifically in mind considers Conrad as impressionist and symbolist. Conrad's renowned metaphor in *Heart of Darkness* likening the meaning of Marlow's episodes not to the kernel of a nut but to an enveloping haze is taken as a representation in miniature of Conrad's combination of symbolistic outer meaning and impressionistic sensory qualities, and Conrad's technique within the story is illuminated by this means. Eloise Knapp Hay traces the development of the term 'impressionism' historically, through painting and literature, and considers Conrad's attitude to it and its influence on his technique as a writer.

Edward W. Said relates Conrad to a specific tradition of ideas through his affinities with Nietzsche. Similarities and affinities between the two are seen as aspects of a common tradition in European literature and thought. Said makes the point that 'Conrad has been systematically treated as everything *except* a novelist with links to a cultural and intellectual past', and concludes that he was sensitively attuned 'to the whole psychological culture of the late nineteenth century'.

Discussion of Conrad's political standpoint, of his concepts of society, inevitably focuses on his political novels, *The Secret Agent* and *Under Western Eyes* and on his essay 'Autocracy and War' and his attitude to things Russian. It was *Under Western Eyes* which received most attention in this context at the conference.

Zdzisław Najder's comparison of Rousseau and Conrad elucidates

Conrad's concepts of man and society, pointing to Conrad's 'opposition-obsession syndrome' in relation to Rousseau's claim for individual uniqueness and the consequent need for freedom, his theory of the 'general will' and the need for the removal of institutions, a syndrome which is revealed not only in his fictional characters and their predicaments but also in Conrad's attitude to democracy, anarchy and revolution. Edward Crankshaw, in 'Conrad and Russia', argues that 'Conrad was a Pole, but it is too often forgotten that he was also a Russian citizen . . . what he renounced in 1886 was Russian, not Polish, citizenship', and taking due cognisance of the possible effects on the young Conrad of his experiences under Russian rule, Crankshaw concludes that his later writings on the subject of Russia were 'the thoughts and feelings, suddenly unloosed after decades of silence, of a man who had been shaken and shocked by the direct impact of evil.' Thus we have both the personal and the intellectual influences in Conrad's life shedding light upon his political convictions.

Two further papers dealing with *Under Western Eyes* shift the emphasis to Conrad as rhetorician and the reader's response to his rhetoric. Andrzej Busza's approach is from the standpoint of ideology and rhetoric. He sees the novel as 'conceived at one level as a polemic and a warning addressed to Garnett and other Western European enthusiasts of things Russian', and claims that this inevitably affects our response to Conrad's insistence that in the novel his intention was ideological, having 'perfect detachment'. Because of this the novel demands a pluralistic approach which neither oversimplifies 'the political stratum of the novel' nor develops 'highly ingenious interpretations' 'in an effort to cope with the ambiguities and complexities of the text'.

Avrom Fleishman's paper, in a sense, goes on to deal with these ambiguities and complexities in detail, examining the plurality of viewpoints within the novel, seeing it as a self-conscious piece of work – its epigram quoted inaccurately from its own text, its text made up of so many different kinds of writing, its main narrator stating in a fundamentally divisive way: 'Words, as is well known, are the great foes of reality . . . the world is but a place of many words and man appears a mere talking animal not much more wonderful than a parrot.'

One paper which stands apart from the rest, and which places Conrad in closer relationship to our own times is M. C. Bradbrook's 'Narrative Form in Conrad and Lowry', which traces parallels between two writers who were equally seamen and exiles and aspired, each according to his own code, to trace the 'interior journey'.

The joint effort of Kenneth W. Davis, David Leon Higdon and Donald W. Rude, 'Editing Conrad', is a significant contribution, representing as it does one of the latest fields of Conrad studies, the establishing of the text in a definitive way. Basing their article on work done at the Textual Studies Institute of Texas Tech University, they present the difficulties and complexities of determining the intention of a writer as meticulous and revisive as Conrad. This work is already bearing fruit in the projected variorum edition of Conrad's works.

The personal relationships in Conrad's life were often significant for his fiction and three essays here consider two of these relationships. James Brand Pinker was Conrad's literary agent from 1899 to 1922 and was of tremendous importance in the support he gave, not least financially. Frederick R. Karl has been editing the Pinker/Conrad correspondence, and in this paper discusses the personal aspect of this relationship and the light it throws upon the development of certain of Conrad's works.

The influence of the effervescent Ford Madox Ford on Conrad's life and works, which arose from collaboration with Conrad and much conversation about technique and purpose, is examined in two papers. Thomas Moser deals particularly with the other side of this relationship – Conrad's influence upon Ford's work, especially *The Good Soldier*, a specific and not perhaps too happy influence. Ivo Vidan examines Ford's *Joseph Conrad, A Personal Remembrance*, a reappraising not only of Ford's reminiscences but also of the literary techniques evolved and employed by both authors, and he ultimately suggests that Joyce was the twentieth century author who carried on where Conrad left off.

Fittingly, I think, we conclude with three papers dealing with Conrad as a Pole, papers which are varied in their approach and in a way again represent the multiplicity of views on Conrad the man and the novelist. Barbara Kocówna in 'The Problem of Language' points out that Conrad spoke Polish, French and English, learning the latter late in life, and sees the problem of language as one intimately linked with the questions of loyalty, involvement and alienation which, as they form part of Conrad's psyche, are part also of his works. Ugo Mursia contributes a chapter to Conrad biography in his account of his search for Conrad's true birthplace, a search which corrects not only later biographers but also Conrad's uncle, Thaddeus Bobrowski. Finally, reversing the picture set up by the conference, Adam Gillon discusses the writer's reception in his native land over the last sixty years, revealing those aspects of Conrad that first impressed – 'a Polish Jack London' – to the present high level of scholastic interest.

I think it can be said that the conference did sum up the abiding interests of Conrad studies, and that it also presaged their future directions. And I must mention that its success depended a great deal upon workers behind the scenes, the committee members, staff at the University of Kent, and those who chaired meetings and contributed to discussions (not least J. C. Maxwell of Balliol who died recently in a road accident) whose presence stands in the background of this book.

Norman Sherry

1 The Conradian Voice

ALBERT J. GUERARD

Let us take two vivid and hateful personages to remind us of differences between two writers who are in some ways akin, Dickens and Conrad. The first is that 'flabby lump of mortality' Rogue Riderhood; he has just been saved from drowning and Dickens takes us very close to him:

> Stay! Did that eyelid tremble? So the doctor, breathing low, and closely watching, asks himself.
> No.
> Did that nostril twitch?
> No.

Those who have saved Riderhood shed tears on seeing an 'indubitable token of life'. But the lump of mortality, regaining full consciousness, is ungrateful:

> "Where's my fur cap?" he asks in a surly voice, when he has shuffled his clothes on.
> "In the river," somebody rejoins.
> "And waren't there no honest man to pick it up? O' course there was though, and to cut off with it arterwards. You are a rare lot, all on you."
> Thus, Mr. Riderhood: taking from the hands of his daughter, with special ill-will, a lent cap, and grumbling as he pulls it down over his ears. Then, getting on his unsteady legs, leaning heavily upon her, and growling 'Hold still, can't you? What! You must be a-staggering next, must you?' he takes his departure out of the ring in which he has had that little turn-up with death.

The other hateful personage is that creature with 'rare hairs hung about his jaws', Donkin of the *Narcissus*: 'the pet of philanthropists and self-seeking landlubbers'. He arrives on board with nothing:

> "No bag, no bed, no blanket, no shirt – not a bloomin' rag but what I stand in. . . Can't 'ee see I 'aven't got no shirt? . . . 'Cos why? . . . The bloody Yankees been tryin' to jump my guts out 'cos I stood up

for my rights like a good 'un. I am an Englishman, I am. They set upon me an' I 'ad to run. That's why. A'n't yer never seed a man 'ard up?' "

The members of the crew give him their compassion and some clothes: 'The gust of their benevolence sent a wave of sentimental pity through their doubting hearts'. But Donkin too is ungrateful. He snarls at the youthful Charley and dances menacingly about the taciturn Finn. He is, in the purest Conradian voice, a contemptible 'votary of change': 'The independent offspring of the ignoble freedom of the slums full of disdain and hate for the austere servitude of the sea'. Later, in the midst of the storm, 'The rage and fear of his disregarded right to live tried the steadfastness of hearts more than the menacing shadows of the night that advanced through the unceasing clamour of the gale.'

So there are two altogether recognisable voices: 'Neither Riderhood in this world, nor Riderhood in the other, could draw tears from them; but a striving human soul between the two can do it easily. . . He takes his departure out of the ring in which he has had that little turn-up with Death.' And 'The independent offspring of the ignoble freedom of the slums full of disdain and hate for the austere servitude of the sea.'

The two voices commenting aloofly on these worthies are cool and contemptuous; but Dickens's is more playful, Conrad's more austere. 'If you are gone for good, Rogue, it is very solemn, and if you are coming back, it is hardly less so.' A quiet, conversational intrusion. Conrad records Donkin's vivid speech, and the fact that 'his shoulders drooped like the broken wings of a bird.' But he is also compelled to withdraw much further than Dickens from the immediate scene, to meditate upon it. The Conradian sentence is often full of abstract moralising modifiers, and may try to alter our common associations, of *freedom* and *servitude* for example. For freedom is ignoble, and servitude is honorably austere: 'The independent offspring of the ignoble freedom of the slums full of disdain and hate for the austere servitude of the sea.'

This is unmistakably a Conradian voice; and, again unmistakably, what Virginia Woolf would have characterised as a masculine one: assured, overbearing, powerful, uttering unanswerable truths, over-riding delicate nuance and exception. It is at its most confident where strong political convictions are at stake, so confident that commas and other punctuated pauses seem out of the question. The rhythm sweeps on and overrides; commas and other punctuated pauses are instruments of hesitation and doubt.

Here is a cablegram sent by Conrad in 1920, without a single 'stop' in it. This commanding voice did not want to stop:[1]

> For Poles the sense of duty and the imperishable feeling of nationality preserved in the hearts and defended by the hands of their immediate ancestors in open struggles against the might of three powers and in indomitable defiance of crushing opposition for more than a hundred years is sufficient inducement to assist in reconstructing the independent dignity and usefulness of the reborn republic.

And here is a letter written in 1899 on the subject of the Boer War, which employs a Conradian variety of sentence structure and length:

> It is always unwise to begin a war which, to be effective, must be a war of extermination; it is positively imbecile to start it without a clear notion of what it means and to force on questions for immediate solution which are eminently fit to be left to time. . . There is an appalling fatuity in this business. If I am to believe Kipling this is a war undertaken for the cause of democracy. *C'est a crever de rire!*

This angry rhetoric, passionate yet composed, complex in syntax – employing both the Conradian periodic sentence and a rolling rhythm – is understandably provoked by his feelings about Russia and Russians, as the 1926 Author's Note to *Under Western Eyes* suggests:

> The ferocity and imbecility of an autocratic rule rejecting all legality and in fact basing itself upon complete moral anarchism provokes the no less imbecile and atrocious answer of a purely Utopian revolutionism encompassing destruction by the first means to hand, in the strange conviction that a fundamental change of hearts must follow the downfall of any given human institutions.

This political assurance was accompanied by an unusual awareness of moral complexities, the certitude often masked deep doubts; the austere ethic could be undermined by sympathy for the outlaw. I argued in *Conrad the Novelist* that the larger structures of Conradian impressionism responded to temperamental needs. The novelist was aloof, evasive, distrustful of others and distrustful of himself, poetic and moralising, bemused by ambiguity. It was very important to his temperament that he should control his distance from his material; that he should be able to penetrate it deeply yet suddenly and safely withdraw, and move from the concrete particular to the very large protective generalisation. Hence the attraction of narrators interposed between the writer and the action; hence the chronological dislocations and sudden time-shifts; hence the shifting visual perspectives and the elaborate drama of conflicting witnesses bringing forward evidence that remains in doubt. We can love the intricacy of Conradian impressionism: for its own sake; or for its power to control the reader's sympathy and judgment, and for its effectiveness in achieving the fullest meanings. But we should also recognise that it catered to the writer's psychological needs: to the demands of his imagination and his temperament. It helped release the richest tonalities of the Conradian voice.

The concept of authorial voice, which has been rapidly gaining currency, remains rather nebulous; and each of us should explain what he means by it. Voice even more than style is the man, though not necessarily the man known to his friends and biographers. It is the expression of temperament at work in the 'lonely region of stress and strife'; it reveals itself most obviously in language and rhythms, in the 'shape and ring of sentences'. It certainly implies that a writer's prose is the expression of a human being, whereas much bureaucratic prose would seem to be produced by a computer or some other machine. Groping to define a writer's particularity, critics tend to fall back on metaphor. They speak of *ordonnance*, of a writer's peculiar *gait*, of timbre, of accent; but most agree that there is something recognisable in every great writer's voice. Can we approximate something similar to the voiceprint which, it appears, will soon be accepted as evidence in courts of law?

How then can we distinguish *voice* from *style*? I define style as language and the conventions of language which are not determined by an author's own temperament and personal exigencies; a certain style may be shared by a number of writers, though each will have his individual voice. A number of eighteenth century poets imitate rather closely Milton's blank verse, as does the Wordsworth of *The Excursion*. Many of the rhetorical devices are the same, yet Wordsworth's long verse paragraphs have their own particular gait. And his double negatives (which usually have the effect of seeming doubly negative) often betray a deep-lying insecurity that is altogether his own. Thus we hear Wordsworth's own voice even when he adopts rather closely a Miltonic style. Style is, more than voice, acquired and conventional. If we look at the very early Conrad, at what he himself called second-hand 'Conradese', we may see voice and style at odds, a voice striving to free itself. The Gallic locutions, the Flaubertian turns of phrase, possibly the French post-positioning of adjectives, are matters of acquired *style*.[2] So too is a Dickensian impulse to rather banal grammatical repetition, such as a series of clauses modified by the word *every*. Thus from 'The Lagoon', which at times seems to rival Max Beerbohm's parody of it:

> At the foot of big, towering trees, trunkless nipa palms rose from the mud of the bank, in bunches of leaves enormous and heavy, that hung unstirring over the brown swirl of eddies. In the stillness of the air every tree, every leaf, every bough, every tendril of creeper and every petal of minute blossoms seemed to have been bewitched into an immobility perfect and final.

We can recognise here Conrad's deep preoccupation with immobilisation, his fear of spiritual paralysis projected onto the visible world, a paranoid landscape: but not his full voice. In *The Nigger of the 'Narcissus'*, written so shortly after, the becalmed *Narcissus* still evokes one instance of Gallic post-positioning, and may remind us also of the Ancient Mariner's ghostly ship. There are even moments of Conradese. But we find here also a more vivid metaphorical eye, and a pace – a voice – which we will encounter many times in later work:

> At night, through the impenetrable darkness of earth and heaven, broad sheets of flame waved noiselessly, and for half a second the becalmed craft stood out with its masts and rigging, with every sail and every rope distinct and black in the centre of a fiery outburst, like a charred ship enclosed in a globe of fire. And, again, for long hours she remained lost in a vast universe of night and silence where gentle sighs wandering here and there like forlorn souls, made the still sails flutter as in sudden fear, and the ripple of a beshrouded ocean whisper its compassion afar – in a voice mournful, immense, and faint. . .

It is not far from here to Lord Jim immobilised on the *Patna*, staring at a bulging bulkhead or at the alarmingly sloping sea:

> I can easily picture him to myself in the peopled gloom of the cavernous place, with the light of the bulk-lamp falling on a small portion of the bulkhead that had the weight of the ocean on the other side, and the breathing of unconscious sleepers in his ears. I can see him glaring at the iron, startled by the falling rust, over-burdened by the knowledge of an imminent death. . . Nothing in the world moved before his eyes, and he could depict to himself without hindrance the sudden swing upwards of the dark skyline,

the sudden tilt up of the vast plain of the sea, the swift still rise, the brutal fling, the grasp of the abyss, the struggle without hope, the starlight closing over his head for ever like the vault of a tomb – the revolt of his young life – the black end.

An even more truly Conradian voice tells us soon that the ship did not sink. That voice is most effectively released when it withdraws into meditative irony and the long historical view, leaving Jim far from us on the deck:

And still she floated! These sleeping pilgrims were destined to accomplish their whole pilgrimage to the bitterness of some other end. It was if the Omnipotence whose mercy they confessed had needed their humble testimony on earth for a while longer, and had looked down to make a sign, 'Thou shalt not!' to the ocean. Their escape would trouble me as a prodigiously inexplicable event, did I not know how tough old iron can be – as tough sometimes as the spirit of some men we meet now and then, worn to a shadow and breasting the weight of life. Not the least wonder of these twenty minutes, to my mind, is the behaviour of the two helmsmen.

We learn how tough old iron can be in one of those startling and characteristic leaps forward in time which suggest absolute authorial control. The old ship is animated as it might have been in Dickens, and given a moment of heroic conscious life:

But she turned her back on them as if in disdain of their fate: she had swung round, burdened, to glare stubbornly at the new danger of the open sea which she so strangely survived to end her days in a breaking-up yard, as if it had been her recorded fate to die obscurely under the blows of many hammers.

So we can make this distinction between *style* and *voice*, between rhetorical structures and mannerisms that a number of writers share at a particular time, and the very recognisable pace, movement, accent, tonality of a great writer's voice.

There is a second essential distinction to be made. This is between the recognisable 'voice' we hear in good prose and the voice of actual speech, whether it be the writer's or someone else's. The distinction is particularly important for writers like Conrad and Faulkner who were incapable of reading their own prose aloud. Conrad's one public reading (the death of Lena from *Victory*) appears to have been virtually incomprehensible; not everyone can be a Dickens or a Joyce, with English as a mother tongue and histrionics a second nature. Yet Conrad

was entirely correct in claiming 'a subtle and unforeseen accord' between himself and the genius of the English language. That is to say,
Conrad had a fine ear for the rich rhythms he could not render aloud;
when writing at the height of his powers, his interior ear and interior
voice were impeccable. The same may be said of Faulkner, whose
breathless readings destroy his lovely polysyllabic flights. It is nevertheless one essential of a good authorial voice that it *can* be read aloud,
that it possesses certain qualities of pleasing speech; that, above all, it
does not seem to emerge from a machine. (In this connection we may
still speculate on the effect of dictation on Conrad's later prose: whether
hearing his own broken speaking voice, rather than that silent interior
voice so free of cacophony, does not account for some of the awkward
short sentences of the late novels. I say this while entirely subscribing
to Thomas Moser's psychological explanation in *Joseph Conrad:
Achievement and Decline*.)

Conrad's authorial voice is then a grave interior one. For this reason
we can detect and hear it, to some extent regardless of the narrative
point of view and whether or not a fictional personage is speaking or
writing. Of course we hear a living voice when Marlow speaks, even
when he speaks rather elaborately, or in the vivid conjectures of
Chance:

> And all this torture for nothing, in the end! What looked at last like
> a possible prize (oh without illusions! but still a prize) broken in her
> hands, fallen in the dust, the bitter dust of disappointment, she
> revelled in the miserable revenge – pretty safe too – only regretting
> the unworthiness of the girlish figure which stood for so much she
> had longed to be able to spit venom at, if only once, in perfect
> liberty. The presence of the young man at her back increased both
> her satisfaction and her rage.

In 'The Secret Sharer', on the other hand, we have a nominally
silent narration in the first person; a grave 'interior speech' which is,
as it were, overheard. Yet the story's elaborate last sentence – difficult
in its syntax, enigmatic in its suggestions, carefully composed throughout – still conveys a voice:

> Walking to the taffrail, I was in time to make out, on the very edge
> of a darkness thrown by a towering black mass like the very gateway
> of Erebus – yes, I was in time to catch an evanescent glimpse of my
> white hat left behind to mark where the secret sharer of my thoughts,
> as though he were my second self, had lowered himself into the

water to take his punishment: a free man, a proud swimmer striking out for a new destiny.

But a very comparable voice is heard even where we are listening to an omniscient narrator, as in the opening chapters of *Lord Jim*: the rich rhythms that can be rendered aloud pleasingly, the composed elaboration of syntax, the shifts from the broad generality to concrete detail and back; and the running rhythm which sometimes gives the impression of a balloon that has been blown up carefully then allowed slowly to collapse. Here is Jim lying in his cabin after being disabled by a falling spar at the beginning of a week of terrible storm:

> The danger, when not seen, has the imperfect vagueness of human thought. The fear grows shadowy; and Imagination, the enemy of men, the father of all terrors, unstimulated, sinks to rest in the dullness of exhausted emotion. Jim saw nothing but the disorder of his tossed cabin. He lay there battened down in the midst of a small devastation, and felt secretly glad he had not to go on deck. But now and again an uncontrollable rush of anguish would grip him bodily, make him gasp and writhe under the blankets, and then the unintelligent brutality of an existence liable to the agony of such sensations filled him with a despairing desire to escape at any cost. Then fine weather returned, and he thought no more about it.

(The struggle of revising this passage is clearly seen in the Tuan Jim sketch in Mr Moser's edition.[3] The initial 'The fact he did not see' moves to the more elevated 'As he had not to look menace in the face' and thence to 'The danger when not seen has the vagueness (of the Impossible) of our imperfect thoughts.' The capitalised abstraction Impossible is cancelled, giving way to the rather banal final form.)

A Shakespearean voice regularly dominates all but the most eccentric comic voices of the characters in the plays; and all the personages of *Absalom! Absalom!* speak flamboyant Faulknerese. So too, though less frequently, with Conrad. We recognise the magisterial, controlling voice, a voice absolutely assured in its rhythms, in a stuffy professor of languages in Geneva, in the sceptical boulevardier Martin Decoud (who is also an angry patriot), in Charles Gould the romantic mining engineer, and even in Holroyd the San Francisco capitalist. All are capable of taking the long, controlled distant view, which they express in balanced periods, and in rhythms which exhaust themselves on the final word.

So the professor of languages, contemplating a solitary Swiss couple taking refreshment:

In the very middle of it I observed a solitary Swiss couple, whose fate was made secure from the cradle to the grave by the perfected mechanism of democratic institutions in a republic that could almost be held in the palm of one's hand. The man, colourlessly uncouth, was drinking beer out of a glittering glass; the woman, rustic and placid, leaning back in the rough chair, gazed idly around.

And so Martin Decoud in *Nostromo*:

There is a curse of futility upon our character: Don Quixote and Sancho Panza, chivalry and materialism, high-sounding sentiments and a supine mortality, violent efforts for an idea and a sullen acquiesence in every form of corruption. We convulsed a continent for our independence only to become the passive prey of a democratic parody, the helpless victims of scoundrels and cut-throats, our institutions a mockery, our laws a farce – a Guzman Bento our master!

Even Charles Gould's periods, though calmer, give this sense of being composed and controlled, powerfully organised rather than improvised. It is once again a question both of running rhythm and of syntax:

Only let the material interests once get a firm footing, and they are bound to impose the conditions on which they alone can continue to exist. That's how your money-making is justified here in the face of lawlessness and disorder. It is justified because the security which it demands must be shared with an oppressed people.

The insatiable American puritan capitalist Holroyd amusingly blends American colloquialism and Conradian rhetoric. In the last of the three sentences below, the Conradian rhythm and irony takes over altogether:

Time itself has got to wait on the greatest country in the whole of God's Universe. We shall be giving the word for everything: industry, trade, law, journalism, art, politics, and religion, from Cape Horn clear over to Smith's Sound, and beyond, too, if anything worth taking hold of turns up at the North Pole. And then we shall have the leisure to take in hand the outlying islands and continents of the earth.

As the Conradian voice may thus be heard across – *à travers* – the voices of individual characters, so it rises above the contingencies of setting and plot. It may record cataclysmic action at sea, typhoons

which send Chinese coolies spinning in the hold and storms that lay a
great iron sailing ship on her side; but also scorched unwrinkled seas
over which the *Patna* moves with a slight hiss, and on which night
descends like a benediction. The voice can convey reflections on the
evil of secret agents in London, autocratic police methods in Russia,
revolutionary exiles in Geneva, self-intoxicated enthusiasts in
Costaguana. The voice, though uncomfortable in the presence of
sexuality, seems equally at home in what are presumably at the
emotional poles of this fictional world, *glamour* and *irony* – the
romantic exotic glamour of the East or of certain moments at sea; the
disdainful irony that rejects wallowing opportunists and revolutionaries.

The Conradian rhythms and jewelled metaphors create the glamour
of the East which his first readers loved:

> . . . a signal fire gleams like a jewel on the high brown of a sombre
> cliff; great trees, the advanced sentries of immense forests, stand
> watchful and still over sleeping stretches of open water; a line of
> white surf thunders on an empty beach, the shallow water foams on
> the reefs; and green islets scattered through the calm of noonday lie
> upon the level of a polished sea, like a handful of emeralds on a
> buckler of steel.

That is from *Karain*. In *Heart of Darkness* the jewels which stand
for historic British ships are also metaphorical stars, set in a night that
is, metaphorically, time:

> The tidal current runs to and fro in its unceasing service, crowded
> with memories of men and ships it had borne to the rest of home
> and to the battles of the sea. It had known and served all the men
> of whom the nation is proud, from Sir Francis Drake to Sir John
> Franklyn, knights all, titled and untitled – the great knights-errant
> of the sea. It had borne all the ships whose names are like jewels
> flashing in the night of time.

This is the pole of glamour, of romantic or exalted feeling. At the
other extreme is the chill irony that can see London as a 'slimy
aquarium from which the water had run off'; that can contemplate an
old horse whose thighs move 'with ascetic deliberation . . . a steed of
apocalyptic misery'; and contemplate Verloc the secret double agent
wallowing in bed and making eyes at the maid: 'His prominent,
heavy-lidded eyes rolled sideways amorously and languidly, the bed-
clothes were pulled up to his chin, and his dark smooth moustache
covered his thick lips capable of much honeyed banter.' From here we

may move to Costaguana and the siesta of the eloquent Gamacho, Commandante of the National Guard, who

> was lying drunk and asleep in the bosom of his family. His bare feet were upturned in the shadows repulsively, in the manner of a corpse. His eloquent mouth had dropped open. His youngest daughter, scratching her head with one hand, with the other waved a green bough over his scorched and peeling face.

What is responsible for the authorial voice we hear in these various passages, regardless of who is speaking and even if no one is speaking at all? We can point to an elevated diction, a language of contemplation often juxtaposed with bright vivid particulars; to pleasing rhythms that run uninterrupted past many natural stopping places, but always with the sense that experience has been ordered and composed; to the elaborate and at times even perverse syntax; and in a general way to a certain gait, a movement of mind, rhythm in the largest sense. Virginia Woolf pondered the internal haunting rhythms that led to the radically different style of *To the Lighthouse*:

> Now this is very profound, what rhythm is, and goes far deeper than words. A sight, an emotion, creates this wave in the mind, long before it makes words to get it; and in writing (such is my belief) one has to recapture this, and set this working (which has nothing apparently to do with words) and then, as it breaks and tumbles in the mind, it makes words to fit it.

Or, as her recent commentator Ellen Rogat puts it: 'Rhythm breaks against and washes over traditional structures because it sweeps up and carries along language, images, associations, from all levels of the mind.' And Virginia Woolf is helpfully close to this concept of voice in the essay 'Women and Fiction': 'And this a woman must make for herself, altering and adapting the current sentence until she writes one that takes the natural shape of her thought without crushing or distorting it.'

There is an important phrase here: the *natural shape of her thought*. I suggest that authorial voice may be determined most of all by characteristic movements of mind. The Faulknerian voice is related to a seemingly incorrigible impulse to absurd qualification and digression, and to the merciless chopping of logic, as the Jamesian voice is to a more elephantine need to qualify and digress. If this is true, then it should be possible to find comparable authorial voices as we move from language to language; and indeed there are certainly moments when *A Hundred Years of Solitude* speaks with the historical ironic voice of *Nostromo*, and Malraux's *The Royal Way* with the tenebrous rhythms and preoccupations of *Heart of Darkness*. Here it would be relevant to think once more of Conrad's own mind moving in its several languages. Mr Najder usefully reminds us of Conrad's relationship to a Polish oratorical style, just as others have made connections between Faulknerese and a bombastic tradition of southern oratory. Certainly some of Conrad's letters in French bemuse us with the unpunctuated running rhythms and grand generalities which seem particularly characteristic of his early writings, whether the eloquence is reflecting patriotic fervour or political disdain.

Nothing can be more wearying than linguistic analysis intruding too technically on criticism. So I will only suggest briefly the directions such analysis might take in trying to define Conrad's movement of mind as expressing an authorial voice. I will confine myself to the variant of that voice as it was energised by political or patriotic feeling; and so return to that cablegram of 1920, that long telegram which has a single basic message: 'For Poles the sense of duty and the feeling of nationality is sufficient inducement to assist in reconstructing the republic' – a direct, economical telegram. But this message is elevated to a high pitch of emotional appeal through a number of characteristic elaborations.

In the first place, the sentence continues without interruption past no less than seven natural resting places where commas or 'stops' might have been expected. The syntactical movement gives the voice no opportunity to fall; the pitch remains evenly high.

Secondly, a number of modifying words or clauses, all of them in some sense meditative, are interpolated. The 'feeling of nationality', for instance, is 'preserved in the hearts and defended by the hands of their immediate ancestors in open struggles against the might of three powers'. These interpolations fall into balancing units.

Thirdly, a number of 'big words', powerful emotive abstractions, contribute to the general elevation: 'imperishable', 'indomitable', 'defiance', 'crushing'; and finally there may be unexpected combinations of words, the unexpectedness placing certain exciting demands on the reader, as the 'independent dignity' of the republic, which, we are reminded, is a 'reborn' republic.

And here, once again, is that telegram whose 'real message' is only twenty words long:

For Poles the sense of duty and the imperishable feeling of nationality preserved in the hearts and defended by the hands of their immediate ancestors in open struggles against the might of three powers and in indomitable defiance of crushing opposition for more than a hundred years is sufficient inducement to assist in reconstructing the independent dignity and usefulness of the reborn republic.

One is reminded of the long and beautiful and highly metaphorical paragraph opening the fourth chapter of *The Nigger of the 'Narcissus'*, the informational content of which can be summarised in four words: *The ship didn't sink.* But the paragraph's elaborations, which initiate a downward modulation from the heroism of old Singleton, who is still at the wheel after thirty hours, also provide a definitive statement of religious scepticism and of ultimate respect for the 'dumb fear and the dumb courage of men obscure, forgetful, and enduring'. Familiar as they are, I will quote again the wonderful ending of Chapter III and that first paragraph of Chapter IV:

Apart, far aft, and alone by the helm, old Singleton had deliberately tucked his white beard under the top button of his glistening coat. Swaying upon the din and tumult of the seas, with the whole battered length of the ship launched forward in a rolling rush before his steady old eyes, he stood rigidly still, forgotten by all, and with an attentive face. In front of his erect figure only the two arms moved crosswise with a swift and sudden readiness, to check or urge again the rapid stir of circling spokes. He steered with care.

IV

On men reprieved by its disdainful mercy the immortal sea confers in its justice the full privilege of desired unrest. Through the perfect wisdom of its grace they are not permitted to meditate at ease upon the complicated and acrid savour of existence. They must without pause justify their life to the eternal pity that commands toil to be hard and unceasing, from sunrise to sunset, from sunset to sunrise, till the weary succession of nights and days tainted by the obstinate clamour of sages, demanding bliss and an empty heaven, is redeemed at last by the vast silence of pain and labour, by the dumb fear and the dumb courage of men obscure, forgetful, and enduring.

It would be tempting to say more about that beautifully dry ironic variant of the Conradian voice we hear in *The Secret Agent*. I turn at random to the opening of chapter nine, and the characteristic irony of negatives: 'Mr Verloc, returning from the Continent at the end of ten days, brought back a mind evidently unrefreshed by the wonders of foreign travel and a countenance unlighted by the joys of home-coming.' Michaelis (opening again at random) characteristically evokes the disease of fatness and the disease of self-intoxicating rhetoric:

> The coals in the grate settled down with a slight crash; and Michaelis, the hermit of visions in the desert of a penitentiary, got up impetuously. Round like a distended balloon, he opened his short, thick arms, as if in a pathetically hopeless attempt to embrace and hug to his breast a self-regenerated universe. He gasped with ardour.

I will not stir the hornet's nest of Norman Holland's ingenious argument that this style represents a defence mechanism against the classic fear of engulfment. I am not one who can throw stones at psychoanalytic readings, though I steadfastly refuse the Jungian label which is occasionally pinned on me. But I do believe stylistic complica-tion – complication of rhythm and especially of syntax – can be a means of composing and controlling very strong feeling: of expressing that feeling, yet keeping it at a necessary distance. A general comment on one of Nelson victories shows Conrad's voice and style coping with very strong patriotic feeling in 'The Mirror of the Sea':

> But in the exulting illusion of irresistible might a long series of military successes brings to a nation the less obvious aspect of such a fortune may perchance be lost to view. The old navy in its last days earned a fame that no belittling malevolence dare cavil at. And this supreme favour they owe to their adversaries alone.

The second sentence, restored to a normal word order, would read thus: 'No belittling malevolence dares cavil at a fame the old navy earned in its last days.' But the actual order, if we number the items of the sentence, is 4, 6, 5, 3, 1, 2: 'The old navy in its last days earned a fame that no belittling malevolence dare cavil at', which makes rather intense demands on our attention.

The voice, then, is that of a temperament, and in the last analysis – while making all necessary distinctions between the writer and the man – I do not think we can entirely separate temperament from the events of one's life, its anxieties and triumphs. The voice in all its evasiveness and richness is as much present in *A Personal Record* as anywhere else; and there too we can see the reluctance to say anything simply. The beauty of even a relatively short Conradian sentence may lie in those modifying clauses, those controlling and evocative digres-sions, those interpolations that are not allowed to break an overarching rhythm. So the question, 'Why should I go to sea?' or, a little more elaborately, 'Why should I undertake the wide seas?' But the modifying clauses added to this simple question state their continuing allegiance to the Polish past and also vividly evoke what life was like at sea: '. . . for why should I, the son of a land which such men as these have turned up with their ploughshares and bedewed with their blood, undertake the pursuit of fantastic meals of salt junk and hard tack upon the wide seas? On the kindest view it seems an unanswerable question.'

Every great writer surprises in one way or another, and Conrad's voice conveys more than its share of unexpected felicities. And greatness is hardly conceivable without the turbulence which is controlled by language or the imaginative flights which are subdued by syntax. But the final characteristic of the Conradian voice I want to stress is control: the temperamental control of its material through lovely running rhythms and through the shifts from long sentences to short and short to long; the control exerted by an often complicated and unusual syntax; and the control exerted by contemplative language.

In spite of some fumblings early on and again towards the end of Conrad's writing career that voice can be heard almost from the beginning and right through to the very end. In *Conrad the Novelist* I detected the first true emergence of the Conradian voice in the manuscript of 'The Rescuer', as the author suddenly takes a distant view of a glamorous past:

> Did you follow with your ghostly eyes the quest of this obscure adventurer of yesterday you shade of forgotten adventurers who in leather jerkins and sweating under steel helmets attacked with long rapiers the palisades of the strange heathen, or musket on shoulder and match in cock guarded lonely forts built upon the banks of rivers that command good trade?

And I hear the voice, though much quieter, in the unfinished *Suspense*:

> His voice was as unexpected when I heard it as your own, signore. The evening shadows had closed about me just after I had seen to the west, on the edge of the world as it were, a lion miss his spring on a bounding deer. They went right away into the glow and vanished. It was as though I had dreamed.

NOTES

1. Conrad gave permission to alter the phrasing for committee publication, and commas were added to another paragraph. The quoted passage is exactly as it exists in the handwritten telegram.
2. The post-positioning, implying as it does a controlling surview of the phrase, may at times be a matter of temperament, e.g. voice.
3. New York: Norton Critical Editions.

2 'Gnawed Bones' and 'Artless Tales' – Eating and Narrative in Conrad

TONY TANNER

In his preface to his wife's *Handbook of Cookery for a Small House* Conrad states that of all the books ever written 'those only that treat of cooking are, from a moral point of view, above suspicion. The intention of every other piece of prose may be discussed and even mistrusted; but the purpose of a cookery book is one and unmistakable. Its object can conceivably be no other than to increase the happiness of mankind.' The tone throughout the short preface is appropriately light, even jocular. But in view of my topic I want to take note of a potentially far-reaching point that Conrad makes.

> Good cooking is a moral agent. . . The decency of our life is for a great part a matter of good taste, of the correct appreciation of what is fine in simplicity. The intimate influence of conscientious cooking by rendering easy the processes of digestion promotes the serenity of mind, the graciousness of thought, and that indulgent view of our neighbours' failings which is the only genuine form of optimism.

Conrad then goes on to designate an opposed realm where the virtues and comforts consequent upon good cooking do not obtain – the wig-wam of the Noble Red Man. In Conrad's version, the Red Indians were great hunters but their domestic life was

> clouded by the morose irritability which follows the consumption of ill-cooked food. The gluttony of their indigestible feasts was a direct incentive to counsels of unreasonable violence. Victims of gloomy imaginings, they lived in abject submission to the wiles of a multi-tude of fraudulent medicine men . . . who haunted their existence with vain promises and false nostrums from the cradle to the grave.

Needless to say Conrad has no evidence for this outrageous state-ment, and no contribution to anthropology is being offered here. What interests me in this slight piece is another example of a characteristic Conradian strategy: the ironic juxtaposition of what I referred to as opposed realms, or more exactly segments of the world in which life in all its cultural aspects – linguistic, religious, ethical, etc. – is structured differently. Examples will be familiar – from west and east, London and the Congo, Switzerland and Russia. The one I am adding is the bourgeois kitchen and the savage's wigwam, with a further related subordinate pair of terms, the cooking of sanity and the diet of un-reason. My source is once again Conrad's preface: 'a sane view of life is, after all, elaborated mainly in the kitchen – the kitchen of the small house, the abode of the preponderant majority of the people . . . a sane view of life can be no other than kindly and joyous, but a believer in patent medicine is steeped in the gloom of vague fears, the sombre attendants of disordered digestion.' Of course the tone is light, eminently domesticated we might say: this is, after all, Conrad writing as Jessie's husband, the sane and contented Western citizen. But if we isolate certain phrases and words from the present context we can see that Conrad is drawing on a vocabulary of opposed states of conscious-ness and mood which in varying forms is operative throughout his major fictional work. On the one hand decency, good taste, correct appreciation, sanity of mind, the preponderant majority, optimism, kindness and joy, all these qualities or states being associated in this context with the small house, the stable edifice of the settled bourgeois; on the other hand morose irritability, unreasonable violence, gloomy imaginings, a haunted existence, vague fears, all associated in this context with the wigwam, the temporary shelter of the restless nomad. Any reader of Conrad will recognise how often he brings mental attitudes and dispositions of these contrasting kinds together, forcing them to contest his fictional space, thus undermining whatever fixed ideas we might have about sanity, good taste, and so on, and impressing upon us the disquieting psychic reality of unreasonable violence, gloomy imaginings, vague fears. If I just cite the juxtaposition of the bland narrator of *Under Western Eyes* and the haunted Razumov it should be clear what I am referring to. And of course this enforced co-presence of differing types of consciousness, different ranges of experience, differing assumptions, values, terminologies, helps to generate that probing and disturbing irony which we associate with Conrad. Although he appears to operate dualistically – London/the Congo – his fiction works to dissolve the dangerous habit of dualistic (i.e. oppositional) thinking. So one effect of *Heart of Darkness* is not to endorse either the West or the jungle but to erode some of the unexamined assumptions which make such either/or thinking possible. I am not suggesting that a comparable ironic energy is at work in his preface to his wife's cookbook – presumably he intended that it should sell rather than that readers should start to question the prevailing vocabulary of the Western kitchen. His wigwam full of groaning dyspeptic Indians is of course a joke – arguably in dubious taste – intended to amuse rather than disturb. But in relating cooking to the whole matter of how we live, Conrad indicates his awareness that what we eat is intimately connected to what we are, in a more than alimentary way.

I want to concentrate on 'Falk', the one piece of fiction by Conrad in which literal cannibalism is the act at the centre of the action (although cannibalism is often referred to elsewhere in Conrad). Not surprisingly the good English cook Jessie Conrad found the story repellent: 'I remember I was quite physically sick when I typed those pages. Sick with disgust at the idea of human beings having been cooked.' (Interestingly enough her cook's imagination is running away with her for there is no reference to humans being 'cooked' in the story – there is indeed a significant silence about the actual deed.) Jessie's reaction is shared by one of the characters in the story, and I must now give a minimal précis of the plot.

The story concerns an enigmatic Scandinavian named Falk who owns the one tug for towing ships out of an unnamed port (based on Bangkok). The narrator of the story recalls a time when his ship was trapped in the harbour because Falk refused to tow him out. The reason for this refusal concerns a girl – unnamed – who is the orphan niece of a German ship-conductor named Hermann, a quintessential bourgeois whose ship is said to resemble a shop. Hermann and the narrator are both waiting to have their ships towed out of the harbour. Falk is desperate to marry the girl but he believes the narrator to be in competition with him, so he forcibly tows Hermann's ship out to sea with the girl on board – it is described as suggesting an act of rape – leaving the hapless narrator landlocked and desperately anxious to get to sea as his crew is falling sick. The position is a kind of stalemate: Falk has the girl out at sea but cannot press his suit because of some unspeakable secret episode in his past. The narrator is trapped in harbour. Appropriately he and Falk have the matter out over a game of cards (games are very important in Conrad), and a kind of bargain is struck. Falk will tow the narrator's ship out if the narrator will help him by acting as some kind of mediator between himself and the Hermann household, or shiphold. In the event the narrator arranges the necessary exposition and clarification. It turns out that Falk once engaged in cannibalism (though he does not call it that) when a ship he was on had broken down and drifted beyond all possible hope of help (as the crew thought) into the polar regions of the southern ice, a white blank zone, effectively a moral void, where simple physical survival became, for Falk, the only issue. By chance he was saved and he has returned to established human society, but though he is in it he is no longer of it – on account of his cannibalism he feels that he is in some way debarred from re-entry. So he lives in eccentric solitude, having something of that aura of a gloomy and haunted existence which Conrad ascribed to life in the wigwam. And indeed his eating habits are unusual. However, he has seen Hermann's niece and he wants her very badly: but first he feels he must tell his story, externalise what he has hitherto kept in isolating interiority. Thus the central scene occurs when Falk avows the facts of his cannibalism in a cabin on Hermann's ship. This is almost a matter of the secrets of the wigwam being disclosed in the security of the bourgeois kitchen, for Hermann would seem to be a good example of that figure of sanity, good humour, optimism and kindness Conrad located in the kitchen of the small house. This confrontation of Hermann and Falk, through the mediation of the narrator and in the presence of the silent niece, is the core situation, the central paradigm, of the book, and I will say a word or two about these figures.

Falk is one of the most arresting figures in Conrad, to be compared and contrasted with Kurtz and Axel Heyst. Unlike most of Conrad's social outcasts and pariahs he was not guilty of a moment's weakness, a sudden collapse of some inner discipline, a fall from the ranks. It was precisely his strength that took him into isolation. It is important that on the voyage which ended in cannibalism he was the man who to the last attempted to maintain order and morale, to give the flagging Captain energy and maintain some organisation and integration on the ship. He was a supreme *maintainer* of the ranks, as long as there were ranks to maintain. His moment of decision came after the other good man on the ship – the carpenter, note – attempted to kill him with a crowbar. That is to say, the builder or mender and upholder of structures had turned into the murderer, and tools became weapons. This is symptomatic of the total collapse and disintegration of normal patterns which I will mention later. After that, self-survival became the only meaningful concern for Falk. The point is that Falk was 'unfortunate' (his word) enough to have to eat human flesh. He feels no guilt about it, yet he feels unclean. He wishes to rejoin human society, but not at the cost of deceit. That is why he insists on telling his story to the girl. Hermann, who is so shocked, seems to be the opposite type to Falk – the man who clings to the shore, whose life is public and orthodox and unhaunted, who stays within the prescribed tastes of the community. Yet in a way he is the real exploiter in the book – he exploits the niece, using her physical labour for his convenience, thus in a sense abusing her body (Falk wants to marry the girl, not to rape her: he respects the cultural binding of the sexual drive). Although when he first hears Falk's story Hermann hysterically dismisses his proposal of marriage, he soon moves from hysteria to prudence and allows the girl to go because she is about to turn from an asset (free labour) into a liability (a mouth to feed). Hermann can also be cruel, devious, and mean. Although everything is so tidy and spotless on his ship, this is only part of the economic system to which he is totally committed. For example, his ship is so clean it is said to look as if it had been 'explored with toothbrushes'. This is not an idle simile, for in a way his bourgeois establishment is a kind of mouth, a clean mouth but a mouth nevertheless, and Hermann is in one way a much more insidious and dishonest kind of 'consumer' than Falk. His reaction to Falk's opening statement – ' "Imagine to yourself that I have eaten man" ' – is notable. He says ' "What for?" ', then later shrieks out ' "Beast" ', and still later says to the narrator ' "Why tell? Who was asking him?" '; utilitarianism, defensive abuse, the preference for concealment – this is the bourgeois mind.

The narrator stands in a different relationship to Falk. For one thing his position is in some ways oddly parallel to the one experienced by Falk. His ship is in trouble, morale is collapsing, men are ill and indeed nearly dying. In addition he has been robbed of his savings – just as for Falk, in another sense, there was finally nothing left for him to draw on. In any case the narrator responds sympathetically to Falk's story with an ' "Ah" of complete enlightenment'. This is why *he* has to take up 'the *rôle* of an ambassador', as he puts it, between Falk and Hermann: the two men live in different countries, different countries of experience, but also different countries of the mind and of character. Hermann's ship is said to be 'world-proof'. Falk looks like a man 'who has fallen out of the world'. The narrator is truly mundane, trying to be in the world as it is, neither refusing it nor having had to step out of it. Hence he is the necessary point of intersection; he is qualified to be the true narrator and translator. The niece, who never speaks, and responds to Falk's story in total silence with total attention, and tears of pure sympathy, is for her part the true listener. She is willing to take in – to assimilate – what Falk had, in a more literal sense, had to assimilate. Hermann wants to extrude it; she can swallow it. That is why she is an appropriate mate for Falk. In these and many other ways, all the main characters are involved in different kinds of hunger, different kinds of devouring and assimilating, different kinds of telling and listening. For the purposes of this paper I simply want to stress the inter-relationship in the story of these three planes of human activity: the biological – eating, hunger, the sexual drive; the economic – there are many references to business, deals, bargains, diplomacy, trading, etc.; and the linguistic, since speaking, talking, translating, explaining are constant and crucial activities.

The connection between hunger and the sexual drive is very explicit in the story. As the narrator says of Falk:

> He wanted to live. He had always wanted to live. So we all do – but in us the instinct serves a complex conception, and in him this instinct existed alone. There is in such simple development a gigantic force, and like the pathos of a child's naive and uncontrolled desire. . . He was a child. He was as frank as a child, too. He was hungry for the girl, terribly hungry, as he had been terribly hungry for food. Don't be shocked if I declare that in my belief it was the same need, the same pain, the same torture.

With this emphatic focus on the 'will to live' Conrad seems to be writing with Schopenhauer in mind, as he did most notably in *Victory*, in which Axel Heyst tries to live out the Schopenhauerian ideal of 'complete denial of the will' – and fails. Interestingly enough, the scurrilous German gossip Schomberg figures in both of these fictions, and both Axel Heyst and Falk are reserved Scandinavians. It is almost as though Conrad was deliberately using a basically similar triangular situation in both of these Schopenhauerian explorations or testings (i.e. the German gossip, the quiet Scandinavian, and a girl who in both cases in different ways is non-lingual). Falk is the direct opposite of Axel. He is the very incarnation of the 'will to live' as described by Schopenhauer – 'indestructible', 'a blind incessant impulse' and so on – and Falk is a survivor. Schopenhauer states that 'will is the thing-in-itself', a phrase used in connection with Falk, and hardly accidentally. In addition Schopenhauer stresses that the sexual drive and its satisfaction is 'the focus of the will, its concentration and highest expression' and that 'next to the love of life' it is 'the strongest and more powerful of motives'. All of which is mutely born out by Falk's behaviour. (It is worth noting that although Schopenhauer rejected suicide as a denial of the will to live, he did allow one species of suicide as being a genuine demonstration of the vanquishing of the will to live – voluntary starvation. This is the one act which Falk absolutely refuses to contemplate.) And in addition to these basic biological hungers, Conrad stresses a related aspect of Falk's behaviour. Not only is he like a child, an early evolutionary product in his appetites (Axel Heyst by contrast comes very late on), he is also a primitive economist. He is, it is pointed out more than once, a 'monopolist', exploiting the fact that he has the only tug on the river. The narrator indeed calls him a 'bloated monopolist', adding that 'It is possible he was unacquainted with the word, but he had a clear conception of the thing itself.' He also says: 'He extracted his pound and a half of flesh from each of us merchant-skippers with an inflexible sort of indifference which made him detested and even feared.' Given the narrator's knowledge of what is to be disclosed, the metaphorical linking of Falk's economic and other appetites can hardly be accidental.

I don't need to make too much of this point but I want to refer to one moment in the story which offers, in grotesque parodic form, a paradigmatic image of the interconnections I have mentioned. When the narrator is desperately trying to find any way to get his ship towed out of the harbour, he is told that there was a pilot called Johnson who had known the river, but who has since taken to drink, married a native, and 'gone to the bad'. Willing to try anything, the narrator seeks Johnson out. He finally finds where he lives (behind a 'mound of garbage') and goes in. Johnson is standing with a banana in his left hand; with his right hand he is flipping silver dollars onto the floor where his native wife, on all fours, is crawling for them. The banana nicely brings together food and sex, and the dollars reveal his – temporary – economic strength. In addition, the whole stance suggests, parodically, the assertion of male power through the ownership of the phallus and through economic supremacy – in general terms, through mastery of the means of production. The woman, also a native, is exploited and humiliated to an animal position of subjection on the floor. Also at this moment Johnson is the man with necessary information which he refuses to divulge, rebuffing the narrator with a drunken version of a gentleman's speech. Thus in a grotesque comic cameo we find the central concerns of the story outlined: the uses and abuses of power, bodily power, economic power, power through language; the banana, the dollar, and the mouth. But let me turn to the setting of the story.

Several of us, all more or less connected with the sea, were dining in
a small river-hostelry not more than thirty miles from London. . .
And through the wide windows we had a view of the Thames. . .
But the dinner was execrable, and all the feast was for the eyes.
That flavour of salt-water which for so many of us had been the
very water of life permeated our talk. He who hath known the
bitterness of the Ocean shall have its taste for ever in his mouth. But
one or two of us, pampered by the life of the land, complained of
hunger. It was impossible to swallow any of that stuff. And indeed
there was a strange mustiness in everything. The wooden dining-
room stuck out over the mud of the shore like a lacustrine dwelling;
the planks of the floor seemed rotten; a decrepid old waiter tottered
pathetically to and fro before an antediluvian and worm-eaten side-
board; the chipped plates might have been disinterred from some
kitchen midden near an inhabited lake; and the chops recalled times
more ancient still. They brought forcibly to one's mind the night of
ages when the primeval man, evolving the first rudiments of cookery
from his dim consciousness, scorched lumps of flesh at a fire of sticks
in the company of other good fellows; then, gorged and happy, sat
him back among the gnawed bones to tell his artless tales of experience – the tales of hunger and hunt – and of women, perhaps![1]

Of course the combining of a banquet and story-telling is as old as
Homer, and familiar from writers like Boccaccio. My interest is in
what Conrad has done with the traditional setting. There is first of all
the obvious grouping of the words 'flavour', 'talk', 'taste', 'mouth',
'hunger', 'swallow', as though Conrad is giving deliberate initial
emphasis to the various inter-permeating aspects of the oral functions.
The second notable feature of the description is the way Conrad uses
the setting to relate the narrative moment to the notional beginning
and end of man. Everything about it seems to portend some terminal
dissolution, since the emphasis is on decay, deterioration, decline
(rotten planks, worm-eaten furniture, chipped plates, and so on). The
waiter and the building alike are 'tottering' with age. Poised pre-
cariously over the mud of the river shore, the dining-room seems on
the verge of returning to the primordial slime, an idea additionally
fostered by references to 'lacustrine dwelling' and 'inhabited lake'. A
kitchen midden is of course a refuse heap (there is a lot of rubbish in
the story), and the hostelry would indeed seem to be close to a final
disintegration. On the other hand prehistoric and antediluvian times
are brought to mind leading to the idea of 'primeval man' just begin-

ning to cook and to narrate, suggesting that the two activites are coeval and inextricably linked. The proximity of 'gnawed bones' and 'artless tales' is a reminder that we engorge the world in the form of food just as metaphorically we devour it with the other sense ('all the feast was for the eyes'), and then disgorge it in the form of words: utterance, or outer-ance (making outer) is thus related to what we may call innerance, the crucial intersection point being the mouth which chews and talks. Of course the use of a group having a rotten meal in an old restaurant as a frame situation for a story about cannibalism is a suitable ironic device. More to the point we can see Conrad, here as elsewhere, exploring current ideas about 'evolution', conflating the prehistoric and the present and perhaps even the post-historic (which will simply be like the prehistoric, all architecture returned to mud and water), as a prelude to a tale which will question the accepted differences and distances between the primeval or primitive and the civilised. Prior to the emergence of the single narrator who tells the story of Falk, the group are said to be discussing a number of topics, including 'break-downs', and although the initial reference is to the breakdown of ships, the story will go on to touch on many other kinds of breakdown – the breakdown of community, of values and rules, of categories, conventions, and ideas, of language, and ultimately the breakdown of the body itself. Two of these breakdowns in particular – of category and of the body – make up my main subject, but for the moment I want to note the rather unusual amount of detail concerning the cooking given in the frame situation – inedible chops, scorched lumps of flesh, gnawed bones, etc. – and move to a point in the narrator's story in which details of cooking become of paramount importance.

The narrator has described how Falk has abducted Hermann's ship and left his, the narrator's, in the harbour. Perplexed by this action, the narrator has gone to Schomberg's hotel and restaurant for some tiffin and perhaps some explanation of Falk's behaviour. He is served with both, both equally foul. Once again inedible chops are on the menu and they are put in front of the narrator at the same times as Schomberg's 'talk gathered way like a slide of rubbish'. Schomberg's hatred for Falk is based on Falk's refusal to patronise his restaurant, and he goes into great detail about Falk's eating habits. Apparently Falk refuses to touch fried or roasted meat ('"a white man should eat like a white man . . . ought to eat meat, must eat meat"' complains Schomberg). He prefers instead rice boiled in a pot, and he eats alone. The narrator says that he could not be bothered about 'Falk's ideas of gastronomy' because 'I could expect from their study no clue to his conduct in matters of business, which seemed to me totally unrestrained by morality or even by the commonest sort of decency.' Of course the clue to Falk's business conduct is precisely to be found in his 'ideas of gastronomy' – as I have mentioned, the biological and the economic are shown to be intimately inter-related – and this becomes clear when Falk finally tells his story: i.e. the two planes merge and emerge at the level of language. Before considering that story I want to draw attention to the range of words relating to different states of food, different kinds of cooking, employed during this conversation with Schomberg – raw, boiled, fried, stale, and by implication roasted and rotten ('rotten meat' is specifically mentioned at a later point when Falk tells how he lived to weep tears of regret at the thought of some rotten meat which had been thrown overboard as a sanitary measure in the early days of the voyage fated to end in cannibalism i.e. what was decreed as inedible, non-food, at one point, at another seems like very desirable food).

At this point let me just recall a few of Lévi-Strauss' ideas concerning the raw and the cooked. I will limit myself to his brief essay on 'The Culinary Triangle'. Starting from the vowel triangle and the consonant triangle, Lévi-Strauss posits a culinary triangle. 'It would seem that the methodological principle which inspires such distinctions is transposable to other domains, notably cooking which, it has never been sufficiently emphasised, is with language a truly universal form of human activity: if there is no society without a language, nor is there any which does not cook in some manner at least some of its food.' The three points of his culinary triangle are the raw, the cooked, and the rotted. But within this abstract triangle there is another, concrete one relating to the fact that 'in any cuisine, nothing is simply cooked, but must be cooked in one fashion or another'. He then sets up the triangle of the roasted, the boiled, and the smoked, but his main emphasis is on the difference between roasting and boiling. His argument, based on the varying degrees of mediation between the raw food and the heat used to cook it, concludes 'the roasted is on the side of nature, the boiled on the side of culture'. Since eating human flesh (the manner of its preparation, *pace* Jessie Conrad, unspecified) Falk, at least in his eating habits, wants to limit himself to 'culture', insisting on the boiled and abhorring the roasted and fried. This might seem a slight point, but it is related to Lévi-Strauss' more general observation that the cooking of any society is a kind of language which in various ways says something about how that society feels about its relations to nature and culture. Seen in this light Falk's gastronomic habits are not an irrelevance but a very important illocutionary utterance connected with a desire to reassociate himself with 'culture'. More generally, I think it does suggest that Conrad was well aware of the basic ideas from which Lévi-Strauss is working – namely that cooking is, with language, a universal phenomenon among men, and that in deciding what is 'food' and what isn't, and then how to cook it to remove it from its natural continuum and, as it were, socialise it, man is exploring and articulating his sense of his complex relationship to both nature and culture. Since he participates in both and belongs wholly to neither realm, man must find this relationship endlessly ambiguous, endlessly engaging. Lévi-Strauss as anthropologist concentrates on how men think about nature and culture and then use the ensuing categories. Conrad as novelist concentrates on how individual men in specific circumstances articulate (perhaps unconsciously) their ambiguous position in nature and culture at a certain moment in time. In particular he was interested in men who, for whatever reason and in whatever set of circumstances, deviate from the prevailing prescriptive classifications and normative categories – whether these be categories of conduct (what 'one of us' should or should not do) or classifications of edibility (what a 'white man' should or should not eat). For it is in such acts of deviation – whether a jump from an apparently sinking ship, or the desperate consumption *in extremis* of a fellow human being – that the apparent stability and binding power of the categories themselves is questioned. Thus, by implication, all the ways in which we describe ourselves to ourselves are available for scrutiny; they can be de-reified, and 'discussed and even mistrusted' to use Conrad's own words.

In this connection let me just refer to Mauss' and Durkheim's book on *Primitive Classification* in which it is stated that 'it would be impossible to exaggerate . . . the state of indistinction from which the human mind developed.' They go on to argue that 'the first logical categories were social categories . . . it was because men were grouped, and thought of themselves in the form of groups, that in their ideas they grouped other things.' Thus classification is 'sociocentric', a projection onto things of ways in which men think about their relations to other men. I stress this because one might infer from this that if a man was in a situation in which all the usual ways of thinking about his relations to other men had 'broken down' so that he no longer conceived of himself as part of a society, a clan, or even a crew, and no longer felt any kind of communality or group solidarity, he might equally find that the habitual classifications of things simply had no meaning. To put it crudely, the completely de-socialised man would find himself in

a completely de-categorised world. This is exactly what happens to
Falk. He fell out of the world and has experienced reality unmediated
through hitherto unquestioned taxinomies. He has confronted, not only
the thing classified, but 'the thing itself'. I am suggesting then that in
Conrad's story the breakdown of categories is intimately related to the
more obvious themes of the breakdown of a ship and the breakdown
of the human body.

To support this suggestion I want to refer to two brief passages in
the narrator's account. When he first took charge of his ship he found
everything in a mess. In particular, a violin case proved to be full of
unreceipted bills and possibly corrupt estimates, with no trace of a
genuine 'fiddle' (I don't know whether Conrad intended the pun); and
an account book – which he hoped would enable him to order the
ship's affairs – turned out to be full of verse, 'rhymed doggerel of a
jovial and improper character'. Apparently a trivial point, but if we
note that what the narrator is encountering here is the wrong things in
the wrong containers, I think it is possible to see this as a minor example
of the failure or breakdown of categories I have been discussing. What
should be the art container or category (the violin case) contains bad
economics (unpaid bills), while what should be the proper economics
container (the account book) contains bad art (dirty poetry). Just as,
on Falk's voyage, the carpenter unexpectedly turned out to 'contain' a
murderer. If we may allow that 'man' and 'food' are two categories
which are usually considered necessarily distinct, then cannibalism too
becomes an example of the wrong things in the wrong categories, i.e.
man shifts into the food category, where he shouldn't be, just as he
ends up in another human stomach, again where he shouldn't be. It is
the most drastic case of the wrong thing in the wrong place, or a
relapse back into that primal lack of differentiation, that indistinction
described by Mauss. (This, incidentally, is, I think, why cannibalism
lies behind the first Greek tragedy, the Orestea trilogy.)

The second passage which interests me in this connection concerns
the narrator's account of Falk's appearance. He looks like a centaur,
'a composite creature. Not a man-horse . . . but a man-boat'. Here
again we have a fusion or con-fusion of usually distinct categories;
man-boat is as much of a taxonomic freak as man-food is a categorical
nightmare, and as much of a surprise as the conjoining of a violin case
and unpaid bills. 'Separated from his boat to me at least he seemed
incompleted. The tug itself without his head and torso on the bridge
looked mutilated as it were.'

Now, related to the theme of the fusion of what should be separate categories is the theme of the fragmentation of what should be a discrete unit, i.e. mutilation. Here again let me recall that at the silent centre of this story is the act of cutting up the human body (fragmentation) to turn it into food (fusion). This theme is very interestingly prepared for by the narrator's earlier description of Hermann's shop-like ship (another slight categorical anomaly – a ship-shop!) In general Hermann is associated with all kinds of compulsive hygiene, and in particular his boat is constantly associated with cleaning and washing clothes. The narrator gives a detailed description of the family washing when it is 'exhibited' to dry.

> It covered the poop entirely. The afternoon breeze would incite to a weird and flabby activity all that crowded mass of clothing, with its vague suggestions of drowned, mutilated and flattened humanity. Trunks without heads waved at you arms without hands; legs without feet kicked fantastically with collapsible flourishes; and there were long white garments, that taking the wind fairly through their neck openings edged with lace, became for a moment violently distended as by the passage of obese and invisible bodies.

What is 'suggested' here – note the word – is the kind of disintegration and mutilation of the human body which, not to dwell on it in too much hypothetical detail, presumably takes place in an act of cannibalism as the body is cut up for purposes of assimilation. But this is not the body, not the 'thing itself', but clothing, the man-made *container* for the thing itself. Clothing is, as it were, an homologous reference to the thing itself, a set of signs which can of course be separated out into different pieces without any harm to the actual body. In this respect clothing is obviously like language, a functional system of references to 'the thing itself'. Note that throughout the story Hermann is associated with clothes, just as Falk is nearly always described in terms of his body presence and posture. With Hermann we are told what he was wearing; with Falk we are told how he was sitting. Falk has participated in the thing itself, the actual mutilation of the human body, not a suggestive dance of signs on a washing line.

Connected to this is their different relationships to language: Hermann is verbose, voluble, hysterical, an over-user of words; Falk is invariably silent, and even when he has to talk he is made to seem almost non-lingual (his speech has no inflexions, and he speaks without emphases). This of course is why he is drawn to the young niece in the way that he is. She too is described as pure magnificent body, with a constant stress on volume, mass, and so on; and she is utterly silent as

well as apparently nameless, as though having no traffic with language.
She too is the thing itself. Language, categories, containers, coverings,
clothes – I am suggesting that these are deliberately inter-connected in
this story. Set over against them is the body, man's corporeal,
'corporate existence'. I stress this phrase used by Conrad in the story
because it brings in the sense not only of the individual human body
(the 'skin-bound organism') but also of a body of men who form some
kind of functioning group which bestows on them their social as
opposed to their physical identity (culturally-interrelated organisms).
Thus one of Conrad's main concerns is to ask what it is that holds
man/men together both physically and socially. And by fixing on the
literal act of cannibalism Conrad can explore in a particularly powerful way what happens when established ways of holding man/men
together 'break down'. At one point the narrator translates *Schiff-
führer* for his listeners. 'That's how they call a Master Mariner in
Germany. I prefer our way. The alliteration is good, and there is
something in the nomenclature that gives to us as a body the sense of
corporate existence.' Thus 'nomenclature', 'body', and 'corporate
existence', are casually though pointedly brought together at the start
of a story which concerns an occasion of their disintegration.

Before moving onto the subject of 'narration', I want to note that
the idea of, or word for, cannibalism recurs frequently in Conrad,
from *Nigger of the 'Narcissus'*, in which Singleton is dignified by a
comparison with a cannibal chief, to *The Secret Agent* in which Stevie
is fragmented into 'what might have been an accumulation of raw
material for a cannibal feast', blown to bits by a metaphor carelessly
dropped earlier in the book. But more important is Conrad's use of
cannibals in *Heart of Darkness*. They are of course admirable figures
in that story: 'Fine fellows – cannibals – in their place. They were
men one could work with.' In addition they are victimised and deprived
on the three levels I have mentioned. They are virtually without food,
thus suffering on the biological level; they are shamelessly exploited
economically – the white men throw their food overboard because it
smells rotten and give them pieces of brass wire as a substitute currency; and they are out of their own language and culture on the ship,
so that their particular concepts and cultural rituals are neither understood nor allowed to operate. The amazing thing to Marlow is why
they didn't eat the white men:

Why in the name of all the gnawing devils of hunger they didn't go
for us – they were thirty to five – and have a good tuck in for once,

amazes me now when I think of it. They were big powerful men, with not much capacity to weigh the consequences. . . And I saw that something restraining, one of those human secrets that baffle probability, had come into play there.

And Marlow then embarks on the long passage pondering the mysteries of 'restraint'; the mystery of what restrains man, and what ensues when normal restraints fail, are central subjects in Conrad. In this story the man without restraint is, of course, Kurtz. It is worth noting in passing that the savage who is killed because he opens the ship's shutters too wide is, rather oddly, compared to Kurtz. 'Poor fool! If he had only left that shutter alone. He had no restraint, no restraint – just like Kurtz.' You will remember that around Kurtz's dwelling there is no enclosure or fence of any kind, the rails have disappeared, there are holes in the roof, what architecture does remain is decaying (remember the river hostelry at the start of *Falk*); there is almost no remaining structure between inside and outside. This is a topographical projection of Kurtz's unshuttered consciousness. He has opened the mental shutters too wide, and in the event he is the real cannibal in the book: not necessarily literally, though the shrunken heads and unspeakable rites hardly rule out that possibility, but metaphorically. Thus Marlow's description of him: 'I saw him open his mouth wide – it gave him a weirdly voracious aspect, as though he had wanted to swallow all the air, all the earth, all the men before him'; and later, 'I had a vision of him on the stretcher, opening his mouth voraciously, as if to devour all the earth with all its mankind.'

In this connection I want to record a fascinating quotation which Norman Sherry includes in *Conrad's Western World*. He confirms that the crews of many steamers on the Upper Congo were mainly from Bangala and were indeed often 'joyfully cannibalistic', like Marlow's crew. He writes: 'The brother of Bapulula (a popular pilot on the mission steamer Peace on the river at this time), when asked if he ate human flesh answered, "Ah! I wish I could eat everybody on earth." ' This, Sherry found in a book by W. Holman Bentley called *Pioneering on the Congo*, published in London in 1910. Whether Conrad had also heard this story, or whether it is just a fascinating coincidence hardly matters. The point is that Conrad goes to considerable lengths to make us see Kurtz as a much more horrifying cannibal than the literal cannibal who may or may not feel like eating everybody (and for the most part cannibalism is not indiscriminate and is usually highly ritualised in cases of extreme 'meat hunger'), but who reveals seemingly inexhaustible reserves of self-restraint. Kurtz wants to eat everything. This is a study of a certain kind of white imperial consciousness which, as it were, wants to engorge the world and transform it into self. With Kurtz it is always 'My Intended, my ivory, my station, my river, my – everything belonged to him. . .' But of course if everything belongs to you, you belong to everything – all slavery is reciprocal. Kurtz wants to consume all that is not-Kurtz; in the event he is consumed by the not-Kurtz. This is why he is a shadow, both satiated and void. Such all-absorbing egoism, in attempting to annex the environment, to subsume all pronouns under the one sovereign possessive personal pronoun 'my', so far from leading to any genuine growth or extension of self can only lead to a dissolution of self back into 'other', a progressive emptying of human substance, a horrifying experience as Kurtz's last words attest. After his misguided and unrestrained attempts at feasting Kurtz is inevitably 'hollow at the core'. Of course this is not all there is to say about Kurtz; he is after all 'a remarkable man'. But I think that Conrad was dramatising in the figure of Kurtz that terrifying drive to annihilate difference, which is too often to be found at the heart of any so-called civilising, imperial drive, or indeed at the heart of society itself (see the treatment meted out to Yanko Goorall in 'Amy Foster' where the community torment and persecute him on account of his 'difference'). This appropriation or nihilation of the other brings us back to cannibalism, but a cannibalism of consciousness which if not restrained will attempt to devour otherness altogether. The destructive potential of such a drive hardly needs underlining.

One of the processes which binds men together, as opposed to breaking them down, is narration, the establishing of a circuit of discourse in a particular way. Conrad's narrative technique in 'Falk' is familiar from the Marlow stories. He starts in the first person plural – 'we', 'us', 'our talk'. This strategy has three important, and illusory, effects. It conceals the solitude of writing behind the communality of conversing; it seems to transform the author into an auditor of a tale not of his making; and it makes the written text appear as a vehicle for speech. Then one of 'us' begins to tell a story – in this case not Marlow but an unnamed narrator. This attempt to make the script simulate the voice is connected to that 'phonocentrism' of Western culture about which Derrida has written, but I do not intend to engage that large topic here. Rather I want to concentrate briefly on one or two aspects of Conrad's deployment of this well-established use of a narrator. When he first introduced Marlow in *Youth* Conrad added a parenthesis: '(at least I think that is how he spelt his name)'. Since

Conrad the writer is in fact bestowing the name this seems a rather odd little trick. It is the kind of thing we are more likely to say as an aside, but in any case it would always be in a context where there is a pre-existent body, already named. In fiction there is only the name, and that I think is what Conrad's little strategy (the namer pretending to vanish before the name) is aimed at concealing: it is part of an attempt to give the illusion of substance where no substance exists, to make the text evoke a corporeal presence. This is related to the more prevailing sense in Conrad of the tension between two feelings: first, the recognition that language can never hold any substantial reality, a realisation which leads in one direction to a sense of both the autonomy and futility of language; and secondly, the recognition that language must constantly attempt to establish some kind of relationship to non-lingual realities, a realisation which leads in the other direction to a sense of the heteronomy and purposefulness of language. This double sense of language is exactly represented in the relationship between Conrad as isolated writer, and Marlow as engaged speaker; and this double attitude towards language's incapacities and obligations – the necessity to tell, the impossibility of telling – is often in evidence when Conrad is exploring the problems of narrating in his fiction.

Very often, for instance, he will associate the attempt to narrate something with mist, fog, dusk, veils, wax, water, etc., phenomena which resist clarity of outline and which suggest desubstantiation, deindividuation, lack of stable definition. Marlow himself often alludes to the problems of narrating and one of his phrases catches exactly the tension I am trying to describe. When he is recounting his exchange with Jewel in *Lord Jim* Marlow describes both his problem with her and with his listeners:

'It is hard to tell you what it was precisely she wanted to wrest from me. Obviously it would be something very simple – the simplest impossibility in the world; as, for instance, the exact description of a cloud. She wanted an assurance, a statement, a promise, an explanation – I don't know how to call it: the thing has no name.'

The exact description of a cloud – that is the impossibility. It is also what is required. The thing has no name. Just as in the case of Marlow's own notional existence, the name has no thing. But the thing must be named, and the name must be thinged: simple impossibilities. Marlow's predicament is both the projection and complement of Conrad's own. The thing must be named in the interests of communality (remember the connection made in the story between 'body', 'nomen-

clature' and 'the sense of corporate existence'). There can of course be
no 'corporate existence' without naming and telling, though Conrad
was aware of the danger of the other extreme – all speech and no body.
Thus Kurtz empties himself into the illusory omnipotence of words.
When he dies Marlow doesn't bother to go and see whatever it might
be that remains. 'The voice was gone. What else had been there?' As
elsewhere in Conrad, we are curiously close to Beckett.

Turning to 'Falk' we may note that not only does the thing have no
name, the narrator has no name (like the niece in *his* story). This odd
withholding of information in Conrad is a matter for separate study;
it goes along with his refusal to name Bangkok, a taking away of an
already given name, and is part of the strategy of despecification
practised so subtly by Conrad. It is also practised by his narrator. Thus
in this story the narrator often uses phrases like 'his name was
Tottersen, or something like that', 'I can't tell now', 'of some sort',
and Conrad is hereby building into his text, albeit on a small scale, a
deliberate imprecision, a sense of approximation, of dubiety, of the
erosion of names and identities, an encroaching inexactness. It is part
of the attempt to make his very art*ful* piece of writing reproduce the
art*less*ness of the told tale. It is a strangely paradoxical procedure,
though not perhaps a rare one, for art has always looked for ways to
conceal, or run away from, its own artfulness. In Conrad's case I think
the motive is to undermine the illusory finality and exactitude of the
written text, to unstabilise its silent impersonal unquestionable
authority, by reintroducing the hesitations of the speaking voice, the
uncertainties and fadings of memory. This is not necessarily part of a
philosophic attempt to impugn completely the capabilities of language
as such. I think it is more an attempt to rephysicalise language, as it
were, to get it off the page and back into the mouth, and make us
aware of how intimately related it is to the body.

This is born out, to my mind, by the unusually detailed descriptions
in 'Falk', not of what people say, but of how people speak. Seldom if
ever is reported speech introduced or concluded with the simple conventional 'he said'. The tone, timbre, volume, are often given, and the
physicality of speaking is constantly brought home to us: to take some
example of words and phrases used in the story, people whoop, yell,
mutter, grunt, make 'loud hospitable ejaculations', talk volubly, set
tongues clacking, babble, mumble, hiss, fume, fret, speak in undertones,
lecture the narrator with 'deafening gibberish', shoot out a string of
words, and so on. At one point Hermann begins 'to mumble and chew
between his teeth something that sounded like German swear-words',

the niece simply 'moves her lips slightly', while Falk makes 'a deep noise in his throat'. Schomberg 'mouths' his gossip, and he in particular is 'unable to hold his tongue'. ('Tongue' is a very important word in Conrad, and it is picked up in the last sentence of the story when the narrator says 'I shouldn't wonder if Schomberg's tongue had succeeded at last in scaring Falk away for good': the dangerous power of the unheld tongue was very real to Conrad. Schomberg is, as it were, the black *alter*-image of the valuable narrator.) In addition, the narrator has varying degrees of trouble with the somewhat Germanic English of the Hermann family – they offer a sort of spectrum of degrees of intelligibility – and he reports that Falk's speech 'was not transparently clear'. In the central scene the niece says nothing, Falk is reluctant to speak, while Hermann says too much (he makes Falk's story seem unreal – language can vaporise action, and destroy truth). It is the narrator who tries to say what is necessary, and this brings in the whole activity of 'translation'; literally of one language into another (as when the narrator has to look up *mensch* and *fressen* after listening to Hermann's rantings), but more generally the translation of sounds into meanings, grunts into words, silence into significance, substance into semantics, or, in the light of my title, the translation of food into narrative, food here comprising the experience consumed through the senses. (The situation is similar to the one Conrad exploits in *Under Western Eyes*.)

Narration takes on a special importance in Conrad as part of the constituting process of man. We must eat to live, but we must also narrate to live. Sartre's Roquentin poses the question in *La Nausée* – live or tell. In Conrad these are not mutually exclusive alternatives; rather, telling is a crucial component of living, at least living with 'a sense of corporate existence'. The idea of living being dependent on narrating may be found in other writers; for instance, John Barth in *Chimera* sees it as the basic meaning of the situation of Scheherazade, and the French critic Todorov makes a similar point about the whole subject of the *Thousand and One Nights* and other story collections, pointing out that from the point of view of the characters 'narration equals life: the absence of narration, death'. For Conrad it is not a matter of biological survival, but of communal survival, though after this study of 'break-down' the very idea of communality can never recover its old stability. But as far as possible experience has to be made assimilable and shareable through narration, even though as it approaches the central core of the experience language fails into silence. The narrator has to 'translate' Falk's unique wordless experience into the vocabulary of people like Hermann, his listeners, and ourselves, not just stating facts but creating a context in which the facts generate meaning. Recalling the terms I mentioned at the start, we may say that he has to bring the anguish of the wigwam into the security of the kitchen, revealing in the process that such a static opposition is a false antinomy, for the wigwam has its sanities, and there is an unreason of the kitchen too: the apparent polarities dissolve into each other. Falk had to eat the uneatable, and in so doing he discovers the radical relativity of cultural categories; the narrator has to speak the unspeakable, and in so doing he encounters the insoluble problematics of utterance. In these two figures Conrad dramatises in an extreme form his sense of the profound paradoxes on which human life – itself a shifting and unstable concept – is founded.

NOTE

1. After giving this paper Professor Emily Dalgarno from Boston University told me that the manuscript of 'Falk' at Yale shows that this paragraph reveals an amount of working over which is unusual in Conrad. In a letter which contains evidence of this working over she informed me that 'it is very unusual to find traces of such laborious and painstaking effort to get a sentence right.' This would seem to add some justification to my decision to single the passage out for special attention.

3 Impressionism and Symbolism in *Heart of Darkness**

IAN WATT

The Preface to *The Nigger of the 'Narcissus'* is usually read as an impressionist document; but much of Conrad's critical position there is also consonant with that of the Symbolists – it is, for instance, very close to Verlaine's *'De la musique avant toute chose'* (*Art poétique*) in making it the supreme aim of literary style to achieve 'the magic suggestiveness of music'. Conrad also wrote in a letter that in *The Nigger of the 'Narcissus'* he had tried 'to get through the veil of details at the essence of life' (27 January 1897);[1] and this avowal of a transcendental perspective later recurs even more explicitly: 'How fine it could be . . .' Conrad wrote to Ford, 'if the idea had a substance and words a magic power, if the invisible could be snared into a shape.'[2]

Conrad expressed this wish to make the idea visible a month before he began *Heart of Darkness*, a work which, among other things, is generally reckoned the supreme example of Conrad's importance in the modern Symbolist literary tradition. Marvin Mudrick, for example, declares with almost pardonable hyperbole that 'After *Heart of Darkness*, the recorded moment – the word – was irrecoverably symbol.'[3] Mudrick's analysis is based on the way Conrad developed 'the moral resources inherent in every recorded sensation'; and he thus surely implies that in *Heart of Darkness* Conrad gave a larger symbolic meaning to an Impressionist recording of particular experience. *Heart of Darkness* is the key work for examining the relation of symbolist and impressionist elements in Conrad for another reason; the fact that the interpretation of its symbolism continues to provoke much critical controversy.

* Portions of this essay were given at the University of Notre Dame (18 April, 1974), at the International Conference on Conrad at Canterbury (18 July, 1974), and at the 1974 meeting of the International Association of University Professors of English at Los Angeles (20 August). I am very grateful both to those who invited me to speak, and to those who took part in the ensuing discussions.

I

At the beginning of *Heart of Darkness* the primary narrator explains that the meanings of Marlow's tales are characteristically difficult to encompass:

> The yarns of seamen have a direct simplicity, the whole meaning of which lies within the shell of a cracked nut. But Marlow was not typical (if his propensity to spin yarns be excepted), and to him the meaning of an episode was not inside like a kernel but outside, enveloping the tale which brought it out only as a glow brings out a haze, in the likeness of one of those misty halos that sometimes are made visible by the spectral illumination of moonshine (p. 48).

Conrad's distinction between the usual story and Marlow's uses a metaphor based on contrasted arrangements of two concentric spheres. In the first arrangement, that of the typical seaman's yarn, the direction given our minds is, to use a term from Newtonian physics, 'centripetal'; the narrative vehicle is the shell, the larger outside sphere which encloses a smaller sphere, the inner kernel of truth; and as readers we are invited to seek this central core of meaning. Marlow's tales, on the other hand, are typically 'centrifugal'; the relation of the spheres is reversed; now the narrative vehicle is the smaller inside sphere, and its function is merely to reveal a circumambient universe of meanings which are not normally visible, and cannot be seen except in association with the story, just as the haze appears only when there is a glow.

Conrad's metaphor clearly implies the complementary, even the symbiotic, relationship of the impressionist and the symbolist aspects of the narrative as a whole. The symbolist aspect mainly depends on the geometric nature of the haze, the outer sphere of larger meaning. It is intangible and theoretically infinite, since, like St Augustine's God and unlike the husk of a nut, it lacks any ascertainable circumference; and yet it depends on the finite glow. Thus the combination of Marlow's two spheres constitutes a symbol precisely in Carlyle's sense of it – 'the Infinite is made to blend itself with the Finite, to stand visible, and as it were, attainable there.'[4]

The impressionist component of the passage is mainly evident in the sensory qualities of Conrad's two spheres. The narrative depicts a meaning which is only as fitfully and tenuously visible as a hitherto unnoticed presence of dust particles and water vapour in what normally looks like a dark void. In this there is a clear parallel with one of the new features of impressionist painting. Claude Monet, for instance, said of the critics who mocked his obscurity: 'Poor blind idiots. They want us to see everything clearly, even through the fog.'[5] The difficulty of seeing is not a gratuitous defiance of the public; haze in Monet – and even more explicitly in Conrad's image – is not an accidental atmospheric interference which stands between us and the 'real' object; the difficulty and the obscurity are essential parts of what the artist is trying to convey.

Much the same idea, and expressed in a similar metaphor, occurs in a classic later statement on the novel in 'Modern Fiction', Virginia Woolf's 1919 essay. There she exempts Conrad, together with Hardy, from her charge against the 'ill-fitting vestments' of the traditional novel, and of the Edwardians, H. G. Wells, Arnold Bennett and John Galsworthy.[6] Her basic objection is that if we 'look within' ourselves we see 'a myriad impressions' quite unrelated to anything that goes on in the traditional novel; and if we could express 'this unknown and uncircumscribed spirit' of life freely, 'there would be no plot, no comedy, no tragedy, no love interest or catastrophe in the accepted style, and perhaps not a single button sewn on as the Bond Street tailors would have it'. For, Virginia Woolf finally affirms, 'Life is not a series of gig-lamps symmetrically arranged; life is a luminous halo, a semi-transparent envelope surrounding us from the beginning of consciousness to the end.'

Virginia Woolf's basic metaphor, the luminous halo, is impressionist in nature; but it is used to describe an aim for the novel very like the characteristic symbolist attempt to reach outwards, to penetrate the semi-transparent, and therefore semi-opaque, envelope of the world outside. With the impressionist painters, the first object of creation is light; and with the symbolists it is most characteristically an inner light of the spirit which illuminates a part of the surrounding darkness.

II

Before applying the description of Marlow's mode of story-telling to a passage from *Heart of Darkness*, a brief historical perspective seems necessary; for, both in their origins and in their later course through modern literature, impressionism and symbolism are essentially manifestations of various general tendencies which first came to prominence in the romantic period; both are anti-traditional assertions of the private individual vision; and they both took their full shape during the epistemological crisis of the late nineteenth century, a crisis most

familiar to literary history under the twin rubrics of the death of God
and the disappearance of the omniscient author.

'Impressionism' as a specifically aesthetic term was apparently
launched in 1874 by a journalist, Louis Leroy, to ridicule the affronting
formlessness of the pictures exhibited at the Salon des Indépendants,
and particularly of Claude Monet's painting entitled 'Impression:
Sunrise'.[7] In one way or another all the main Impressionists, from
Monet to Renoir, made it their aim to render the appearance of objects
as they saw them under particular atmospheric conditions, an aim
which, as E. H. Gombrich has shown, allots the impressionists a decisive
role in the process of art's long transition from portraying what all men
know to portraying what the individual actually sees.[8]

This transition is recorded in the history of the word 'impression'
and its cognates, a history which embodies in more general terms the
growing disjunction between public systems of knowledge – what all
men know – and the ephemeral indefiniteness of private experience –
what the individual actually sees. The concentration of philosophical
thought upon epistemological problems from Descartes and Hume
onwards made the relation between individual sensation and ascertainable truth increasingly problematic; and the disjunction found more
radical expression at the end of the eighteenth century, when the
increasingly pervasive authority of a mechanistic and sensational
psychology in effect drove the religious, imaginative, emotional and
aesthetic orders of being into the private and internal world of the
individual. After the romantics this process took a more deeply sceptical
direction, which was most memorably expressed in the famous
Conclusion to *The Renaissance* (1868–73), where Pater speaks of how
'each mind keeping as a solitary prisoner its own dream of a world'
can actually experience directly only 'the passage and dissolution of
impressions, images, sensations . . .'

The critical thought of Pater, and of the nineties, are both embodi-
ments of a fusion between various Impressionist and Symbolist
tendencies which had reached their fullest expression in France. The
French Impressionists and Symbolists were exactly contemporary;
Verlaine, Rimbaud and Mallarmé wrote during the heyday of the
Impressionist painters in the seventies, although symbolism as a conscious movement came a little later – in poetry when Jean Moréas
wrote his manifesto in 1886, and in painting at the Café Volpini
exhibition in 1889. Compared to the views of earlier painters and
writers, there were many parallels between the attitudes of the adherents
of symbolism and impressionism both in painting and poetry; they

fully agreed in rejecting intellectual conceptualisation and established artistic traditions in the name of expressing a directly-apprehended personal and subjective vision.

In one important respect, it is true, the impressionists and symbolists took logically opposite directions. The Impressionist painters began with the outside world as it appeared to their own subjective perception, whereas the Symbolist painters wished, as Moreau put it, to 'clothe the idea in perceptible form'; in effect the two schools differed in approaching their task from different ends of the same newly-intensified polarity between individual consciousness and external reality.[9]

In literature the symbolists, and especially Mallarmé and later Valéry, while just as opposed to logical conceptualisation as any Impressionist, nevertheless wanted to get larger ideas into literature somehow, although they were ideas of a very special kind; ideas which belonged only to the inner world of the consciousness, which could only be summoned through the portals of the creative imagination, and which were only manifested to the senses of the artist or his audience in the shape of symbols.

Here symbolism must be seen as part of the same historical process which produced the individualist and subjective direction of impressionism, since the imagination and the symbol are distinctively romantic and post-romantic preoccupations. The process by which the individual mind attributed a larger intellectual or emotional meaning to particular objects and events was hardly a problem in earlier periods, because the whole universe was generally assumed to constitute a fixed order in which every item had its communally-agreed meaning – most obviously in mythology which gave a spiritual role to everything in the external world. Men could hardly be consciously concerned with symbolism when the larger meaning of objects was already established, as with the cross, for instance, or the apple. But the Romantic writers felt impelled to assign their own personal symbolic meanings to natural objects, to mountains, birds and flowers; and they did so by creating new orders of meaning which were not those of the established orthodoxies but of the individual imagination. After Blake and Wordsworth it was commonly assumed that the poet had access to previously unknown immanent connections between the external world and spiritual reality.

This general epistemological assumption is reflected in one of the characteristic expressive idioms of modern literature. The post-romantic symbol is likely to be private rather than public; but it is not

intended to stand for a single and definable concept. Even the poets
who were most attached to esoteric or transcendental beliefs tended in
their writing to rely primarily on the many natural connotations of
their images; Shelley's skylark, Keats's nightingale, or the swans of
Mallarmé and Yeats – none of these are univocal or allegorical symbols;
their meanings arise from the varied inherent suggestions of the poetic
object, and only to the extent that these are mobilised in the poem so
that the reader concretely experiences all the implications of seeing
and not seeing, singing and not singing, soaring and not soaring. The
essential meaning of these symbolic images is established in a way quite
unlike those traditional in allegory, a way that bears out Yeats's contrast between a symbol, which was 'the only possible expression of
some individual essence, a transparent lamp about a spiritual flame',
and allegory, which was 'one of many possible representations of an
embodied thing or familiar principle, and belong[ed] to fancy and not
imagination . . .'[10]

Yeats's metaphor of the lamp and the flame for the inherent, natural
and personal way that object and meaning come together in modern
symbolism, is fairly close to Conrad's metaphor of the two spheres;
and both of them implicitly require a special kind of symbolic interpretation from the critic.

The significance of any particular symbolic object or its verbal sign
is usually established either by arbitrary convention, as in algebra, or,
more commonly, by an extension of its normal properties. Thus we
understand that 'the apple of my eye' means a beloved object merely
by an extension of our knowledge that an apple has the properties of
looking beautiful and being good. As with many other objects, however, the apple has also been assigned various conventional or allegorical
meanings which can only be understood by reference to specific bodies
of knowledge. The story of Discordia at the wedding of Peleus and
Thetis, for instance, is the item of special knowledge required to interpret the conventional phrase an 'apple of discord'. This distinction
between the two kinds of symbol can be summarily expressed by the
neologisms *homeophor* and *heterophor*: 'the apple of my eye' is a
homeophor because we can arrive at its symbolic meaning by an
imaginative extension of the *same* or *similar* properties as are normally
possessed by the object; the 'apple of discord' is a *heterophor* because
its symbolic meaning is carried by *something else* – in this case by
another body of knowledge.

There are obviously many historical reasons why allegory should
have gone out of general favour in a period characterised by less and

less community of belief in any body of knowledge, and thus why modern literature should predominantly rely on *homeophoric* symbolism. It also follows that, in fiction as well as in poetry, modern writers should typically have developed an expressive idiom which activates this kind of symbolic response.

To begin with, the symbolic images described by Yeats can only carry multiple suggestions to the extent that they evoke all the potencies of particular individual experience; and the symbolist method therefore makes much the same primary demand as impressionism or imagism[11] in requiring the writer to render the object with an idiosyncratic immediacy of vision which is freed from any intellectual prejudgment or explanatory gloss. The reader must also feel that he is in the presence of an unfamiliar hierarchy of attention – it is, for instance, the emphasis on some details and the absence of others which makes it clear that the birds in the poems of Mallarmé or Yeats are presented not for their ornithological or autobiographical interest, but for some other purpose, some larger complex of connecting values and meanings. These values and meanings are not stated, but only the hypothesis of their hidden presence, it seems, could explain the special emphases with which the writer's perceptions are conveyed; the obtrusive disparity between a particular image and the significance apparently attributed to it creates a semantic gap which we feel called on to fill with our own symbolic interpretation.

One logical result of this semantic gap, and more generally of the characteristic idiom and objectives of impressionism and symbolism, has been to give a much more important, but also a much more difficult, role to the literary critic. He is faced with the task of explaining to the public in discursive expository prose a literature whose authors deliberately kept their works as free as possible from rational or conceptual definition. He confronts an incompleteness of utterance, an indeterminacy of meaning, a seemingly unconscious or random association of images, which simultaneously demand and defy logical exegesis. In the fiction which belongs primarily to the impressionist school, such as that of Stephen Crane, or to its imagist and later heritages, such as that of Hemingway, the idiosyncratic sequence of vivid particularities asks to be construed and translated into the realm of public discourse; but once translated into that expository language not much is left, and its residue of general meaning is likely, in the critic's rendition of it, to seem both meagre and ambiguous. The difficulty is even greater for writing with a strong symbolist element, where there is, in addition, a semantic gap to be bridged, and an intangible unifying essence to be discovered. In either case the critic is asked to provide a commentary which will transcend the very epistemological problems which dominate the expressive idiom of the literature he is analysing; no wonder, then, that the modern critic is prone to an excessive metaphysical abstraction in aims and language, and to a notorious compulsion for extravagant symbol-hunting.

This last tendency, which was particularly powerful during the apogee of the prestige of literary criticism in the fifties, seems to have been partly based on the idea that the essence of symbolism lay, not in its attempt to suggest the larger possibilities of meaning behind individual experience, but in its use of an essentially esoteric purpose and method. In the case of *Heart of Darkness* this *heterophoric* approach often concentrated its attention on the episode where Marlow receives his appointment from the Trading Company, to which, at long last, we can turn.

III

A narrow and deserted street in deep shadow, high houses, innumerable windows with venetian blinds, a dead silence, grass sprouting between the stones, imposing carriage archways right and left, immense double doors standing ponderously ajar. I slipped through one of these cracks, went up a swept and ungarnished staircase, as arid as a desert, and opened the first door I came to. Two women, one fat and the other slim, sat on straw-bottomed chairs, knitting black wool. The slim one got up and walked straight at me – still knitting with down-cast eyes – and only just as I began to think of getting out of her way, as you would for a somnambulist, stood still, and looked up. Her dress was a plain as an umbrella-cover, and she turned round without a word and preceded me into a waiting-room. I gave my name, and looked about (pp. 55–8).

Marlow is ushered into the presence of the Director, and then

In about forty-five seconds I found myself again in the waiting-room with the compassionate secretary, who, full of desolation and sympathy, made me sign some document. I believe I undertook amongst other things not to disclose any trade secrets. Well, I am not going to.

I began to feel slightly uneasy. You know I am not used to such ceremonies, and there was something ominous in the atmosphere. It was just as though I had been let into some conspiracy – I don't know – something not quite right; and I was glad to get out. In the outer room the two women knitted black wool feverishly. People were arriving, and the younger one was walking back and forth introducing them. The old one sat on her chair. Her flat cloth slippers were propped up on a foot-warmer, and a cat reposed on her lap. She wore a starched white affair on her head, had a wart on one cheek, and silver-rimmed spectacles hung on the tip of her nose. She glanced at me above the glasses. The swift and indifferent placidity of that look troubled me. Two youths with foolish and cheery countenances were being piloted over, and she threw at them the same quick glance of unconcerned wisdom. She seemed to know all about them and about me too. An eerie feeling came over me. She seemed uncanny and fateful. Often far away there I thought of these two, guarding the door of Darkness, knitting black wool as for a warm pall, one introducing, introducing continuously to the unknown, the other scrutinising the cheery and foolish faces with unconcerned old eyes. *Ave!* Old knitter of black wool. *Morituri te salutant.* Not many of those she looked at ever saw her again – not half, by a long way.

Several critics have made the two knitters a primary basis for a large-scale *heterophoric* interpretation of *Heart of Darkness* in which Marlow's whole journey becomes a symbolic version of the traditional descent into Hell, such as that in the sixth book of Virgil's *Aeneid*,[12] or in Dante's *Inferno*. Marlow certainly presents his experience in the general perspective of the pagan and Christian traditions of a journey to the underworld; this is sufficiently explicit when he talks of the knitters 'guarding the door of Darkness', and of the two youths 'being piloted over'. But it is surely only a primary assumption that there was a single kernel of truth to be extracted, that a thorough-going *heterophoric* interpretation was a good idea, which could have impelled one critic to assert that there is 'a close structural parallel between *Heart of Darkness* and the *Inferno*', and proceed to make the Company Station Limbo, the Central Station the abode of the fraudulent, and Kurtz both a 'traitor to kindred' and a Lucifer.[13]

Marlow goes on to make some further *heterophoric* references; but they are also surely intended merely to place the two knitters in the ageless perspective of the heartless unconcern of spectators at an ordeal which may be fatal to the protagonists. This unconcern is also evoked by the *tricoteuses* callously knitting at the guillotine, and by the crowds at the Roman circus to whom the gladiators address their scornful farewell in Marlow's rather pretentious interjection: '*Ave!* old knitters of black wool, *Morituri te salutant.*' These parallels, however, are surely as local in function as the earlier historical allusions to Drake and Franklin; once made, they are dropped, if only because keeping the parallel going would detract both from the immediacy of the narrative and from its freedom to evoke other associations and suggestions.

Certainly, if we are seeking an interpretation which makes *Heart of Darkness* as a whole an essentially *heterophoric* work, we are likely to alert our attention too exclusively to clues of a specific kind. Why does Conrad give us only two fates? Which one is Clotho the spinner? and which is Lachesis the weaver? Did the Greeks know about knitting anyway? Where are the shears? What symbolic meaning can there be in the fact that the thin one lets people *in* to the room and then *out* again – a birth and death ritual, perhaps? Thus preoccupied, however fruitfully or unfruitfully, our attention will hardly be able to respond fully in the immediate *homeophoric* suggestion of how the thin knitter 'got up and walked straight at me – still knitting with downcast eyes – and only just as I began to think of getting out of her way, as you would for a somnambulist, stood still, and looked up. Her dress was as plain as an umbrella-cover . . .'

If we submit ourselves to the vivid impressionistic particularity of these details their connotations take us far beyond our primary sense of the fateful, uncanny and impassive atmosphere of the scene to a larger awareness of a rigid, mechanical, blind, and automatised world: the thin knitter does not speak or see or even move in relation to others; her shape recalls an umbrella and its tight black cover; there has been no effort to soften its hard and narrow ugliness with rhythmic movements, rounded forms, or living colours. It is not her reminding us of the classical Fates that really matters, but that she is herself a fate – a dehumanised death in life to herself and to others, and thus a prefiguring symbol of what the Trading Company does to its creatures.

A full analysis of the scene would no doubt reveal an inexhaustible network of expanding symbolic suggestions; one incidental reason for the vogue of *heterophoric* criticism may be that it bypasses the endless and necessarily tentative explication which is theoretically entailed by symbolist writing. Here, however, there is room only for a very summary illustration of how the typical features of the impressionist and symbolist expressive idiom combine to illuminate one of the general themes of *Heart of Darkness*.

The impressionist elements in the rendering of the scene are present

in the way we see it entirely and manifestly through Marlow's remem-
bering mind, and without any canonical gloss by an omniscient author.
This limited and subjective nature of the report is made most explicit
when Marlow says of the tycoon, 'He shook hands I fancy'. Marlow's
comment enforces our awareness that we are inside a consciousness that
d ͏ͪͦͭ notice or understand much of what is happening in the world
o   d. This has the effect of legitimising and emphasising
ᵥ   nal details do emerge. The older knitter, for example,
ᵧ   and her flat cloth slippers, becomes a stark visual image
ᴄ   ɪd spiritual deformity combined with imperturbable self-
            , an image which recalls the grotesque crones of Dégas or
            utrec.

            tinise the whole episode to see what is and is not recorded
            the pattern in his hierarchy of attention becomes apparent.
            ɪch that would be mentioned in an autobiography, or a
            ʌel; we are not given, for instance, the name of the city,
            ᴇ company, or the details of Marlow's contract. Here, as
            ɪ's method follows the symbolist injunction, as expressed
            'Nommer un objet, c'est supprimer les trois quarts de la
            poème . . . le suggérer, voila le rêve.' Marlow reports
            the briefest and most general terms; for instance, the
            ly a 'pale plumpness' because big bureaucrats typically
            don't exercise outdoors, are featureless and somehow
            ɪ the other hand, the very incompleteness and apparent
            ʌhat details are given forces the reader to extract what-
            nbolic intimations he can. There must, we feel, be a
            ʌow's attention to particulars is so intermittent; if he
            he external and the factual it may be because he is
            ᴛhe internal and the moral; and so we come to see
            ʌlow essentially registers with increasingly agonised
            ᴊs inward reaction to an initiation into what is perhaps
            ᴜl of modern mysteries – how the individual confronts a
            ᴄracy, and in particular how he gets a job from it.
            ᴊegins his rites of passage with a representative ecological
            approach through unfamiliar streets and arid staircases;
            ɪarshalling from waiting-room to grand managerial sanctum;
            ty-five seconds later, a more rapid return thence through the
            ᴛages, with a delayed and demoralising detour for medical
            ɪation. The sequence of routinised human contacts is equally
            ɪl: the impassive receptionists; the expert compassion of the
            ᴅential ⸌ ᴄretary; the hollow benevolence of the plump tycoon;

the shifty joviality of the clerk; and the self-congratulation of the medical examiner.

When the scene ends Marlow is left with a sense of doubly fraudulent initiation: the Company has not told him what he wants to know; but since Marlow has been unable to formulate the causes of his moral discomfort, much less voice any protest or ask any authentic question, his own tranced submission has been a double betrayal – indirectly of the Company and directly of himself.

This prefigures one of the larger and more abstract themes of the story – the lack of any genuinely reciprocal communication anywhere. For instance, Marlow's most extended dialogue at the Company's offices is with the doctor. In part it merely typifies this particular aspect of bureaucratic initiation: the routinised insult ('Ever any madness in your family?'); the pretence of disinterested devotion to scientific knowledge (measuring Marlow's cranium); and the pretendedly benevolent but actually both impractical and deeply disquieting counsel ('Avoid irritation more than exposure to the sun'). Such details might be said to operate partly in a centripetal way, since they point to specific later issues in the narrative, to Kurtz's skull and those on his fenceposts and to Marlow's physical and mental collapse at the end; but the details also have larger and more expansive centrifugal overtones. The horrors of the modern secular hell are not merely the affronting mumbo-jumbo of the medical priesthood; Marlow has illuminated the haze which hangs like a pall over the society of which the doctor, the clerk, the knitters and the pale plumpness are representatives; and we are led outwards to see the complete impossibility of genuine communion with anyone else's intellectual or moral centre.

Beyond that again we are left with an overpowering sense of Marlow's fateful induction into the vast overarching network of the silent lies of civilisation. No one will explain them – not in the Company offices, certainly – if only because the jobs of the personnel depend on their discretion, and because the division of labour restricts each individual to knowledge of a very small part of the system: none of the people there seem to have been to Africa for instance. The great corporate enterprise has made itself, and it has no voice; yet men cannot help attributing moral meanings and intentions to all its appearances because they are the only available manifestations of a power which controls their lives.

The semantic gap exists at higher thematic levels. Marlow doesn't fully understand the meaning of what is happening; there is no Virgil in sight, much less a Beatrice; and no one will help him, or even admit that the problem exists. Later the narrative reveals that this gap extends throughout Marlow's world, and we see that the silent, lethal madness of the civilisation for which the Trading Company stands enacts the intellectual and moral impasse whose narrative climax is to be the forced lie to the Intended. This gap, in turn, can be seen in a much wider perspective as a reflection of the same impasse, the same breakdown of the shared categories of understanding and judgment, as had originally imposed on Conrad and his peers among the artists of the period, the indirect, subjective, and guarded strategies that typify the expressive idiom of impressionism and symbolism.

Conrad wrote in the preface to *The Nigger of the 'Narcissus'* that his aim was 'before all, to make you *see*'. One could argue that the distinctive aim, not only of Impressionist painting but of much modern literature is, to put it a little more explicitly, 'to make us see what we see'. For this, the essential requirement in our reading and our criticism is surely a primary commitment to the literal imagination. In this case it involves a receptiveness to the whole scene which can discern in the knitters symbolic meanings which are essentially *homeophoric* extensions of their own inherent qualities, and which combine to extend these symbolic meanings in a centrifugal way which extends far beyond the literal vehicle of the narrative.

The opposite kind of critical reading gives priority to an esoteric interpretation of particular objects – knitters are *heterophors* for the fates – and combines them into a centripetal interpretation of the work as a whole: *Heart of Darkness* is essentially about a descent into hell, or into the unconscious. One suspects, incidentally, that this kind of criticism has also had unfortunate side-effects for literature. Some recent novelists write fiction as if it was supposed to fit a *heterophoric* prescription in mythological acrostics, or engineer gratuitous semantic gaps so that they can be bridged by symbol-finding critics – *Last Year at Marienbad* is a likely candidate.

As regards *Heart of Darkness*, such criticism is surely contrary to the implications of the primary narrator's image, which asks us to reach out, not in, to expand, not to narrow the range of meaning. *Heterophoric* criticism, on the other hand, inevitably bypasses much of the narrative because it burrows beneath it in quest of a single edible kernel of truth presumed to be hidden deep below the surface. It is surely curious, and saddening, to reflect that there have appeared a dozen or more studies which take a *heterophoric* view of the knitters, and none which see them, and the scene in which they figure, as *homeophoric* symbols of the great corporation and the civilisation for which it stands.

IV

It would certainly be lengthy, and it would probably be inconclusive, if one attempted to assess how close the affinities of *Heart of Darkness* are to the general spirit and methods of the French symbolists. Many difficulties arise from the extreme diffuseness and variety of the symbolist tradition, and from the inherent differences between literary genres – a symbolic image obviously cannot have the same autonomous and controlling importance in a long prose narrative as in a short poem. Another major difficulty is that Conrad's most explicit theoretical comments are, as usual, puzzling and unhelpful.

In 1918 Conrad wrote to a critic that 'all the great creations of literature have been symbolic.' This might mean no more than that Oedipus or Don Quixote portray universal human characteristics and situations: one of the commonest uses of the term 'symbolic' means little more than 'representative'. Here, however, Conrad seems to imply something rather more specific, for he goes on:

> A work of art is seldom limited to one exclusive meaning and not necessarily tending to a definite conclusion. And for the reason that the nearer it approaches art, the more it acquires a symbolic character. This statement may surprise you, who may imagine that I am alluding to the Symbolist School of poets or prose writers. Theirs, however, is only a literary proceeding against which I have nothing to say. I am concerned here with something much larger . . .[14]

The fact that Conrad implies a polar opposition between a work of art, which is symbolic, and other modes of discourse, which have exclusive meanings and definite conclusions, certainly starts from a view of literature similar to that of the French Symbolists. But, while disclaiming the symbolist doctrine, Conrad characteristically abstains from any further explanation of his own views.

In 1902, when the publication of *Heart of Darkness* in book form had provoked further discussion, Elsie Ford made various objections to what Conrad called 'my pet Heart of Darkness'. He allowed only one of them: 'What I distinctly admit is the fault of having made Kurtz too symbolic or rather symbolic at all.'[15] Conrad probably meant only that he would have liked Kurtz to be more convincing as a character; perhaps Conrad came to regret the experiment he had made, and felt that he had failed in trying to combine some general symbolist aims with more traditional fictional values and methods, although one notes that characterisation is hardly the strong point either in the novels of Villiers de l'Isle Adam and Huysmans, or in the plays of Maeterlinck and Jarry.

Another clue to the essential nature of Conrad's achievement is supplied by the fact that Henry James did not much like *Heart of Darkness*. In her unpublished diary, Olivia Garnett reports Elsie Ford as saying that James 'objected to the narrator mixing himself up with the narrative in *The Heart of Darkness* and its want of proportion.'[16] James's phrase about Marlow's 'mixing himself up with the narrative' surely discloses a myopic resistance to the technique of *Heart of Darkness* which only James's invariable veneration for his own methods can explain. Marlow is certainly very different from the Jamesian central intelligence; in effect he flouts what James thought the essential objection to the first-person method – the fact that the narrating 'I' has 'the double privilege of subject and object.'[17] But if James believed that there was an 'object' to be clearly seen, Conrad did not; it is precisely because Marlow is both subject and object that *Heart of Darkness* prefigures how the modern novel was to reject, much more fully than did James, the assumption of full authorial understanding, and, in its formal posture at least, restrict itself to showing an individual consciousness in the process of trying to elicit some personal order or meaning from its impressions of past and present experience. If we see Conrad as decisively closer to us than James, it is surely because he gave much more radical expression to the sceptical and subjective attitudes which also characterised the impressionist and symbolist movements; and in the context of these traditions we can recognise *Heart of Darkness* as a landmark in the literature of modern solipsism.

Conrad shrank from all literary schools and doctrines, and he was certainly not a symbolist with a capital 'S'. The available evidence at most strengthens the view that he is closer to the symbolist tradition than any previous English novelist, and especially close in *Heart of Darkness*, although two later short stories, 'Tomorrow' and 'The Secret Sharer', are near contenders. Conrad's earlier work had already shared some of the general features of French symbolism – the simple plots, the musical, suggestive and poetic nature of the prose, the intensity of attention to physical objects. *Heart of Darkness* added some further elements of similarity: the spiritual voyage of discovery, especially through an exotic jungle landscape, which was a common symbolist theme, in Baudelaire's 'Le Voyage' and Rimbaud's 'Bateau Ivre', for instance; the pervasive atmosphere of dream, nightmare and hallucination, again typical of Rimbaud, and especially of 'Une Saison

en Enfer'; the very subject of Kurtz recalls, not only Rimbaud's own
spectacular career, but the general symbolist fondness for the lawless,
the depraved and the extreme modes of experience; and in *Heart of
Darkness* Conrad is making his supreme effort, in Baudelaire's phrase
about Delacroix, to reveal 'the infinite in the finite'.[18]

This intention is suggested in the title. What is most characteristic
about the symbolist tradition is certainly not the use of particular
objects and acts as *homeophoric* symbols, a use which is almost equally
common among the impressionists and imagists. Thus in his Imagist
Manifesto Ezra Pound defines an image as 'that which presents an
intellectual and emotional complex in an instant of time', and makes
the ringing polemic affirmation 'the natural object is always the
adequate symbol'.[19] Insofar as any specific feature of Symbolist literature can be identified, it is more probably the centrifugal way in which
the meaning of the work as a whole is conceived. Thus the Symbolist
poets often made their titles suggest a much larger and more mysterious
range of implication than the work's overt subject apparently justified –
one thinks of the expanding effect of T. S. Eliot's *The Waste Land* for
example, or of *The Sacred Wood*; and this centrifugal direction in the
title was sometimes produced by an obtrusive semantic gap – a coupling
of incongruous words or images that forced us to look beyond our
habitual expectations.

Such is the final effect of Conrad's title. Compared with the particularity of Conrad's earlier and more traditional titles such as
Almayer's Folly and *The Nigger of the 'Narcissus'*, *Heart of Darkness*
strikes a very special note; we are somehow impelled to see the title as
much more than a combination of two stock metaphors for referring to
'the centre of the Dark Continent' and 'a diabolically evil person'.
Both the nouns are too densely charged with physical and moral
suggestion; and together they generate a puzzle which compels us to
expect something beyond our usual moral and literary experience; the
words do not name what we know, but ask us to know what has, as yet,
no name. The more concrete of the two terms, 'heart', is attributed a
strategic centrality within a formless and infinite abstraction, 'darkness'; the combination defies both visualisation and logic. How can
something inorganic like darkness have an organic centre of life and
feeling? How can a shapeless absence of light compact itself into a
formed and pulsing presence? And what are we to make of a 'good'
entity like a heart becoming, of all things, a controlling part of a 'bad'
one like darkness? *Heart of Darkness* was a fateful event in the history
of fiction; and to announce it Conrad had hit upon as haunting,

though not as obtrusive, an oxymoron as Baudelaire had for poetry with *Les Fleurs du Mal.*

NOTES

1. G. Jean-Aubry, *Joseph Conrad: Life and Letters*, 2 vols. (London, 1927), I, 200.
2. Cit. Jocelyn Baines, *Joseph Conrad: A Critical Biography* (London, 1960), p. 223; November 1898.
3. 'The Originality of Conrad', *Hudson Review*, II (1958), 545–53. *Heart of Darkness* is taken as a major example of the Symbolist novel in William York Tindall's *The Literary Symbol* (New York, 1955), pp. 86–91.
4. *Sartor Resartus*, Bk. III, ch. 3 (Oxford, 1913, p. 158).
5. Jean Renoir, *Renoir, My Father*, trans. Randolph and Dorothy Weaver (Boston and Toronto, 1958), p. 174.
6. *The Common Reader* (London, 1938), pp. 145–59.
7. Jacques Letheve, *Impressionistes et Symbolistes devant la presse* (Paris, 1959), p. 63.
8. E. H. Gombrich, *The Story of Art*, 12th ed. (London, 1972), p. 406.
9. Albert Skira and Jean Leymarie, *Impressionism*, 2 vols. (Cleveland, 1955, 1959), II, 86–8, and Guy Michaud, *Message Poétique du Symbolism* (Paris, 1947), pp. 165, 123–4, 143–4.
10. Cit. Frank Kermode, *The Romantic Image* (London, 1957), pp. 112–13.
11. On the complexities of Pound's view of the relationship of imagism to impressionism, see Herbert N. Schniedau, *The Image and the Real* (Baton Rouge, 1969), pp. 34–5. For this reference, and much else, I am indebted to Donald Davie.
12. Lillian Feder, 'Marlow's Descent into Hell', *Nineteenth-Century Fiction*, 9 (1955), 280–92.
13. Robert O. Evans, 'Conrad's Underworld', *Modern Fiction Studies*, 2 (1956), 56–62.
14. G. Jean-Aubry, *Joseph Conrad: Life and Letters*, 2 vols. (London, 1929), II, 205.
15. Letter of Conrad to Elsie Ford, 3 December 1902 (a transcript courtesy of Frederick Karl).
16. Thomas C. Moser, 'From Olive Garnett's Diary: Impressions of Ford Madox Ford and His Friends, 1890–1906', *Texas Studies in Literature and Language*, 16 (1974), 525 (5 January 1903). James apparently thought ' "The End of the Tether" the finest of the stories' in the *Youth* volume.
17. In the Preface to *The Ambassadors* (Henry James, *The Art of the Novel*, ed. Blackmur [New York, 1934], p. 321).
18. *Oeuvres complètes*, ed. Ruff (Paris, 1968), p. 404.
19. 'A Stray Document' (1913), in *Make It New* (London, 1939), p. 337.

4 Impressionism Limited*

ELOISE KNAPP HAY

'It was not important that things be beautiful [for the impressionist]; what he sought to discover was their identity – the signs by which he should know them.'

Henry James in *A New England Winter* (1884)

'. . . the latent dangers of the impressionist practice . . . [are] the tendency to simplification and the neglect of a certain faculty for lingering reflection.'

Henry James on Sargent in 1886

Impressionism, a magic word that conjures visions of the fresh, true and beautiful in art, has come to bear meanings it did not possess for writers and painters when the movement was alive. For Conrad as for James, impressionism was very different from what it became, for instance, in 1932 when Joseph Warren Beach classified Conrad as an impressionist. While both Conrad and James would have accepted the Impressionist painters' principle that a true artist deals only with accurate sense perception, rejecting academic rules and fixed conceptions, both novelists found the Impressionist painters and writers who followed them (like Maupassant and Crane) to be deficient in one important respect: they rejected depth 'analysis' and the probing of hidden human 'mysteries'.

Ford was wrong, then, when he claimed after Conrad's death that Conrad 'accepted' the stigma of 'impressionist'.[1] More accurately, Ford claimed in 1914 that certain 'maxims' which he called 'impressionism' had been 'gained mostly in conversation with Mr Conrad'.[2] We see Conrad's hand and hear his voice in these maxims, but it is hard to reconcile Ford's use of the word 'impressionism' with Conrad's derisive use of the term. ('Impressionism' is spelled with an initial capital in this essay only when it refers to the movement in painting.)

One answer to the riddle would be to consider that in addition to French Impressionism, which Conrad (as we shall see) ridiculed, there was an older English movement that rarely went by the name. Through

* This essay first appeared in a different form in the *Journal of Aesthetics and Art Criticism*, xxxiv, 2 (1976).

Walter Pater's criticism, James and Conrad became sympathetic with this tradition. Further light is thrown by discovering a possible link, missing between Ford's 'maxims' and Conrad's unkind words about impressionism. The missing link might be found in an essay titled 'Impressionism in the Novel' by Ferdinand Brunetière in 1879.[3]

Brunetière's essay began as a searching review of Alphonse Daudet. In Conrad's later essay on Daudet (1898), he treats Daudet much as he treated Crane – as a wonderful secondary writer with a gift for seeing 'only the surface of things . . . for the reason that most things have nothing but a surface.' Almost echoing Brunetière, Conrad adds: 'it is . . . sometimes very hard to forgive . . . this making plain of obvious mysteries'[4] – a remark that paraphrases another famous critic of impressionism, Paul Gauguin.

If we put together all that Conrad said about impressionism, we see three fairly distinct phases in his attitude: the first in his disgust at a collection of Impressionist paintings in 1891; the second when he met Crane and gave qualified praise to his art in 1897, soon afterwards writing his Preface to *The Nigger of the 'Narcissus'*; and the third at the end of his life when he curiously reversed himself – after years of denigrating the movement – and began to aim for the same effects that he had earlier questioned.

Conrad undoubtedly read Brunetière before reading Pater. Brunetière was Marguerite Poradowska's editor at *La Revue des Deux Mondes* in the early 1890s while she – 'Tante Margot' – was Conrad's only literary confidante. Conrad mentions him twice in letters to her (later also in *A Personal Record*, Chapter 5), and speaks of himself as a member of Brunetière's 'Daudet cult'. If Conrad read Brunetière's essay on Daudet and impressionism, he probably did so after 1883, when it made one chapter in a book of Brunetière's titled *Naturalism in the Novel*. Like Zola before him, Brunetière saw impressionism as one *sort* of naturalism, and indeed the painters saw themselves as naturalists. Brunetière commends the impressionists for rejecting Zola's squalid vision; also for correcting Flaubert (progenitor of naturalism) in his 'disdainful impassivity' as between author and characters. Nearly echoing Brunetière, Conrad at different times said he never sought in art anything but 'a form of the Beautiful'. His method as between author and characters, he said, 'aimed essentially at the intimacy of a personal communication'.[5]

For Brunetière the main attraction of Daudet's impressionism was that it was able 'before all to open our eyes to seeing the distinctive trait, to accustom our hands to rendering this primal aspect of things for the eyes of others . . . that is the first point.'[6] It was also the most important point in Conrad's Preface to *The Nigger of the 'Narcissus'*.

There were other 'truths' that Brunetière found among the 'errors' of literary impressionism. He praised the impressionist's power to present the raw data of chaotic experience and then make sense out of it. Meaning is not *imposed* on experience but found in it. One finds instances of this everywhere in Conrad – for instance in Marlow's gradual 'reading' of incomprehensible sensations after the *Judea* explodes.[7]

Brunetière goes on to praise Daudet's use of 'the picturesque imperfect tense' instead of the usual narrative preterite, thus immobilising a scene in a painterly tableau, while allowing other actions to overtake it and pass out of sight. One thinks of Conrad's group immobilised aboard the *Nellie*, listening to Marlow's Congo story. Such unconventional handlings of time lead to an effect that Henry James called 'superposition'. William James gave the name 'stream of consciousness' to the disordered sequences of temporal impressions. Pater had earlier described experience as a 'flood' on which 'impressions, images, sensations' overtake one another, pass, and dissolve in a 'perpetual weaving and unweaving of ourselves'.[8] As Ford said in 1924, life does not narrate but makes impressions on our brains.[9]

Brunetière says the impressionist does not create characters, 'he encounters them' – again a 'maxim' of Ford's impressionism. Conrad's ambiguous narrator, mingling alternately with crew and officers of the *Narcissus*, achieved this effect; also the other one Brunetière demanded, of counteracting Flaubert's impassivity. Conrad's narrator 'lives' and 'suffers with' his characters.

Brunetière remarks that Daudet and the literary impressionists often suppress parts of speech normally demanded by logic or convention. The lost connectives in conversation – so loved by James and Ford – are examples of this, as are the lost syntactical referents that have been found troublesome in Conrad's writing.[10]

Another impressionist trait, says Brunetière, is the translation of feelings and thoughts into 'the language of sensation'.[11] In *Under Western Eyes*, Razumov's eye falls on the statue of a running youth, just as Haldin's escape and his own threatened life confront him as irreconcilable. The ekphrasis is a telling example of Conrad's labours in this method, as is Kurtz's allegorical painting.[12]

Thus far one could almost invent Brunetière from Ford's maxims for impressionism. What one cannot find in Ford is that Brunetière – and Conrad after him – had almost as much to say against the 'errors' of

impressionism as for its 'truths'. Brunetière saw impressionism as one
more manifestation of the tendency in modern literature to substitute
physical sensation for inward experience. 'It is no longer literature',
he says, 'if language forces itself to evoke not the ideas of things but
the things themselves.'[13] The spectre of Butor's *'chosisme'* is already
taking shape. Conrad seems also to confront it when he speaks of his
concern with *'les valeurs idéales'*. Indeed the 'unconventional grouping
and perspective', on which he said his art depended, are methods of
forcing the reader to look *deeply* into *things*.[14] Conrad's whole relation
to the impressionist movement is a comment on Brunetière's final
tirade against it. The great writers in all times, Brunetière says, 'did
not play at being artists, or dilettantes, of the undulating . . . surfaces
of things; they went straight to the bottom of things first [*ils allaient au
fond des choses*].'[15]

The three phases I find in Conrad's attitude toward impressionism
begin appropriately with his reactions to the Impressionist painters.
Conrad was related to a minor Impressionist painter, Paul van Ryssel,
as the painter called himself. In real life he was the medical doctor
Paul Gachet, blood cousin of Marguerite Gachet Poradowska – 'Tante
Margot' – *encore*. In 1890 Van Gogh died virtually in Gachet's arms.
The following year, in Paris, Conrad visited Mme Poradowska and
found her walls hung with a superb collection of Impressionist paintings. She was staying in Gachet's apartment, and he had acquired them
during the twenty previous years, out of charity for his unsalable fellow
painters. When his collection was given to the Louvre in the 1950s, it
included paintings by Monet, Renoir, Pissarro, Sisley, Van Gogh, and
Cézanne. After seeing these paintings, Conrad returned to London
and wrote to his cousin: 'I do not like to think of you in the Doctor's
apartment. It is too nightmarish with that collection of paintings by
the School of Charenton.'[16] 'Charenton' meant, of course, the school
of madmen, like the Marquis de Sade and Van Gogh.

How closely Conrad's reactions imitate Henry James's! In 1876
James had reviewed the second Impressionist Exhibition in Paris for
the *New York Tribune*. Calling the painters 'the Irreconcilables', he
wrote:

the effect was to make me think better than ever of all the good old
rules which decree that beauty is beauty and ugliness ugliness. . .
[The Impressionists] are partisans of unadorned reality and absolute
foes to arrangement, embellishment, selection. . . Let [beauty] alone,
they say, and it will come at its own pleasure; the painter's proper

field is simply the actual, and to give a vivid impression of how a thing happens to look, at a particular moment. . .[17]

Two years later James argued that 'a picture is not an impression but an expression – just as a poem or a piece of music is.'[18] But within four years, James wrote in *The Art of Fiction*: the novel is 'in its broadest sense, a direct impression of life'. The novel's value, he added, 'is greater or less according to the intensity of the impression'.

Conrad's evolution followed a similar course, beginning fifteen years later than James's. After initial revulsion in 1891, Conrad wrote his quasi-impressionist Preface to *The Nigger* (1898). Explicitly refusing to connect himself with any *isms*, Conrad here nevertheless defined all art as 'an impression conveyed through the senses'.

The Preface betrays a bias, again like James's, against the breezy surface effects and rejection of chiaroscuro in Impressionist painting – and with some justice, since the painters themselves declared it their purpose to study the effects of light on surfaces, repudiating the Academy's stress on sculptural plasticities. Perhaps pointedly, Conrad's Preface twice mentions that fiction must have not only 'the colour of painting and the magic suggestiveness of music' but also 'the plasticity of sculpture'. In fact, like Conrad at this time, the post-impressionist painters – from Seurat and Cézanne through Picasso – were all trying to discover the stillness, solidities, depths, and multiple perspectives that the Impressionists rather deliberately foreswore. Conrad's view in this second phase of his attitude toward impressionism is clear from what he said about Stephen Crane.

Conrad said that it was Edward Garnett, in an article of 1898, who recognised Crane as 'chief of the impressionists'. Garnett's essay owes nothing to Brunetière. It reflects rather what Mallarmé (addressed by Hugo as '*mon cher poète impressionniste*') had written in 1876 about the French painters: their 'results'

appear to have been attained at the first stroke. . . That which I preserve through the power of Impressionism is . . . the power of having recreated nature touch by touch. I leave the massive and tangible solidity to its fitter exponent, sculpture. I content myself with reflecting on the clear and durable mirror of painting, that which perpetually lives yet dies every moment. . .[19]

Similarly Garnett wrote of Crane (*pace* Brunetière): 'We would define him by saying he is the perfect artist and interpreter of the surfaces of life. . . To dive into the hidden life is, of course, for the artist a great temptation and a great danger . . . the artist, seeking to interpret life, departs from the truth of nature.'[20]

Conrad, in this second phase, did not go so far as Garnett in admiring Crane. In 1897 he had written to Garnett, 'Crane's thought is concise, connected, never very deep – yet often startling. He is *the only* impressionist and *only* an impressionist.'[21] That Conrad did not consider himself an impressionist, as Beach (following Ford) claimed, was still clear in 1900 when Conrad wrote thanking R. B. Cunninghame Graham for a book of stories: 'they are much more than mere Crane-like impressionism but even as impressionism these sketches are well nigh perfect.'[22]

Conrad had thus moved from a phase of despising impressionism as a school of madmen to recognising it as an appealing, superficial movement in the arts, a style that gave back pure, bright, surface effects of nature, as in the 'clear and durable mirror' of Mallarmé. Yet Conrad's letters at this time insist that brilliant surfaces are incapable of capturing what he repeatedly called 'the inner truth' or 'flesh and blood' of life.[23]

His own labours to fathom experience cost him more than he ever wanted to pay, these same letters show. Garnett may have been thinking of Conrad when he said that 'the artist seeking to interpret life departs from . . . nature.' John Rewald confirms that this was the opinion of the Impressionist painters: 'Nature [for them] was no longer an object susceptible of interpretation; it became the direct source of pure sensations.'[24] From 1898 until Conrad wrote *The Rover*, he saw an important half-truth in this doctrine, but never a whole truth. He wished to collaborate with Crane in 1898, perhaps hoping to steal a bit of his fire without being burned. His reasons for turning then to Ford for collaboration suggest the same search for help in achieving the swift mastery of words over impressions. With such an ally, he said, he could then 'descend into [his] own little hell' for his main work.[25]

The power in himself that Conrad named insistently was what he called 'analysis'. This seems a direct echo from Maupassant's 1887 Preface to *Pierre et Jean*, where Maupassant divides modern novelists into those who are 'objective' and those who are 'partisans of analysis'. Plainly Maupassant's sympathies are with objective writers (like himself and Flaubert), who render life 'as it is' – manifested 'under the facts of existence'. 'Analysis' was a word often used also by painters who criticised Impressionism. Cézanne and Gaugin sought the very thing that Maupassant rejected. As Conrad virtually said of Crane, Cézanne said of Monet, 'He is only an eye but, my God, what an eye!'[26] Cézanne, like Conrad, was determined to seek 'structure beneath richly nuanced surfaces'.[27] Gauguin too criticised the Impressionists this way. He said, they 'look for what is near the eye, and not at the mysterious heart of thought.'[28]

The same reaction away from 'objective' impressionism was marked by Proust.[29] What Conrad found most remarkable in Proust was his use of 'analysis', and indeed Proust (who is a post-impressionist like Cézanne) commented on this himself.[30]

Proust reminds us of another aspect of impressionism important both to him and to Conrad, the quality called 'temperament'. Conrad often spoke of writing as the 'temperamental handling of personal experience'. Rewald points out how important the word 'temperament' was for Baudelaire and Zola. Baudelaire said of Manet, 'he *has* temperament, that is the important thing.'[31] Zola searched among painters for what *he* called 'creation seen through the medium of a powerful temperament.'[32]

Perhaps struck by these remarks, Pater soon afterwards wrote: 'What is important is not . . . a correct abstract definition of beauty for the intellect, but a certain kind of temperament. . .'[33] Beauty is a response of temperament to certain kinds of impressions. For Pater in 1873, 'what is real in our life fines itself down to a single sharp impression.'[34]

Conrad's Preface to *The Nigger* (affected by Pater, as Baines has shown) connects impressions with temperament, but then goes on to stress that the artist's appeal is always from one temperament to another. Brunetière also made this point, as cited above (p. 55). For Conrad, the artist thus achieves two ethical as well as aesthetic results: first, attachment to the earth, which often otherwise seems alien, and secondly 'the solidarity of all mankind'. Conrad adds that the artist's power may extend further still, to give us that 'glimpse of truth' for which the reader has 'forgotten to ask'. Whereas Pater treated the recording of impressions, through temperament, as fully justified by a heightened awareness of life, Conrad redirects the current of this modern Epicurus into a Stoic's ethic, worthy of Zeno, but modern in its suggestion of man's strangeness in nature.

Pater's impressionism is a necessary supplement to the mainstream of impressionism in France. It is a direct and natural development from seventeenth-century English empiricism and the later philosophy of David Hume. In France impressionism represented not a development but a revolt – against the main philosophical tradition of Descartes. French impressionism expressed itself first among painters revolting against the sacrosanct Academy. The movement therefore became associated with lunacy and *la vie bohème*. This was not true in England if one looks at the tradition of Hume, as Ford (looking only toward France) was not minded to do. The word 'impressionism' was coined by John Rogers in 1839, referring to Hume's tradition.

Hume's great question was 'How do I move from the hard facts of sense data to certain knowledge?' The question would make a good second epigraph for *Lord Jim*. In 1921 Conrad told Louis Lenormand that the great novel still to be written would be about 'the decline of men who have reached a sense of certitude'.[35]

Hume concluded that man's pursuit of certainty will never be satisfied, but such certainty as is necessary to life could be derived from sense impressions. As the first sentence of his *Treatise of Human Nature* read, 'All perceptions of the human mind resolve themselves into impressions and ideas.' Ideas are poor seconds in the pursuit of truth, however, since ideas are only the residue of impressions. Hume established thus that impressions are the generative force behind all knowledge. Pater merely poeticised an 'impressionism' elaborated over a century earlier. It was already accepted when William Hazlitt pronounced, 'I think what I feel. I cannot help receiving certain impressions from things; and I have sufficient courage to declare . . . what they are.'[36]

The combined force of Hume and Pater, perhaps corrected by Brunetière, may have moved Conrad towards the near-impressionism of his second phase. The third and last phase of his interest was brief, and marked by a curious reversal of his earlier stand on Crane's impressionism. In 1919, Conrad wrote that Crane was 'the chief impressionist of our day', acknowledging the phrase as Garnett's. But in 1898, Garnett had also written, Crane was 'never great in the sense of so fusing . . . a whole, that the reader is struck dumb as by an inevitable revelation.' Now, in 1919, Conrad insists contrarily that Crane 'had a wonderful power of vision . . . that seemed to reach, within life's appearances and forms, the very spirit of life's truth.' To Garnett's argument that Crane was 'the perfect artist and interpreter of the surfaces of life', Conrad (who has the old article beside him) answers, 'His impressionism of phrase went really deeper than the surface.'[37] But, discounting that, Conrad had reasons bearing on his present fiction that would adequately explain the reversal of his early stand on Crane's impressionism.

We know that in writing *The Rover*, Conrad prided himself on at last achieving a novel that was deftly objective and short, a novel from which 'analysis' was absent and all search for 'the truth of life' ended in the palpable 'facts of existence'. A year after publishing *The Rover*, Conrad was more than ever concerned with achieving 'objectivity', similar to the impressionism he once deprecated in Crane but which now, as the essays on Crane show, he considered more than ever desirable.

This was when he met Lenormand in Corsica, while there hoping to capture impressions for the writing of *Suspense*. The problem with his writing, he confessed to Lenormand, was this: *'Je me trouve trop conscient.'* Throughout his career he had made the same complaint. But now he adds a new note. Denying that he wishes to look below the surface of things, he backs away from discussion of the deeper meanings of his great novels. 'I am only a story-teller,' he says. 'I do not want to go to the bottom of things. I want to consider reality as something rough and crude over which I let my fingers play. Nothing more.'[38] The key phrase in this disclaimer – *'aller au fond'* – was precisely the phrase used by Brunetière for the power wanting in impressionism.

Perhaps Conrad had come to believe it was better not to look too deeply into things. Or perhaps, now that impressionism was dead all over Europe, he wanted to praise it. His view of it, as of Stephen Crane, was elegiac; and he was always good at elegies. Also this change of heart toward *'L'École de Charenton'* was like nostalgia for his middle years, when literary 'schools' and *isms* were lively issues, and when he knew, or thought he knew, the great difference between surfaces and what lay beneath.

NOTES

1. *Joseph Conrad, A Personal Remembrance* (London, 1924), p. 182. Ford's and Conrad's references to Stephen Crane's impressionism may be related to discussion of the subject (fortunately indexed) in Jean Cazemajou's *Stephen Crane* (Paris, 1969).
2. Ford Madox Hueffer, 'On Impressionism', in *Poetry and Drama* (Paris, June and December, 1914), II, 167–75 and 323–34.
3. Ferdinand Brunetière, 'Impressionnisme dans le roman', in *La revue des deux mondes* (Paris, 15 November 1879), pp. 446–59; reprinted in the same author's *Le roman naturaliste* (Paris, 1883). Where translated, the translations are mine.
4. 'Alphonse Daudet', in *Notes on Life and Letters* (London, 1921), p. 28.
5. Conrad's references to Brunetière are in *Lettres de Joseph Conrad à Marguerite Poradowska*, ed. René Rapin (Genève, 1966), pp. 157–8. His remarks on his own art are in 'A Familiar Preface' and in his letter to Richard Curle of 14 July 1923.
6. 'Impressionnisme dans le roman', in *Le roman naturaliste*, pp. 89–90.
7. Brunetière, loc. cit.; Edward Said, *Joseph Conrad, The Fiction of Auto-*

biography (Cambridge, Mass., 1966), pp. 107–8; and Ian Watt in a paper delivered at Warsaw in 1972, to be included in a forthcoming book.

8. Brunetière, pp. 90–1; Walter Pater, 'Conclusion' to *The Renaissance* (New York, 1919), pp. 195–6; William James, *The Principles of Psychology* (1890), Chapter IX.

9. Ford, *Joseph Conrad, A Personal Remembrance* (London, 1924), pp. 181–2.

10. Brunetière, p. 92. Ian Watt, commenting on this in a letter to me of 18 June 1974, writes of one puzzling passage: 'Conrad was thinking in terms larger and more subjective than his syntax allows.'

11. Brunetière, p. 92.

12. Conrad seemed to envy Stephen Crane his power to express human experience purely as sensation in the first lines of 'The Open Boat': 'None of them knew the colour of the sky.' See 'Stephen Crane', *Last Essays* (London, Dent, 1940), pp. 102–3.

13. Brunetière, pp. 104–5.

14. Letters of 18 March 1917, to Sidney Colvin; and 14 July 1923 (both in Jean-Aubry, *Life and Letters*).

15. Brunetière, p. 108.

16. *Lettres de Joseph Conrad à Marguerite Poradowska*, p. 87. I have translated from the French.

17. Henry James, 'The Impressionists', in *The Painter's Eye*, ed. J. L. Sweeney (New York, 1956), pp. 114–15.

18. *The Painter's Eye*, p. 28.

19. Quoted in John Rewald, *The History of Impressionism* (New York, 1973), pp. 372–4.

20. Edward Garnett, *Friday Nights* (London, 1922), p. 206. This volume contains both the 1898 articles and a new assessment of Crane.

21. Letter of 5 December 1897, to Garnett (*Letters from Joseph Conrad*, Indianapolis, 1928, p. 119).

22. *Joseph Conrad's Letters to R. B. Cunninghame Graham*, ed. C. T. Watts (Cambridge, England, 1969), p. 130.

23. Technical facility could even interfere with truth in art, Conrad held. See for instance his letter of 1899 to Galsworthy (in *Life and Letters*, I, 270–271), where he says, 'Technical perfection, unless there is some real glow to illumine and warm it from within, must necessarily be cold.' And explaining why there seems to be no 'flesh and blood' in James's fiction, Conrad says that James writes 'perhaps with too much perfection of *method*'.

24. Rewald, pp. 284 and 330.

25. Letter of October, 1898, to W. E. Henley, quoted in Baines's *Joseph Conrad* (London, 1959), pp. 217–19.

26. For Conrad's own struggles with 'analysis', several times mentioned in his letters to Garnett, see also his letter of 4 October 1906, to Pinker (in the Berg Collection): offering to shorten *The Secret Agent* if an editor wished, he writes, 'I can take out 2 to 3 thousand words if so desired – analysis.' See also his letter of 31 May 1902, to Blackwood, quoted in Baines, p. 284. Cézanne's remark about Monet is cited in Peter and Linda Murray, *A Dictionary of Art and Artists* (London, 1960), p. 277.

27. Rewald, p. 558.

28. Rewald, pp. 574–5.

29. See Proust's objection to the 'realism' of the Goncourts – so similar to Conrad's objection to Arnold Bennett's realism – in Proust's *Contre Sainte-Beuve* (Paris, Gallimard, 1971), p. 642.

30. Conrad's remarks that Proust 'pushed analysis to the point where it became creative' and 'his is a creative art absolutely based on analysis', are in a long letter of 17 December 1922, to Scott Moncrieff in *Life and Letters*, II,

290–2. Proust's most precise remark comes in *A la recherche du temps perdu* (Paris, 1954), III, p. 880; 'L'impression est pour l'écrivain ce qu'est l'experimentation pour le savant, avec cette différence que chez le savant le travail de l'intelligence précède et chez l'écrivain vient après. Ce que nous n'avons pas eu à déchiffrer, à éclaircir par notre effort personnel, ce qui était clair avant nous, n'est pas à nous.' Walter Pater had said something very similar in his Conclusion to *The Renaissance* in 1873: 'experience seems to bury us under a flood of external objects. . . But when reflection begins to play upon those objects . . . each object is loosed into a group of impressions – color, odor, texture – in the mind of the observer. . . Analysis goes a step farther still, and assures us that those impressions of the individual mind . . . are in perpetual flight . . .'

31. Letter to Mme. Paul Meurice of 24 May 1865, quoted in Rewald, p. 54.

32. From an essay of Zola on Proudhon, quoted in Rewald, p. 143.

33. Pater, Preface to *The Renaissance*.

34. Pater, Conclusion to *The Renaissance*.

35. Louis Lenormand, 'Note sur un séjour de Conrad en Corse', in *La nouvelle revue française*, XXIII (December, 1924), 670. Translation mine.

36. William Hazlitt, Preface to *A View of the English Stage* [1818], in *Works* (London, 1930–4), V, 175.

37. 'Stephen Crane' reprinted in *Notes on Life and Letters*, p. 50. It seems possible that private jokes between Conrad and Garnett about 'Stevie' (as they called Crane) may have come into the portrait Conrad drew after Crane's death of Winnie Verloc's half-witted brother Stevie, who like Crane had an unusual attachment to horses, a weak lower lip, and an unrestrained temperament. Garnett's perfidy in divulging the joke would have been sufficient cause for Conrad's indignation.

38. Lenormand, p. 669 Translation mine. Conrad's remark was instigated by Lenormand's 'discovery' of Freudian meanings in *Almayer's Folly* and *Lord Jim*. Psychoanalysis, as then understood, seems to have given Conrad more reason to side with the enemies of analysis.

5 Conrad and Nietzsche

EDWARD W. SAID

Conrad and Nietzsche were disaffected and yet admiring students of Schopenhauer. Each was temperamentally in agreement with Schopenhauer's pessimistic philosophy, although each – in similar ways – was critical of its principal arguments. Nietzsche did not believe that the Will was blind, nor did he think that it was simply a Will to live. Rather he saw the Will as inclining always to the acquisition of power; so too Conrad, for whom such men as Kurtz, Gould and Nostromo were nothing if not wilful and deliberately egoistic over-reachers. What troubled Nietzsche about Schopenhauer was the latter's weakening before the amoral picture of the world he had drawn. Whereas Nietzsche acknowledged life's uncompromising and inescapable disdain for either man or morality, he felt that his once-revered teacher had devised a cowardly retreat from life by preaching stoic withdrawal. Nietzsche's repeated statements of this criticism are echoed by Conrad's treatment of Heyst in *Victory*, whose code of philosophic disengagement from life is articulated only to be violated by Lena, Schomberg, Mr Jones, and the others. These, plus a lifelong interest in Wagner, are part of a common cultural patrimony shared by Nietzsche and Conrad.

There are a number of superficial resemblances between the Professor in *The Secret Agent* and what is often referred to as the extreme nihilism of Nietzsche's philosophy. As the embodiment of an attitude uniting a total moral purity with the will to absolute destruction the Professor, it is true, seems like one result of Conrad's interest in radical paradoxes of human character – a result perhaps refined, or even inspired, by a reading of Nietzsche. In his letter of 26 October 1899 to Garnett (written before *The Secret Agent*) Conrad speaks of having received a copy of Garnett's essay on Nietzsche;[1] so far as I know Conrad simply mentions the essay twice and never again refers to it. But from his tone – for instance, the passing reference to Nietzsche in 'The Crime of Partition' – it is arguable that Conrad was familiar with Nietzsche as the author of such ideas as the will to power, the

Overman, and the transvaluation of all values. There may be more circumstantial evidence of actual borrowings to show how Conrad not only read but made use of Nietzsche, but turning it up is not what I consider to be the most interesting or useful way of considering the two writers together. Rather they are best read in terms of a common tradition of which Nietzsche, always determined to spell things out in the smallest detail, is in many ways the apogee. That such a tradition exists is a fact of European literature and thought, and even though Conrad is a good deal less explicit about it than Nietzsche, I think that one can find evidence for it in the fiction nonetheless.

Since my main concern is with showing similarities and affinities between the two writers I can only touch rather inadequately on the methodological and historical question of why and in what manner Conrad and Nietzsche together belong to this tradition. In other words, everything I shall write here might very well be put into serious doubt by any rigorous attempt to define the common field of play inhabited by Conrad and Nietzsche. Even to say that they both inhabit a common field is, at least for Conradian criticism, to say something fairly unusual. Conrad has been systematically treated as everything *except* a novelist with links to a cultural and intellectual context. His politics, aesthetics, and morality have not been analysed as the products of thought, with roots in an intellectual ambiance, but rather as a series of accidents that happened to a Pole writing in England between the nineties and 1924. Why this critical failure is so, for a novelist whose cultural range is after all so impressively vast, is a subject for analysis in itself. Here I shall limit myself to describing the connections between Conrad and Nietzsche's thought, connections quite interesting enough for their own sake.

For want of a better label to give the tradition to which I referred above, I shall call it the radical attitude towards language. For Nietzsche, no less than for Conrad, the life of language was the first fact of the writing life, of what Conrad named the life of 'the worker in prose'. In his early work, for example a set of notebooks dating from January to July 1875, Nietzsche used the title 'philologist' to apply to great artists and thinkers capable of seeing and articulating the sharpest truths, Goethe, Leopardi, Wagner, Schopenhauer. As his thought developed through the late seventies and up to 1888 Nietzsche returned constantly to the connection between the characteristics of language as a form of human knowledge, perception, and behaviour, and those fundamental facts of human reality, namely will, power and desire. All through the great series of works he produced from *Human, All Too*

Human (1878), through *The Gay Science* (1882), *Thus Spake Zarathustra* (1883–92), *Beyond Good and Evil* (1886), *Genealogy of Morals* (1887), *Twilight of the Idols* (1889), up to and including the extraordinary set of posthumously published notes entitled *The Will to Power* (1883–88), Nietzsche examined language for its concealed duplicity, and its alliance with power and rank, which he called perspective. As early as 1873 he described truth in linguistic terms as follows:

> What, then, is truth? A mobile army of metaphors, metonyms, and anthropomorphisms – in short, a sum of human relations, which have been enhanced, transposed, and embellished poetically and rhetorically, and which after long use seem firm, canonical, and obligatory to a people: truths are illusions about which one has forgotten that this is what they are; metaphors which are worn out and without sensuous power; coins which have lost their pictures and now matter only as metal, no longer as coins.[2]

Nietzsche's moral and historical transvaluations depend very greatly upon insights such as this, which are a form of perspectival interpretation, treating language as a tyrannical epistemological system.

Although he developed this position, with all its complex self-irony (since Nietzsche was perfectly aware that his own work too was a perspectival fact of language) beyond any other writer, the position itself is not original with Nietzsche. Rather one ought to see it as a logical development out of the new philology of the early nineteenth century, and of course out of the so-called higher criticism of the Bible later in the century. Nietzsche's affiliations with his philological antecedents are too detailed to list here, but one main line of descent from them can be pointed out. That is the discovery – made by numerous investigators including Bopp, Grimm, von Humboldt and the two Schlegels – that there is no such thing as a first, or original, language, and nor is there a first text. All human utterances are connected to each other, but not genealogically as to a first language (most commonly believed to be the Hebrew spoken by God and Adam in Eden); the connections between utterances are formal, lateral, adjacent, complementary, systematic. In short, every utterance is a controlled, disciplined, rule-coordinated variation on some other utterance. While it is unique to human beings, language is an order of repetition, of creative repetition, not of original speech. Thus every utterance interprets a prior utterance, is an interpretation of an interpretation which no longer serves. More urgently still Nietzsche saw human history as a battle of interpretations; for since man exists without hope of getting to the first link in the chain of interpretations he must present his own interpretation as if it were a secure meaning, insteady merely of one version of the truth. By doing so he forcibly dislodges another interpretation in order to put another in its place. The struggle between interpretations historically grasped is what Nietzsche considered the genealogy of *morals* to be all about. As to the function of interpretation in a world of increasing becoming, Nietzsche has this to say in 1885-6:

> 'Interpretation', the introduction of meaning – not 'explanation' (in most cases a new interpretation over an old interpretation that has become incomprehensible, that is now itself only a sign). There are no facts, everything is in flux, incomprehensible, elusive; what is relatively most enduring is – our opinions.[3]

The extent to which such a view was carried by Nietzsche can be gathered from section, subtitled 'Our new "infinite" ', of *The Gay Science*:

> But I should think that today we are at least as far from the ridiculous immodesty that would be involved in decreeing from our corner that perspectives are permitted only from this corner [Nietzsche here rejects the position that takes all other positions as mere interpretation, implying that this one is truth and not interpretation]. Rather the world has become 'infinite' for us all over again, inasmuch as we cannot reject the possibility that *it may include infinite interpretations.*[4]

If from one point of view therefore language heightens the 'pathos of distance'[5] between the user and brute reality, from another point of view language makes common, betrays, coarsens human experience. Nietzsche's thesis from *The Birth of Tragedy* on was that *melos* is a more authentic expression of reality than *logos*. The more highly developed consciousness is, the more likely then that language will exceed simple communication between men (need and distress cause men to want to communicate, and this desire increases to a point where the power of communication is really an accumulated subtlety exceeding actual need) and will be poor with regard to the 'incomparably personal, unique, and infinitely individual'.[6]

This difficult paradox, that language is at once excess and poverty, stands very near the heart of Nietzsche's work, and, I believe, plays a considerable role in Conrad's handling of narrative language and technique. This view of language as perspective, interpretation, poverty, and excess is the first of three ways in which Conrad and Nietzsche can be brought together. Elsewhere I have commented on Conrad's habit of employing reported, or secondary, speech by which to convey the tale;[7] in this he is like Nietzsche averring that all language is an interpretation of an interpretation. Moreover the transformation of narrative time from the linear to, in Conrad's major work, the multiple, bears witness to Nietzsche's general obsession with the past, and to the observation made in *Wir Philologen* that man is 'a multiplication of many pasts'.[8] Yet despite this conviction such Conradian narrators as Marlow are always reminding their audience that what is being said can never capture the true essence of the action that took place. Though Conrad's stated aesthetic rested on his avowal to make the reader see, with few exceptions what the reader remembers is a sustained effort to make words tell, even as it is frequently evident that words are ultimately inadequate, so special and eccentric is the experience.

I do not think it is incorrect to understand the peculiar genius of Conradian narrative – especially in such standard-setting works as *Heart of Darkness* – as in many ways arriving at a number of the same discoveries formulated by Nietzsche. Of course Conrad's tone is rarely like Nietzsche's; no one should underestimate the difference between the startling aphoristic gaiety cultivated by Nietzsche and Conrad's frequent solemnity and affected garrulity, which often seems at a loss for exactness. (There are occasional similarities: for example, the *Schadenfreude* of 'An Outpost of Progress' or the cutting sarcasm of *The Secret Agent*). Yet to be stopped by the difference is no more correct than speaking indiscriminately of their common nihilism. Both writers are too uncommonly detailed in their technique and in the presentation of their views for that. But what has often passed for an adequate literary account of the Conradian, or for that matter the Jamesian, interest in narrative presentation, the use of multiple point of view, the overlaying of one narrative by another, the enveloping of an inner by an outer frame – all this seems, I think, better accounted for when Nietzsche's work is read as relying upon a set of working attitudes towards language shared in common with Conrad. And of these attitudes the one seeing utterance as inevitably and endlessly leading to another, without recourse to a single originating or unequivocally privileged first fact – this is, I think, the major point in common. What matters in Conrad is what Nietzsche called interior 'polyphony of effort':[9] Kurtz and Jim and Nostromo are finally no more important than the meditation and the reflection and the language they stimulate.

They are posited in a way as fundamentally unknowable. It is left for the narrative to deliver them, not in themselves, but as they are from many perspectives. Narrative does not explain, it introduces plural meanings where none had been before – at the heart of darkness. One passage from *The Gay Science* describes the Conradian enterprise in *Heart of Darkness*.

> What is originality? *To see* something that has no name as yet and hence cannot be mentioned although it stares us all in the face. The way men usually are, it takes a name to make something visible for them. Those with originality have for the most part also assigned names.[10]

What Marlow does in the tale is precisely – or as precisely as he can – to name something which has no name; he does this in order for it to be seen. This too is Kurtz's distinction at the end: to have judged, identified, named the horror even if that horror is less a thing than a thing said. The economic literalness of how Conrad does this is remarkable indeed, the more so I think in that it resembles Nietzsche's way too. More often than not Conrad's narratives are delivered by men whose professional standpoint in life is learned, contemplative, even medical in the sense that a physician is a doctor whose compassion includes the capacity for understanding as well as the perspective seeing humanity as an affliction. These narrators, reporters, conveyors of special insights not only tell a story, they also inevitably create an audience even as they fashion their tale: *Lord Jim* and *Heart of Darkness* are perfect examples, with their select group of listeners, and their carefully devised barriers between one or another temporal, declarative and physical level. Is not this exactly a major fact of Conrad's style, this elaborate strategy for the controlled play of meaning in language, this scenic design for utterances delivering and withholding 'original' truths? Here is Nietzsche discussing the process:

> One does not only wish to be understood when one writes; one wishes just as surely *not* to be understood. It is not by any means necessarily an objection to a book when anyone finds it impossible to understand: perhaps that was part of the author's intention – he did not want to be understood by just 'anybody'. All the nobler spirits and tastes select their audience when they wish to communicate; and choosing that, one at the same time erects barriers against 'the others'. All the more subtle laws of any style have their origin at this point: they at the same time keep away, create a distance, forbid

'entrance', understanding, as said above – while they open the ears of those whose ears are related to ours.[11]

Yet even to those 'related' ears there are mysteries which Conrad's language does not finally reveal, for all its effusiveness and breadth. His narratives are dotted with disclaimers such as 'there are no words for the sorts of things I wanted to say'. These, I think, are appeals from *logos* to *melos*, from what Nietzsche called the net of language to a lyrical domain that words cannot penetrate. 'We have emancipated ourselves from fear of reason, the ghost that haunted the eighteenth century: we again dare to be absurd, childish, lyrical – in one word: "we are musicians." '[12] The virtuosity of Conrad's language, even when it has offended critics by its untidy sprawls and rhetorical emptiness, regularly carries with it eloquent indications that language is not enough. 'Compared with music all communication by words is shameless; words dilute and brutalize; words depersonalize; words make the uncommon common.'[13] The lyrical evocativeness of the scene between Marlow and Kurtz's intended unmistakably gestures towards that mysterious musical realm of intoxication, unreason and danger:

> . . . and the sound of her low voice seemed to have the accompaniment of all the other sounds, full of mystery, desolation, and sorrow, I had ever heard – the ripple of the river, the soughing of the trees swayed by the wind, the murmurs of the crowds, the faint ring of incomprehensible words cried from afar, the whisper of a voice speaking from beyond the threshold of an eternal darkness.[14]

The second rapprochement between Nietzsche and Conrad is their sense of intellectual adventure and with it, their discovery of the inevitable antitheses everywhere to be found in human existence. In Conrad, the form of his tales enacts the dialectic between two opposed impulses, one, that of what Nietzsche calls the man who wants knowledge, and who 'must again and again abandon the *terra firma* where men live and venture into the uncertain'; and two, 'the impulse which desires life [and which] must again and again grope its way toward a more or less secure place where it can find a purchase.'[15] In *The Mirror of the Sea* Conrad described these impulses as landfall and departure, experiences of the sea with obvious pertinence to such excursions into the unknown as *Heart of Darkness*, or such wilful adventures as those of Jim and Nostromo and returns to 'civilisation' and life as are contained in Marlow's retrospective ruminations.

But even this dual movement from one antipode to the other is rooted in the sort of logic formulated in linguistic terms that makes the violent postscript of Kurtz's report not so unacceptable an aberration as it appears. In *Beyond Good and Evil* Nietzsche argued that the distinctions between such qualities as good and evil or such concepts as cause and effect are 'pure concepts, that is to say . . . conventional fictions for the purpose of designation and communication – *not* for explanation.'[16] A better way of understanding these concepts is by psychology – Nietzsche everywhere employs psychology in conjunction with metaphors of depth and penetration – which alone can enter the place where one can see how values are *created* by strength of will, no matter how contradictory is the material from which they are made. Words bear evidence of this kind of creation; at no point can a word be said necessarily to refer to a fixed concept or object like 'good' or 'reasonable'. Similarly, Marlow's journey into the heart of darkness is everywhere characterised by dislocations in psychological sense caused by the displacement of habitual values, objects, meanings from one place to another. At bottom, literally, much of the strangeness in the tale is attributed to Kurtz, whose power has been precisely to create free from the logical, social, and grammatical constraints holding back everyone else. This is also Jim's achievement in Patusan. Language – as Nietzsche first found out in his early studies of Greek civilisation – enables the cohabitation of total opposites, as when it is possible for a modern philologist to envision Greek tragedy as one aspect of Wagner's art work of the future. Underneath words seethes a potential will to power, bringing forward evil with knowledge or an insight such as 'and this also was one of the dark places of the earth'. Nietzsche's thesis, argued for the first time in *Human, All Too-Human* is that the sheer honesty of the free spirit pays no heed to conventions separating things or words from their opposite. Every coin has another face; this must be acknowledged, just as Kurtz's light of progress is sustained at exactly the same level and with the same degree of intensity as the darkness.

It would be inadvisable, I think, to call this second rapprochement between Conrad and Nietzsche their common nihilism. For one, Nietzsche's nihilism is no simple thing; indeed he makes numerous distinctions between types of nihilism, between pessimism, romanticism, decadence, and nihilism, and it is altogether unclear to me whether even in Book One, 'European Nihilism', of *The Will to Power* he applies the adjective 'nihilistic' to himself. There is not much doubt on the other hand that both he and Conrad believed the world to be devoid of anything except spectacular value. Such a belief, to quote

Nietzsche, is 'the last form of nihilism . . . [and] includes disbelief in any metaphysical world and forbids itself any belief in a *time* [as opposed to *becoming*] world. Having reached this standpoint, one grants the reality of becoming as the *only* reality, forbids oneself every kind of clandestine access to afterworlds and false divinities – but *cannot endure this world though one does not want to deny it*.[17] As to the world itself, there is a striking resemblance, accidental I am sure, between Conrad's famous letters to Cunningham Graham, dated 20 December 1897 and 14 January 1898, on the knitting machine, and this last item in *The Will to Power*:

> This world: a monster of energy, without beginning, without end; a firm, iron magnitude of force that does not grow bigger or smaller, that does not expend itself but only transforms itself; as a whole of unalterable size, a household without expenses or losses, but likewise without increase or income; enclosed by 'nothingness' as by a boundary; not something blurry or wasted, not something endlessly extended, but set in a definite space as a definite force, and not a space that might be 'empty' here or there, but rather as force throughout, as a play of forces and waves of forces, at the same time one and many, increasing here and at the same time decreasing there; a sea of forces flowing and rushing together, eternally changing, eternally flooding back, with tremendous years of recurrence, with an ebb and a flood of its forms; out of the simplest forms striving towards the most complex, out of the stillest, most rigid, coldest forms towards the hottest, most turbulent, most self-contradictory, and then again returning home to the simple out of this abundance, out of the play of contradictions back to the joy of concord, still affirming itself in this uniformity of its courses and its years, blessing itself as that which must return eternally, as a becoming that knows no satiety, no disgust, no weariness: this, my *Dionysian* world of the eternally self-creating, the eternally self-destroying . . . without goal. . . . *This world is the will to power – and nothing besides!* And you yourselves are also this will to power – and nothing besides![18]

Nietzsche had expressed similar views in *The Gay Science*, section 109, cautioning against attributing 'aesthetic anthropomorphisms' – that is, 'order, arrangement, form, beauty, wisdom' – to the world.[19]

So far as the writer is concerned such a view of the world entails no simple acceptance of it, but rather an acknowledgment that values are created, just as words in a text are also created, by human force. Conrad's confession that writing for him was the conversion of force into words bears this acknowledgment out. A more problematic consequence, however, is that a highly patterned many-levelled narrative structure of the type I discussed earlier is also an act of will, in which the care expended upon making the structure firm runs the risk of being effaced when the distinctions sustaining the structure collapse into equals. This occurs notably in the final sentences of *Heart of Darkness* where Conrad uses exactly the same words to describe the setting at the Thames estuary that he had used for the African scenes. In other words we can find instances of repetition whose function is to reduce the difference between one value, one place or time and another, to an absolute identity. In *Nostromo*, for example, all the men – for all their differences in character and temperament – are slaves of the recurrent power of the silver mine.

This alternation between difference and repetition brings me to my third and final instance of the similarity between Conrad and Nietzsche. Conrad's narratives for the most part (this is especially true of the earlier work up till *Under Western Eyes*) flirt quite deliberately with enigma and 'inconclusive experience'. What starts out as a tale bearing hope for some conclusion, some teleology, turns out either not to reveal the secrets for which the reader searches, or it minimises the distinction between the exceptional, masterful egoistic hero and 'us', the comparatively herd-like remainder of mankind. In both cases of course Conrad's method, I said earlier, is to employ reported, or secondary speech. Such a narrative tactic has the effect of transforming novelty into recurrence; as Nietzsche said, 'the great dice game of existence . . . must pass through a calculable number of combinations.'[20] Here both Nietzsche and Conrad are part of a very pervasive nineteenth-century European tradition of philosophic repetition to be found in Kierkegaard, Marx, and later, Freud; paradoxically, there are as many different philosophies of repetition as there are philosophers describing repetition, so it would be wrong to impose a strict identity of views upon Conrad and any one of the others. But what demands notice is this tendency in Conrad – and in Nietzsche insofar as his view of the world as repeatable force coincides with Conrad's – to move his characters and his narrative structures unceasingly from a reliance on novelty, exceptionality, egoism, exoticism to a perspective where after all they are repetitive instances of some common all too-human pattern. So in *Heart of Darkness* we recognise that the tale's difficulty is precisely the unmediated co-presence in it of the untoward and the altogether unprecedented, with the familiar, the habitual and the ordinary. This co-presence is situated on every level, on that of action, language, and character. How much of Marlow's discomfiture in Africa is due to seeing, for example, routine office duties performed in the remotest jungle as if in a London office. The narrative pries the habitual from its normal surroundings and applies it to new ones, which in turn must be apprehended and described by a language telling us that things are not so different after all: must we not remember that here is another one of Marlow's 'inconclusive experiences', that 'this also was one of the dark places of the earth', and so on?

'There are moments when one's past came back to one, as it will sometimes when you have not a minute to spare to yourself; but it came in the shape of an unrestful and noisy dream, remembered with wonder amongst the overwhelming realities of this strange world of plants, and water, and silence.'[21] The alternation is typically Conradian: from present, to past, to present again – never forward into the dawn, as we would have moved in Nietzsche's case. Whereas Nietzsche attached the greatest explicit importance to conceiving eternal recurrence as an aspect of the future, Conrad's obsession with the past kept him in a tighter orbit of past and present, one repeating the other without respite. The two great European writers separate at this point. One can speculate that Conrad's deepest commitment as a writer is to the narrative form, which of itself finds the recurrence of past and present normal and congenial. Nietzsche, the superb aphorist who worked in the mode of LaRochefoucauld, Chamfort and Lichtenberg uses language to thrust and probe further from what is expected, despite the wholly admitted belief in eternal recurrence. Conrad is the less daring of the two, although – and this is one of those seeming contradictions of art that Nietzsche was a genius enough to appreciate, even as he denigrated the novel – he is no less of a European event than his contemporary Nietzsche. No one could have written such works as *Heart of Darkness*, with their suggestive dramatisation of changes in state of mind, and have not been sensitively attuned to the whole psychological culture of late nineteenth-century Europe. It is hard to fault Conrad, as D. H. Lawrence did, for not going far enough. After all, both Conrad and Nietzsche permanently modified our confident sense of aesthetic and psychological direction. Why it was done differently by a novelist and a philosopher, and how it was done are questions that should not be confused. But as we answer both questions separately we cannot deny *that* it was done.

NOTES

1. Edward Garnett, *Letters from Joseph Conrad, 1895–1924* (Indianapolis: Bobbs-Merrill Company, 1928), pp. 157, 158.
2. *The Portable Nietzsche*, ed. and trans. Walter Kaufmann (New York: Viking Press, 1966), pp. 46–7. Wherever they are available I cite Kaufmann's excellent translations. On one occasion I cite another translation, but have also used the German text edited by Schlechta.
3. Friedrich Nietzsche, *The Will to Power*, trans. Walter Kaufmann and R. J. Hollingdale (New York: Vintage Books, 1967), p. 327.
4. Nietzsche, *The Gay Science, with a Prelude in Rhymes and an Appendix of Songs*, trans. Kaufmann (New York: Vintage Books, 1974), p. 336.
5. Nietzsche, *Beyond Good and Evil: Prelude to a Philosophy of the Future*, trans. Kaufmann (New York: Vintage Books, 1966), p. 201.
6. *Gay Science*, pp. 298–9.
7. Edward W. Said, 'Conrad: The Presentation of Narrative', *Novel*, Vol. 7, No. 2 (Winter 1974), 116–32.
8. Nietzsche, 'We Philologists', trans. William Arrowsmith, *Arion*, New Series 1/2 (1973–4), p. 299.
9. Nietzsche, *Menschliches, Allzumenschliches*, in Volume I of *Werke*, ed. Karl Schlechta (Frankfurt: Ullstein, 1972), p. 464.
10. *Gay Science*, p. 218. See also pages 221–2.
11. *Gay Science*, p. 343.
12. *Will to Power*, p. 524.
13. *Will to Power*, p. 428.
14. Conrad, *Heart of Darkness* in *Youth and Two Other Stories*, Vol. XVI of *Complete Works* (Garden City: Doubleday, Page and Company, 1925), p. 159.
15. 'We Philologists', p. 308.
16. *Beyond Good and Evil*, p. 29.
17. *Will to Power*, p. 13.
18. *Will to Power*, p. 550.
19. *Gay Science*, p. 168.
20. *Will to Power*, p. 548.
21. *Heart of Darkness*, p. 93.

6 Conrad and Rousseau:
Concepts of Man and Society

ZDZISLAW NAJDER

The objective of this essay is not a quest for sources. That Conrad read Rousseau does not need to be proven; how well he remembered his works and how strongly he felt Rousseau's influence when writing his own novels does not concern me here. What I am attempting is not a genetic inquiry, but an exploration in the history of certain ideas. Nor is it a comprehensive study of the Conrad–Rousseau relation, which would have required a fuller discussion of various aspects and diverse components of Rousseau's thought and means of expression.

Rather, comparing Conrad with Rousseau is supposed to serve three purposes: firstly, to elucidate, by way of a contrastive analysis, Conrad's concepts of man and society; secondly, to place Conrad within the mainstream of European moral and socio-political thought which, in turn, will make it possible to determine his position on the map of philosophical and political tendencies of his day; and finally to clarify the intellectual structure of those works of Conrad which can be interpreted in terms of his opposition to Rousseau's ideas.

The political issues raised in Conrad's fiction attracted scant notice during his lifetime. He was also gravely disappointed by lack of public response to 'Autocracy and War', his longest piece of political journalism. But within the last thirty years Conrad as a political writer has been given a growing consideration. Still, the conceptual framework of his thought, the sources and implications of his fundamental ideas of man, society, and historical process, and the relation of his beliefs to the main currents of European political philosophy have not been much explored. Conrad's political convictions remain to a large extent insufficiently defined.

In the thirties the label 'conservative' was affixed to Conrad – and it stuck. In spite of what Professors Howe and Kettle wrote later on Conrad's realistic presentation of social and political conflicts,[1] 'conservative' is an epithet still used almost automatically in characterising Conrad's views. Professor Avrom Fleishman was the first to challenge this simplicistic opinion, but I believe that he has not done so on well-chosen grounds. Fleishman places Conrad within what he calls 'the Burke tradition'. Indeed, there are evident affinities between Conrad's and Burke's attitudes. But there are also serious differences both in their views and in their conceptual framework. For instance, where Conrad writes about the nation or humanity, Burke has the state or society; in fact, in his understanding of the nation Burke is closer to Rousseau than to Conrad. Moreover, to place Conrad within the Burke tradition, that is within the tradition of the thinker generally considered to have been the father of modern conservatism, makes it rather awkward to account for, or even to point at, those elements of Conrad's thought which do not belong to and indeed clash with this tradition.[2]

Two other objections may be raised. The whole concept of 'the Burke tradition' is rather vague, because Burke was a polemicist, not a systematic thinker. Also, interpreting Conrad in terms of Burke and his followers leads us away from the more immediate, continental sources of Conrad's ideas – which, even if we leave aside his Polish background, I believe account for most of the analogies with Burke's 'organic' approach to society. It was certainly no accident that Conrad would switch to French almost invariably when writing on philosophical or political problems; there can also be no doubt that he knew French history more intimately than English.

Beside Rousseau, the only other thinker with a similar scope of interests Conrad knew and referred to was Carlyle. But, in spite of superficial resemblances, Conrad was even more radically opposed to and less influenced by Carlyle than Rousseau.[3] More importantly, Carlyle is too shallow, shrill, and idiosyncratic a thinker to be really useful as a comparative counterpart. Also, he was not the father to but only a stepson of a certain political and intellectual tradition, and therefore a comparison with him will drive us into a side-alley of the history of ideas.

Not that the comparison with Rousseau himself presents no difficulties. It is well known that he was a man of split personality and that his writings, even his developed theories, abound in contradictions. Rousseau the sentimentalist disappears with hardly a trace in his *Social Contract*; his philosophy of the individual seems to conflict with his philosophy of the state. Moreover, the Rousseau of the *Considérations sur le gouvernement de la Pologne* is much more outspoken than his later adversary Burke on the issue of national feelings and traditions – but the Rousseau of *The Social Contract* understands the nation in the purely abstract terms of an agglomeration of the loyal inhabitants of a state. I am not, however, going to dwell on these contradictions (of which Conrad might have been completely unaware) and shall conveniently talk only about those theories and aspects of Rousseau which have exerted most influence and thus can be taken, at least in the historical sense, as most characteristic of him.

Rousseau appears twice in Conrad's works: in *A Personal Record*, with reference to *The Confessions* and *Émile*, and in *Under Western Eyes*, where a reference to *The Social Contract* is made and where a monument of Jean-Jacques plays quite an important role – one exile watching another exile.

Commenting upon *The Confessions*, Conrad ironically shrugs off Rousseau's 'thoroughness in justifying his own existence' and calls him – also ironically, I presume – 'an artless moralist'.[4] And indeed, to a writer so passionately concerned with the problems of moral responsibility, *The Confessions* must have appeared as primarily an exercise in self-exculpation. The theoretical foundations of this auto-apology are laid in one of the opening sentences of Rousseau's memoirs: 'I am not made like any of those I have seen; I venture to believe that I am not made like any of those who are in existence.'[5] Why is Jean-Jacques different? Because he is exceptionally sensitive, has natural good impulses, 'worships freedom, abhors restraint, trouble, dependence'. The outspoken advocate of equality assures us that he is not 'one of those low-born men' without 'a real sentiment of justice'. The claim to uniqueness is thus coupled with a claim to goodness. The seat of goodness is his heart, whatever the evidence of his actions may say. The man who has told us the memorable story of how he accused a girl who was in love with him of stealing a ribbon he had stolen himself, replies in this manner to criticism of the way in which he disposed of his five children:

> Is it possible that my warmheartedness, lively sensibility, readiness to form attachments . . . my natural goodwill towards all my fellow-creatures, my ardent love of the great, the true, the beautiful, and the just; my utter inability to hate or injure . . . the sweet and lively emotion which I feel at the sign of all that is virtuous, generous, and amiable; is it possible, I ask, that all these can ever agree in the same heart with the depravity which, without the least scruple, tramples underfoot the sweetest of obligations? No! I feel and loudly assert – it is impossible.

Rousseau's position boils down to this: I am unlike anybody else, and therefore I should be judged by special standards; I am well-intentioned and sensitive, therefore I cannot do evil. Any account of the moral principles advocated by Conrad must include the exact opposite of Rousseau's position, and the moral stance of many Conradian heroes represents the antithesis of Rousseau's peculiar 'great moral lesson'; 'to avoid those situations of life which bring our duties into conflict with our interests'. This, Conrad would say, is stark moral cowardice. In his life, Conrad also made compromises; but to proclaim such a programme would, in his eyes, amount to making moral cowardice a norm.

Conrad's gibe – in the quoted fragment of *A Personal Record* – at confessions as a 'discredited form of literary activity' acquires a peculiar significance in view of his own frequent use of this very convention. His heroes quite often indulge in confessions of two different types. The first is a straightforward disclosure of a painful or otherwise important experience, an 'opening of one's heart to a friend', as we have in 'The Lagoon', 'Karain', 'An Anarchist', Jukes' letter in *Typhoon*, *Chance*, and finally in *The Shadow Line*, which is subtitled *A Confession*. The function of such a confession is to unburden one's soul by communing with another person. The frequency and the psychological role of this type of confessions derives possibly, as Professor Thomas Moser suggested to me, from Conrad's Catholic background.

The other type is an apologetic confession: its objective is not so much to communicate, as to justify oneself. Chapters four to eleven of *Lord Jim*, 'Falk', and large parts of *Under Western Eyes* contain, or are based on, confessions of this kind.[6] In fact, in *Under Western Eyes* we have also a third type of 'confession': Razumov's secret report to the Russian police, the scornful and conceited missive which this 'man of reason', driven by best intentions, composes under the benevolent effigy of Rousseau. He feels perfectly safe when he writes it on a solitary islet devoted to the philosopher who maintained that man is innately good and that democracy is an excellent system but suitable only to people who are sufficiently mature.

Different as their subjects are, Jim's confessions to Marlow in the first part of the novel, and Razumov's confessions in his diary, have in common not only their self-exculpating purpose, but also the way in which the arguments are developed. Both Jim and Razumov point to the peculiarities of their respective situations, which make it nonsensical to demand from them a 'conventional' kind of behaviour. Both stress their good intentions and their reasonableness. In the early chapters of the novel, Jim explains away his desertion of the *Patna* by arguing that to remain on board was practically pointless and that he never intended to shirk his duty. Razumov's explanation of his betrayal of Haldin follows a different course; he uses historical, political, and philosophical arguments to support his decision – but the essential argument is the same: he was tricked by the circumstances, he did the only sensible thing, his motives were pure and non-egoistic. Thus in both cases we encounter a characteristically Rousseauian type of self-justification by reference to the exceptionality of one's situation and (in Razumov's case) personality, and to one's good intentions.

In the latter part of the novel, Jim changes his attitude and simply admits that he was afraid. Razumov also throws away his mantle of self-righteousness and makes a true, non-apologetic, confession to Miss Haldin, in this way bowing to the demands of 'conventional conscience'.

Conrad's ethic of fidelity and constraint, of duty, honour, and human solidarity, was directly opposed to that of Rousseau, and was rooted in a fundamentally different concept of human nature.

Bertrand Russell was the first to comment on this contrast:

> His point of view, one might perhaps say, was the antithesis of Rousseau's 'Man is born in chains, but he can become free.' He becomes free, so I believe Conrad would have said, not by letting loose his impulses, not by being casual and uncontrolled, but by subduing wayward impulses to a dominant purpose . . . Conrad's point of view was far from modern. In the modern world there are two philosophies: the one, which stems from Rousseau, and sweeps aside all discipline as unnecessary; the other, which finds its fullest expression in totalitarianism, which thinks of discipline as essentially imposed from without. Conrad adhered to the older tradition, that discipline should come from within. He despised indiscipline, and hated discipline that was merely external.[7]

The first of the cited sentences contains a glaring misquotation; another misses the fact that both mentioned philosophies exist side by side in Rousseau's thought – but Russell's point is still valid and deserves amplification.

' "Man is born a coward" ', says the French lieutenant in *Lord Jim*. ' "It is a difficulty, parbleu! It would be too easy otherwise. But habit – habit – necessity – do you see? the eyes of others – voilà. One puts up with it." '[8] The 'older tradition' voiced here goes far back to ancient Greece. Man is naturally, spontaneously, neither virtuous nor strong;

he has to be educated and given examples to follow; he must work on himself, but cannot be morally self-reliant. To Aristotle's dictum that man outside society is either god or beast, Conrad adds in *Heart of Darkness* that a man who wishes to be a god becomes inevitably a beast. Kind emotions and good intentions have a limited ethical value: were not both Kurtz and Charles Gould men of good intentions? And though a man can rise to greatness, he cannot put a simple trust in himself because of his inherent frailty.

In *The Social Contract* Rousseau admitted that his main problem in that work was how to preserve the ideal of freedom and at the same time to impose discipline. His extreme moral individualism and emotionalism made constraint in the form of a strongly authoritarian social doctrine virtually a necessity, while his hypothesis of the noble savage and his optimistic idea of the innate goodness of man made an absolutist approach easier and seemingly safe. The outcome was his ideology of a totalitarian democracy: totalitarian because it pre-supposed a sole and exclusive truth in politics, democracy because it left, at least ostensibly, the search for this truth to all citizens at once. But when a counterbalance to the excesses of individualism was established, it led, both in Rousseau's theory and in the later revolutionary practice, to a total abrogation of the rights of the individual to state mechanism.[9]

Although *The Social Contract* is not short of contradictions, its general drift of its arguments cannot be mistaken. Unfortunately, many readers become so fascinated by Rousseau's rhetoric, so enchanted by the famous and superbly demagogic first sentence ('Man is born free, but he is everywhere in chains'[10]), that they miss the more sinister but inevitable implications of the treatise. What are the main points of Rousseau's doctrine?

Contrary to what might be expected from an apologist of individualism, the concept of society used by Rousseau is quantitative rather than qualitative: a society is simply an agglomeration of units, not an organic whole, and men's powers, wills, interests and personalities are conceived of and represented quantitatively, in form of numbers and fractions. They can be added or subtracted, multiplied or decreased without apparently undergoing an essential change. His vision of society is therefore one of a multitude of atoms. This multitude enters into a social contract which consists of the 'total alienation by each associate of himself and all his rights to the whole community'. This community of ciphers is capable of possessing a 'general will'. The general will is described in terms which are at the same time mathematical and metaphysical. It does not represent an opinion of the majority, nor does it have any empirical counterpart – but it is, nevertheless, composed of a sum of all interests, from which the conflicting individual interests have been subtracted. The general will cannot err and is absolutely binding on all citizens of the state. 'Whoever', says Rousseau in one of his most remarkable statements, 'refuses to obey the general will shall be constrained to do so by the whole body, which means nothing other than that he shall be forced to be free.' (We have here an archetypal instance of double-speak.) No parties, representing divergent opinions, should be permitted. For different peoples different types of government are appropriate; the more populous a state, the stronger should be its government. No wonder that Hegel, the philosopher of the Prussian authoritarian state, thought highly of Rousseau's political teachings; but Rousseau's programme of social atomisation combined with a powerful central government was fulfilled only in our century.

Rousseau's belief that a removal of institutions will bring about a change, and a change for the better, in men, seems to have been particularly disturbing to Conrad. He made at least one obvious allusion to this 'strange conviction', in his Note to *Under Western Eyes*. And his notorious dread of anarchy may be traced back to his knowledge of Rousseau's doctrine and its results during the French Revolution. The vision of a mob 'liberated' from all traditional constraints and authorities, unruly and heedless but easily swayed by the cleverest demagogue, appalled Conrad.

But it would be a gross distortion to present Conrad's relation to Rousseau simply in terms of a negative reaction. In his attitude towards Rousseau's ideas we are rather dealing with an opposition-obsession syndrome: although Conrad's reaction to Rousseau was predominantly negative, the ideas he condemned left on him an indelible imprint. It is obvious that the doctrine of the general will must have been repugnant to Conrad, but more important is the fact that he saw radical social change, the modern nation-state, and democracy itself in characteristically Rousseauian terms. Although he chose to become a British subject, he envisaged democracy neither in the way in which many English theorists saw it – as a system gradually introduced from above, with the electorate being broadened out – nor in the Jeffersonian manner, as a system of government by equal and fully enfranchised individuals. Rather, democracy meant for him – as for a typical French conservative – a mechanistic government by the mob, with an inbuilt tendency to autocracy. Only by taking this into account can we explain, for instance, Conrad's vitriolic outburst against the Reform Bill and the results of the 1885 elections in his letter to Joseph Spiridion.[11] I do not know whether he ever read *Democracy in America*, but he apparently took as a *fait accompli* the threat of a new kind of democratic oppression which had troubled de Tocqueville.[12] To use modern terminology, he equated all democracy with its totalitarian form. And in contemporary social democrats he saw direct exponents of Rousseau's pernicious ideology – minus any national sentiments the author of *Émile* might have had.[13]

Characteristically, Conrad criticised the modern democratic or semi-democratic state on two counts. Firstly, in a way Rousseau would agree with, for depersonalising and emasculating its citizens, for turning them into cogs of a huge socio-economic machinery; and secondly, for achieving what Rousseau had demanded, in other words for getting rid of traditional bonds and institutions, for atomising the human community. The typical products of modern society, Conrad suggests, are economic robots and moral anarchists.

Under Western Eyes provides ample evidence of Conrad's opposition-obsession syndrome in relation to Rousseau. To begin with, Rousseau figures there in two roles: as a distinguished native of Geneva, an illustrious patron of Swiss democracy, exiled during his life-time but now honoured by the monument which plays such an important part in Razumov's actions; and as a patron of the revolutionary emigrants. Both roles are well-grounded in facts, because Rousseau signed his *Social Contract*, later to become a theoretical basis for revolutionary movements, 'a citizen of Geneva'. The first Rousseau is treated with a double-edged irony. The scoffing remarks about Swiss democracy have to be referred to him; and he provides a symbolic shelter for the *agent provocateur* Razumov. The ideology of revolutionary upheaval induced by terror and destruction is an object not only of implicit irony, but also of direct criticism, raised somewhat naively by the narrator but given authorial support by the fact that most professional revolution-aries are presented as rather despicable figures.

Although the career of their leader, Peter Ivanovitch, owes some-thing to that of Bakunin, he also resembles Rousseau – an 'inspired man' as well – not only in his irrationalism and declared feminism (combined with ruthlessness towards those women who are dependent on him), but primarily in his being maintained by an aristocratic lady. He is supported by his elderly lover, Mme de S—, just as Rousseau was supported by his mistress Mme de Warens, and later by Mmes Dupin, d'Epinay, d'Houdetot, and several others.

The opinions on Russia expressed in *Under Western Eyes* sometimes seem to echo Rousseau. Thus when the teacher of languages says that Russia has what she deserves, he could easily have been made to quote Rousseau's theoretical rule that 'The sovereign by the mere fact that it is, is always all that it ought to be.' More specifically, Rousseau maintained that Russia, with her natural historical tradition broken by Peter the Great, had lost her ability to develop normally,[14] an idea which is also reflected in the novel.

However, the main advantage of looking at *Under Western Eyes* from the angle of Conrad's relation to Rousseau is that it not only makes us realise to what extent this is a novel of ideas – in a manner similar to *The Magic Mountain* – but also puts us on the right track in looking for the historical origins of those ideas. Thus the declaration of Mr de P—, the Minister of State, that 'the thought of liberty has never existed in the Act of the Creator. From the multitude of men's counsel nothing could come but revolt and disorder; and revolt and disorder in a world created for obedience and stability is sin. It was not Reason but Authority which expressed the Divine Intention' echoes, surely not by accident, the views of Joseph de Maistre, one of the most outspoken and influential conservative critics of Rousseau and the Enlightenment.[15] De Maistre's voice can be heard also in Razumov's dispute with Haldin, when he pits historical tradition against radical change, and in Razumov's five principles, which he puts down after Haldin's arrest:

History not Theory.
Patriotism not Internationalism.
Evolution not Revolution.
Direction not Destruction.
Unity not Disruption.

Another conservative philosopher who was greatly influential in Russia – Hegel – is echoed by Razumov when he says that what was needed for 'the travail of maturing destiny' of Russia was 'not the conflicting aspirations of a people, but a will strong and one . . . not the babble of many voices, but a man – strong and one!' 'The logic of history made him unavoidable.'[16]

Neither are the narrator's critical remarks on Russia, her people, and her system of government, invented ad hoc; they reflect opinions voiced by many Polish writers (notably Mickiewicz, whom Conrad twice quotes[17]), by some Russian dissenters (particularly Chaadayev[18]), and by the Marquis de Custine, author of the justly famous *Russie en 1839.*[19]

Thus Conrad replays, mainly in Razumov's internal monologues but also in the narrator's commentary, the actual debate, which lasted throughout the whole of the nineteenth century, between the apologists of Holy Russia, Orthodoxy, and tsarist autocracy and the liberal-minded 'occidentalists', who saw Russia as the centre of barbaric reaction in Europe, a nation strangled by a monstrous spiritual and political tyranny. This gives *Under Western Eyes* its solid historical foundations, and tallies with the fact that Conrad apparently conceived it as an anti-Dostoevsky novel. The statement that 'In Russia, the land of spectral ideas and disembodied aspirations, many brave minds . . . turned to autocracy for the peace of their patriotic conscience as a weary unbeliever, touched by grace, turns to the faith of his fathers for the blessing of spiritual rest' alludes, among others, to Dostoevsky, who, after the social and intellectual radicalism of his early years, turned into a leading reactionary thinker. (Incidentally, Dostoevsky clearly belongs to the Rousseau tradition in his moral psychology and his approach to religion.)

We find in *Under Western Eyes* the conservative position more fully presented than the revolutionary programme, which remains only vaguely defined. But there can be no doubt that Conrad condemns both alternatives. Generally speaking, the negative side of his political views is more easily discernible than the positive: we come to know pretty well what he was against; what he was for we find only adumbrated in his work. It appears that his ideal society would be one that was deeply rooted in national history, that observed basic liberties stemming from the recognition of man's dignity, and that was organically integrated and structuralised by a hierarchy of obligations. It is worth remarking that, whatever its origins, this vision does not differ from the idea of society presented in the writings of his father.

This, at least, should make us pause before calling Conrad a conservative. To what extent is this designation, so commonly applied to Conrad, adequate? 'Conservative' is, of course, a vague term which can be applied to many kinds of political, moral, and cultural opinions and attitudes. As Conrad was neither a professional politician nor a publicist, the most sensible approach seems to be one of analysing his 'style of thought', as understood by Karl Mannheim. In his classic essay on 'Conservative Thought' Mannheim characterises the conservative style of thought, as opposed to that of the eighteenth century Enlightenment, liberal-progressive, 'natural law' philosophers. He shows how it stresses the importance of the following ideas:

1 History, life, the nation, as opposed to reason;
2 The irrationality of reality;
3 The individuality of phenomena rather than their universal validity;
4 Society as an organism;
5 Social wholes which are not sums of their parts; 'belonging' to such wholes;
6 A dynamic conception of reason.[20]

Now with the possible exception of the sixth point Conrad's thought runs along the same conceptual lines. Moreover, his concept of man is qualitative, as opposed to the characteristically quantitative idea of man used by most radicals, and he stresses the superiority of experience over all theories. (Here again *Under Western Eyes* provides an excellent example: Razumov had it all thought out – but his theories collapse in the face of reality, both personal and moral.)

But there are also in Conrad's work four factors which conflict with the conservative style of thought. Firstly, political problems are for him essentially moral problems; in this, as in several other respects, he stands at the opposite pole to Carlyle. Conservatives would, typically, separate the two spheres. Secondly, he rejects the sumpremacy of the state, the government, all established official institutions, even the law, over traditional values and over individuals and their spiritual claims. Thirdly, the postulate of equality as a component of liberty – which evoked the strongest protests from conservatives – is evidently acceptable to him. And fourthly, his attitude to property is as scornful as any revolutionary's.

Passing from the general categories of a style of thought to the concrete presentations of social reality in Conrad's work, we face the same puzzling dilemma: the author of *Nostromo* and *The Secret Agent* can hardly be described as a conservative; but how can we describe his political attitude, if not as conservative? Not only in the two novels mentioned, but also in, for instance, *The Mirror of the Sea* and 'Autocracy and War', we can discern an acute consciousness of the need for fundamental social and political change, an awareness of widespread injustice and corruption, and a strong disapproval of the status quo. This 'conservative' was an outspoken critic of contemporary bourgeois society and of a system which gives first place and free play to 'material interests'. It is remarkable that his criticism reminds us more of those romantic and 'feudal' critics of the capitalists who were so vocal at the beginning of the nineteenth century, than of contemporary radical attacks on the prevailing social and economic stratifications. But, unlike those conservative critics of capitalism and industrialism, Conrad was no apologist for the feudal system, which was also due for an essential change. How can one explain this dilemma? And how can one account for the fact that when Conrad postulates change, evolution, reform, his does not start from the present, but from a point in the past, before the plague of material interests had spread, and before other pernicious forces of the present had begun their work of corruption.

The answer is to be found in Conrad's peculiar political background. It is a peculiar characteristic of nineteenth century Polish political thought that its dominant trends are at the same time progressive and traditionalist.[21] All Polish patriotic thinkers had to be traditionalist, or even conservative, because they wanted to restore their partitioned country. The restoration of national independence was the principal belief, the first point on the agenda, of everybody who did not acquiesce in Poland's annihilation. To accept the present as the basis for change would have meant to resign from the national dream, to renounce the glories of the past. This conservative impulse was strengthened by a constant need to preserve the remnants of the old order in the form of language, tradition and customs. But, despite everything, Poles remained in the vanguard of international radical movements throughout the nineteenth century, fighting on innumerable barricades, and supporting or even leading revolutionary movements in Italy, Hungary and France – including the ill-starred Paris Commune, in which the commander of the armed forces was Jarosław Dabrowski, an old companion of Conrad's father and uncle in their underground work.

The long and winding path we have taken since our initial comparison of Conrad and Rousseau has not been chosen at random, but has been determined by the implications of the concepts we have analysed. We have not fully explored the similarities and the contrasts between the two men; one more, at least, deserves to be mentioned. Both Rousseau and Conrad were members of a new class: the intelligentsia. Both lived outside the basic socio-economic strata of their societies, both lived off their work, both felt broader intellectual and political responsibilities, and both were critical of the societies in which they lived. Both were, for many years, footloose wanderers, and both were expatriates; but although Conrad spent almost his entire life without any concrete communal bonds, he was not, like Rousseau, spiritually rootless. Although he did not envisage any social groups in which he could put his trust, he never broke his mental bond with the human community. In his traditionalism and his heroic clinging to an *ideal* fellowship, *ideal* institutions, an *imagined* tradition, he seems to have been a characteristically Polish intellectual.

The difficulty of defining his politics reflects his own political dilemma. Conrad passionately rejected autocracy and authoritarianism as contrary to all that he valued most in man. But he had strong objections to democracy which, he thought, 'had elected to pin its faith to the supremacy of material interests'.[22] The bulwarks of liberty seemed to be at the same time the strongholds of materialism and social atomisation. To a European intellectual of today this dilemma looks disturbingly familiar.

NOTES

1. A. Kettle, *An Introduction to the English Novel* (London: Hutchinson University Library, 1953), vol. II, 67–81. I. Howe, *Politics and the Novel* (New York: Horizon Press, 1957), pp. 76–113.
2. A. Fleishman, *Conrad's Politics: Community and Anarchy in the Fiction of Joseph Conrad* (Baltimore: Johns Hopkins University Press, 1967). Fleishman compounds his difficulties by committing numerous factual errors in describing Conrad's Polish background. And Rousseau was *not* a theorist of the organic state (see p. 231).
3. Conrad is linked to Carlyle by Fleishman, loc. cit., pp. 62–4. One has to beware of such accidental analogies in analysing Conrad's philosophical views. For example the affinity with Schopenhauer has been exaggerated: Conrad shared neither his ethics nor his epistemology, the two notable elements of Schopenhauer's thought. The similarities with Jean-Marie Guyau in ethics and Émile Boutroux in the philosophy of knowledge seem much more significant.
4. *A Personal Record*, Dent Collected Edition, p. 97. (All further references are to this edition.)
5. The Modern Library edition (New York: Random House), p. 3. All quotations are from this edition.
6. There are others in Conrad's work: in *Nostromo*, 'The Secret Sharer', in 'The Nature of a Crime' (written in collaboration with F. M. Ford), scattered throughout *Almayer's Folly* and *An Outcast*, etc.
7. *Portraits from Memory* (London: Allen & Unwin, 1956), pp. 82, 84.
8. J. Conrad, *Lord Jim*, p. 147.
9. See J. L. Talmon, *The Origins of Totalitarian Democracy* (London: Mercury Books, 1961), pp. 38–49.
10. *The Social Contract*, trans. by Maurice Cranston (Harmondsworth: Penguin, 1968), p. 49. All quotations are from this edition.
11. G. Jean-Aubry, *Joseph Conrad: Life and Letters* (London: Heinemann, 1927), v. I, 84.
12. See A. de Tocqueville, *De la Démocratie en Amérique*, IV, 6.
13. It is worth noticing that while Conrad seems to have been quite well read in political philosophy of the eighteenth and early nineteenth century, he knew little of contemporary political writers. If he ever read Marx, he managed to hide this fact completely; and his letter to R. B. Cunninghame

Graham of 8 February 1899, in which he bands together Jaurèr and Liebknecht as socialist annihilators of the national idea, shows his ignorance both of Jaurès's attitude and of Marx's own outspokenly pro-Polish stand.

14. *The Social Contract*, II, 8, pp. 89–90.
15. Especially *Les Soirées de Saint-Pétérsbourg* and *Étude sur la souveraineté*. De Maistre spent fourteen years (1803–17) in St Petersburg as ambassador of the King of Sardinia.
16. *Under Western Eyes*, pp. 8, 61, 66, 33, 35.
17. For details see Z. Najder, *Nad Conradem* (Warsaw, 1964), pp. 167–8.
18. Ibid., where striking analogies with other Russian thinkers are discussed. Conrad could not have read Chaadayev, but de Custine (see next note) tells his story and offers a resumé of his first *Philosophical Letter*. See also A. Walicki, *The Slavophile Controversy* (Oxford University Press, 1975) and Raymond T. McNally, *Chaadayev and His Friends* (Tallahassee, 1971).
19. I have no doubt that Conrad read Astolphe de Custine. *Russie an 1839* was one of the most famous books on Russia; it was written by a fairly conservative Roman Catholic, but was sharply critical of both the regime and the people. On several specific points there are parallels between de Custine and Conrad: they both mention, for example, the conservative temper of the nation, resignation as a Russian national trait, drunkenness, cynicism, etc. On de Custine and Polish influence on his work see George F. Kennan, *The Marquis de Custine and His Russia in 1839* (Princeton University Press, 1971).
20. K. Mannheim, *Essays in Sociology and Social Psychology* (London: Routledge and Kegan Paul, 1953), pp. 74–118.
21. See J. Szacki, *Ojczyzna, naród, rewolucja* (Warsaw, 1962), pp. 13–14, 26–30.
22. J. Conrad, *Notes on Life and Letters*, p. 107.

7 Conrad and Russia

EDWARD CRANKSHAW

I can offer no discoveries about Conrad. What I should like to do is to look at certain aspects of Conrad's life and work, which are common knowledge, and ask whether by modifying certain assumptions and suggesting a changed emphasis here and there we may, perhaps, come a little closer to him than before.

It is now very widely accepted that Conrad's profound concern with problems of moral failure, of desertion, of betrayal, in a large part sprang from guilt feelings about his own abandonment of Poland – a Poland helpless under an alien tyranny. When at sixteen, the argument runs, he went off to France and the sea, he was taking the first step, no doubt unconsciously, towards the abandonment of the land for which his ancestors, indeed his own father and mother, had suffered and died. That abandonment was made absolute eleven years later when he became a British citizen. And it was the sense of guilt implanted by this act that was the inspiration of much of his writing, and, most clearly of all, *Lord Jim*. Jim's fatal jump to safety echoed the young Korzeniowski's flight from Poland.

I suppose the most extreme exponent of this theory has been Gustav Morf, who was categorical on the subject in *The Polish Heritage of Joseph Conrad*, published in London in 1930. *Lord Jim*, he assured us, 'is more than a novel, it is a confession'; and he goes on to analyse the novel in Freudian terms. '*Lord Jim* is more than a psychological novel', he concludes, 'it is a psychoanalytical novel written before psychoanalysis was founded. It appeared in 1900, the very year when Freud published his first book, *The Interpretation of Dreams*, which indirectly helps us to explain the novel.'

Perhaps it does. But unless handled with extreme care, it also helps to obscure it. Thus, for example, Morf's insistence, which he italicises, on the similarity between the name of the sinking ship, the *Patna*, and the Polish name for Poland, *Polska* – to say nothing of the equation of Jim's father, an English parson, with Conrad's father, 'a great religious idealist' in Morf's words – seems to go too far.

This is not a criticism of Morf, who offered many valuable insights.

I cite him here because he was, as far as I know, the first to suggest the over-riding importance in Conrad's work of guilt feelings of a very simple kind – all centred on Poland. It is a conception which, I believe, has been too readily absorbed into the canon, even if few would go all the way with Morf. Conrad was not a simple man, and his feelings were not simple either. Furthermore, one may ask why it should be so readily assumed that he should be expected to feel guilty – seriously and enduringly guilty – as the consequence of a very reasonable action of a kind fairly commonplace in nineteenth century central Europe, as in our own day. Certainly Conrad himself could write: 'It would take too long to explain the intimate alliance of contradictions in human nature which makes love itself wear at times the desperate shape of betrayal'. And this sentence from *A Personal Record* has been taken as a direct and exclusive reference to Poland. It could well be that Conrad did in fact have in mind the past reproaches of certain of his compatriots, but only, I feel sure, in a corner of his mind. His eye, as always, was fixed on a farther and wider horizon, on nothing less than the insoluble questions posed by human existence, warm, eager, deeply flawed, aspiring but corruptible, lost in the immensity of a hostile universe.

I do not for a moment suggest that feelings of guilt formed no part in the make-up of this extremely complex man. It would be surprising, too, if long before the violent attack on his desertion by his stay-at-home compatriot, the novelist Eliza Orzeszkowa, in 1899, Conrad had not looked back on his own tragic land and, in some moods, asked himself whether, to put it flatly, he had done the right thing in cutting himself off from the working out of Poland's destiny. How far, how deeply, this may have gone could be argued for ever – and for ever inconclusively. I do not propose to start now. But at this stage I think we should remind ourselves of the Polish reality in the years between 1875, when the young Korzeniowski set out for Marseilles, and 1886 when he became a British citizen.

Conrad was indeed a Pole, but it is too often forgotten that he was also a Russian citizen, a subject of the two successive Alexanders, II and III. As a subject of the Tsar he was liable for conscription into the Imperial army. What he renounced in 1886 was Russian, not Polish, citizenship. His own country did not exist: it was partitioned between the three monarchies, Russia, Prussia and Austria. Conrad transferred his formal allegiance from the dully reactionary Alexander III to Queen Victoria during the third administration of Mr Gladstone. What sort of a betrayal was this?

And what could he have done if he had stayed in Poland under Russian rule? There were only two possibilities. He could have participated in the clandestine, foredoomed, in the circumstances absurd, politics of revolt, an utterly hopeless cause since the crushing defeat of the 1863 insurrection which his father had helped to prepare. Or he could have collaborated with the occupying power.

I do not apologise for using that term. It is easy for us to think of collaborators with contempt, but it may be very wrong all the same. Of course, there is collaboration and collaboration. Those French men and women, for example, who actively played up to the Germans in the last war, seeking favour at the expense of their compatriots who resisted or who held themselves as far as possible aloof (negative collaborators, one might call them), no doubt deserved all that some of them got. But people of that kind, unprincipled careerists, sycophants, place-seekers, look for advantage in that sort of way in all societies in all countries. Their behaviour is equally base whether they are demeaning themselves for the sake of advancement before their own superiors or before the representatives of an occupying power. The presence of an occupying power does, however, force the whole population, active resisters apart, into collaboration in the more or less negative sense. Every individual in Russian Poland who lived quietly and got on with his own job was in this way a collaborator, in that he helped to make it possible for the enemy to govern. There was no escape from this. Even those splendid Polish women who demonstratively went about in mourning for their country after the crushing of the earlier rebellion in 1830 had to collaborate in a negative sense in order to survive. The only non-collaborators were men like Conrad's father who actively conspired and rebelled, risking their own lives and bringing down the wrath of Russia on their fellow countrymen – a line of conduct which Conrad came to deplore because of its futility. Uncle Thaddeus Bobrowski, on the other hand, was himself a negative collaborator, who sought to make life easier for his compatriots by subduing his own feelings. He was conscious enough of the problems involved in this line of conduct to urge his nephew, who lacked, as he saw it, the level-headedness essential for the collaborationist's role, to get out and keep out.

Given this background it seems to me inconceivable that Conrad could have been overcome by a sense of guilt and betrayal to the extent that has sometimes been imagined. Nostalgia for the might-have-been he certainly experienced; twinges of doubt and self-accusation also; and overpowering sympathy for those left behind. And obviously the vehemence of his rejection of revolutionary violence of any kind was stimulated by the desperate futility of his father's insurrectionist and conspiratorial activity and embittered by the divided loyalties implicit in this rejection.

But it seems to me that the real agonising – and this comes out again and again in his writings – was centred not upon his own personal relationship with Poland but on something at the same time broader and more fundamental: an intellectual and emotional problem brought home to him by the experience of his own people which caused him to brood for ever on the very nature of evil as an irresistible force. Firstly, what did it mean? Secondly, how could one face the irresistible without bringing down vengeance on the heads of the innocent and yet salvage personal integrity, honour, one's own soul in defeat? It seems to me that, acute as Conrad's feelings about Poland as such quite evidently were, we should look at Jim in particular and the novels as a whole against this far wider and more generalised complex of problems. And I believe that Russia provides the clue.

When he began publishing in 1895, at thirty-seven, the consciousness of evil in Western Europe was less immediate than at any time in its history. The prevailing mood still reflected the scarcely questioning optimism and faith in material progress symbolised by the Great Exhibition of forty-four years earlier – an apotheosis that Conrad himself specifically derided. England had not been involved in any major war since the end of the Crimean adventure. The appalling slaughter of the American Civil War was far away. And although Prussia had fought and beaten Austria in 1866 and France in 1870, it was widely assumed that the universe had been tamed and that the continental monarchies would sooner or later inevitably yield to the all-conquering rectitude of liberal ideas and the secret ballot. Even the Bulgarian atrocities were a thing of the past. The sense of the power of evil as an arbitrary force had dwindled. The idea that it might be the dominant force was inconceivable. There was no sense of doom. There was hope. There was more than hope. There was confidence.

How different for the Poles! The Poles, as a nation and as individuals, were really up against it – '*it*' being the naked and inescapable fact of arbitrary violence, of the power of evil roaming free and able to strike where it willed; more than to strike: to crush, in a way the English had not known since the sixteenth century. The Poles, all of them, lived, existed, under some sort of alien rule. Some were lucky under the comparatively beneficent rule of Austria. Others had to cope with the harsh, brutal, but predictably orderly rule of Prussia. But the

Russian Poles, Conrad's Poles, were exposed to the constant threat of an alien and arbitrary tyranny which seemed to belong to another world.

A good deal has been written about Conrad's attitude towards Russia, especially, of course, in connection with *Under Western Eyes*. But nobody has yet given, it seems to me, sufficient weight to the role of Russia in shaping his whole outlook. And perhaps this is because it is impossible to appreciate the full weight of the impact of Russia on a speculative Western mind unless one has experienced it directly in one's own life.

Conrad experienced it very directly indeed. There is nothing new in the idea that the origin of Conrad's conception of evil may be traced to his childhood memories of Russian rule. But even Sir Victor Pritchett, who has shown awareness of this has not, I think, appreciated the enduring force of these memories. Others, notably the Polish emigré-writer, Gustav Herling-Grudzhinsky, are inclined to minimise their importance because, they think, the boy Conrad was too young when he left Russian Poland to have received strong and lasting impressions. I have nothing but respect for Mr Herling, who himself survived the most appalling experiences in Stalin's labour-camps and afterwards wrote, long before such revelations became approved reading in the West, a classic account of his experiences entitled *World's Apart*. Mr Herling seems to think that Conrad based his whole conception of Russia on the cloudy memories of childhood impressions fortified with a little reading fifty years later. It is easy to see how a man who suffered dreadfully in his own body and soul under the Soviet penal system might at first sight find in Conrad's highly stylised and understated argument in *Under Western Eyes* the work of a man remote from Russian reality. It is not so easy to understand how such a view could survive a second reading, or why Herling should discount the importance of childhood experience – or, indeed, why he should assume that Conrad had not been thinking and brooding a great deal about Russia, and adding to his historical understanding of that portent, during the intervening years.

Mr Herling, it also seems to me, goes even farther astray when he complains of the superficiality and inadequacy of Conrad's presentation and treatment of the currents of revolutionary thought, of the revolutionary psychology, at the relevant period – the first years of this century, that is. This, too, he finds, is an indication of Conrad's remoteness from Russian reality.

It would be interesting to discuss Conrad and his revolutionaries at length, but it would take us too far from the matter in hand. What I do want to urge, however, is that Conrad was only minimally concerned with the psychology of individual revolutionaries, still less with the niceties of their ideological variations. In fact, I am sure that he understood such matters much more than Mr Herling supposes. He did not understand everything, of course: who at that time, outside the various parties and factions, did? But he understood a good deal, was not deeply interested, and had no need of such detail for the purposes of his novel. I am sure that Dr Hay hits the truth in her admirable book, *The Political Novels of Joseph Conrad*, but is a little diffident in offering it, when, after quoting both Pritchett and Herling, she observes that Conrad may very well have been deliberately loose and inaccurate to show his contempt for the whole revolutionary circus. In this connection, it is worth noting that when he needed to display contrasting revolutionary types for a particular purpose, as he did when creating the character of Michaelis in *The Secret Agent*, he exhibited a fully adequate understanding of the relevant aspect of Marxism – as opposed to anarchism, populism, or whatever:

> Michaelis by staring unwinkingly at the fire had regained that sense of isolation necessary for the continuity of thought. His optimism had begun to flow from his lips. He saw Capitalism doomed in its cradle, born with the principle of competition in its system. The great capitalists devouring the little capitalists, concentrating the power and the tools of production in great masses, perfecting industrial processes, and in the madness of self-aggrandisement only preparing, organising, encouraging, making ready the lawful inheritance of the suffering proletariat. . . . The future is as certain as the past – slavery, feudalism, individualism, collectivism. This is the statement of a law, not an empty prophecy.

To say that a man who could write those words and oppose them to the destructive mania of Professor Yundt and the apocalyptical ravings of Comrade Ossipon knew nothing of contemporary revolutionary thinking simply will not do.

It is a long way from Peter Ivanovich, 'the heroic fugitive' of *Under Western Eyes*. It is meant to be a long way. In *Under Western Eyes* Conrad was not remotely concerned with describing or analysing current revolutionary thought among the Russian emigrés in Switzerland (who, at that time, of course, included Lenin himself). He was not concerned with current affairs at all. He was writing about Russia – and not, as has been argued, in an abstract and generalised way but, rather, in the most immediate and concrete manner possible. He was distilling certain aspects of Russia, to arrive at the pure spirit as he understood it. And he brought the essential corruption of Russia, its irrationalism, its fathomless cynicism, etc., to life no less vividly than Mr Herling in his own fine book – pretty well the whole of that book about life in Stalin's camps being implicit already in *Under Western Eyes*, from the terrible scene when the decent and rational student Razumov beats up the drunken coachman to the character of Nikita, the thug who bursts Razumov's eardrums – and is accepted as a necessary evil and an equal by his idealistic comrades. He brings the nobility of Russia to life as well.

Dr Hay is right when she refers despondently to the multiplicity of the sources upon which Conrad may have drawn for his Russian characters. But she need not have despaired. An exploration of the sources for those novels and tales which embody particular aspects of Conrad's own experience, an exploration already carried out in great style by certain perceptive critics known to us all, is valuable and revealing. But the only source that really matters when it comes to *Under Western Eyes* is Russia itself – and the general idea of what Conrad called Utopian revolutionism as one aspect of Russia.

He himself tells us all we need to know in the preface to *Under Western Eyes*. The novel, he says, is 'as a whole an attempt to render not so much the political state as the psychology of Russia itself.' And he approached this task, he goes on to say, with 'a profound sense' that 'the obligation of absolute fairness was imposed on me historically and hereditarily by the peculiar experiences of race and family.'

There were, of course, limitations to that fairness. Peter Ivanovich and Madame de S. are, in Conrad's own words, considered as 'fair game'. They are 'the apes of a sinister jungle', universal charlatans of a destructive kind and a peculiarly Russian flavour. The fairness is limited to the people of Russia. And these include Prince P, Razumov's putative father; Counsellor Mikulin; the warm-hearted and devoted revolutionary fanatic, Sophia Antonovna; as well as the sacrificial assassin, Victor Haldin. They include, above all, of course, the marvellous girl, Natalie Haldin. Natalie may have been shaped by visions of martyred Polish women, but her special quality is as unmistakably Russian as the quality of Counsellor Mikulin himself – or of the ineffable Mr Vladimir in *The Secret Agent*. It is a tremendous fact, it seems to me, that Conrad could recognise this Russian quality of nobility, recreate it and pay homage to it. It is a very important fact. It must have severely complicated his whole attitude towards Russia, as he saw it: an arena 'of tyrannical lawlessness which, in general human terms, could be reduced to the formula of senseless desperation provoked by senseless tyranny.'

When it came to the tyranny itself there was no question of fairness entering into it. The autocracy was evil. And all the human characters, as distinct from the caricatures, in *Under Western Eyes* are presented as victims. Again, to quote from the preface, 'all these people are not the product of the exceptional, but of the general – of the normality of their place, and time, and race.' And, he goes on,

> The ferocity and imbecility of an autocratic rule rejecting all legality and in fact basing itself upon complete moral anarchism provokes the no less imbecile and atrocious answer of a purely Utopian revolution-ism, encouraging destruction by the first means to hand, in the strange conviction that a fundamental change of hearts must follow the downfall of any given human institutions. These people are unable to see that all they can effect is merely a change of names.

Conrad was born a Russian citizen, and a Russian citizen he remained for twenty-eight years. He lived in the direct shadow of St Petersburg until he was ten years old, when his father took him to Austrian Poland. When he was three, in 1861, an only child, his father – poet, novelist, dramatist, a romantic extremist, a rebellious nationalist who was driven also by a religious sense of the holy mission of Poland – was arrested and sent into exile with his wife and child. His arrest almost certainly postponed his death: had he lived he would have been a leader of the 1863 insurrection and almost certainly killed; as things were, when the shooting started he was safely in Russian hands.

At first he was sent to Vologda in the northern forests. I wonder how many Conradians have visited Vologda? I have had that privilege. It was, still largely is, a wooden town with streets and sidewalks of logs built on a swamp in the back of beyond, a station on the railway run-ning east from St Petersburg, or Leningrad, to the Urals. The people of the surrounding district are very poor indeed, and the summer climate is wretched and unhealthy into the bargain. It was this climate that killed Conrad's mother. St Petersburg would have let her die at Vologda, but the local authorities, more humane, took action to save her; and it was now that Apollo Korzeniowski encountered at first hand that unexpected manifestation which became familiar to so many Poles exiled in pre-revolutionary Russia – the kindness and persistent initiative of a surprisingly large number of provincial governors. Many of these, of course, were tyrants, and corrupt at that. But others behaved with great decency when a hard case was brought to their notice (itself, of course, largely a matter of chance). They could do nothing to over-ride the central bureaucracy in the way of institutional reforms, but they could, and frequently did, intervene to make life easier for the exiles dumped down in their provinces.

The Korzeniowskis were lucky in their governor, who managed to get the little family transferred, under parole, to the more salubrious centre of Chernikhov, much nearer home, in the Ukraine. This was in the summer of 1863 and the Polish insurrection was then at its height. But this did not prevent another kindly governor from giving leave to Evelina Korzeniowski to take her small son on a long visit to her brother, Thaddeus Bobrowski. It was too late to save Evelina whose tuberculosis was far advanced. She died a year after rejoining her husband in his exile. The great rebellion had been broken by then and the punishments followed. Two of Apollo's brothers had been involved in the revolt, one was killed, one exiled to Siberia. Apollo, his own life in ruins, was alone at Chernikhov with his seven-year-old son.

It seems to me very odd to think that the impressions of this time could be other than deep, sharp, and enduring. I am not suggesting that the man would have remembered everything or that the boy would have understood the meaning of all that was going on around him. But by the time his mother died he must have been very conscious of the existence of an alien power, remote and impenetrable, inscrutable to use one of his favourite words, yet ever present and bearing down cruelly on his family circle, dislocating the life of every day, the cause of bitterness and tears and curses. Conrad was taken out of Russian Poland when he was ten to breathe the freer air of Austrian Poland, first to Lvov (Lemberg as it was then more widely known), then to Cracow. Apollo Korzeniowski was then a broken man. He applied himself as well as he could to the education of his son, but he would all too easily lose himself in bitter and despairing brooding. He survived his wife by only four years, dying in May 1869; and the eleven-year-old Conrad, quite old enough now to know what was going on, and to understand well enough a great deal of what lay behind it, had to walk at the head of an immense funeral procession which was a patriotic demonstration.

Russia had killed first his mother, then his father – to say nothing of other relatives and family friends. How can one imagine that the sense of Russia as a source of evil was not burnt into him? And, of course, he had the artist's memory. Consider to this account in *A Personal Record* of his setting out with his mother to return into exile after their three months stay with Uncle Thaddeus. The time was the winter of 1867 and Conrad was six:

> I remember well the day of our departure back to exile. The elongated, bizarre, shabby travelling-carriage with four post-horses standing before the long front of the house with its eight columns, four on each side of the broad flight of stairs. On the steps, groups of servants, a few relations, one or two friends from the nearest neighbourhood, a perfect silence, on all the faces an air of sober concentration; my grandmother all in black gazing stoically, my uncle giving his arm to my mother down to the carriage in which I had been placed already...

And so on until 'In the distance, halfway down to the great gates, a light, open trap, harnessed with three horses in Russian fashion, stood drawn up on one side with the police captain of the district sitting in it, the vizor of his flat cap with a red band pulled down over his eyes.'

The memory of that police captain must have been always with him, a symbol of the power that had destroyed – or provoked the self-destruction – of both his parents by the time he was eleven. It was not a thing to be talked about. Indeed, he was not to utter a word about it in public until just on forty years after his mother's death. Then, in 1904, the humiliation of Russia by the Japanese, the shattering of the brazen monolith by a new and unconsidered power arising in the east, broke down his reserves, released his so long pent-up feelings; and the distinguished novelist, weaver of tales of sea and jungle, shocked many of his admirers with the intensity and violence of that remarkable essay, 'Autocracy and War'.

> The Russian autocracy as we see it now is a thing apart. It is impossible to assign to it any rational origin in the vices, the misfortunes, the necessities, or the aspirations of mankind. That despotism has neither an European nor an Oriental parentage; more, it seems to have no root either in the institutions or the follies of this earth. What strikes one with a sort of awe is just this something inhuman in its character. It is like a visitation, like a curse from Heaven falling in the darkness of ages upon the immense plains of forest and steppe lying dumbly on the confines of two continents: a true desert harbouring no Spirit either of the East or the West...

And again:

> The Government of Holy Russia, arrogating to itself the supreme power to torment and slaughter the bodies of its subjects like a God-

sent scourge, has been most cruel to those whom it allowed to live under the shadow of its dispensation. The worst crime against humanity of that system we behold now crouching at bay behind vast heaps of mangled corpses [he is referring to the murderous and suicidal fighting against the Japanese] is the ruthless destruction of innumerable minds. The greatest horror of the world – madness – walked faithfully in its train. Some of the best intellects in Russia, after struggling in vain against the spell, ended by throwing themselves at the feet of that hopeless despotism as a giddy man leaps into the abyss. An attentive survey of Russia's literature, of her Church, of her administration and the cross-currents of her thought, must end in the verdict that the Russia of today has not the right to give her voice on a single question touching the future of humanity, because from the very inception of her being the brutal destruction of dignity, of truth, of rectitude, of all that is faithful in human nature has been made to the imperative condition of her existence. . .

And he moves into terrible prophesy:

A brand of hopeless mental and moral inferiority is set upon Russian achievements; and the coming events of her internal changes, however appalling they may be in their magnitude, will be nothing more impressive than the convulsions of a colossal body. As her boasted military force that, corrupt in its origin, has ever struck no other but faltering blows, so her soul, kept benumbed by her temporal and spiritual master with the poison of tyranny and superstition, will find itself on awakening possessed of no language, a monstrous full-grown child having first to learn the ways of living thought and articulate speech. It is safe to say tyranny, assuming a thousand protean shapes, will remain clinging to her struggles for a long time before her blind multitudes succeed at last in trampling her out of existence under their millions of bare feet.

These are not the thoughts and feelings of a man with a dim, far-off memory, his knowledge brushed up with a little ad hoc reading. They are the thoughts and feelings, suddenly unloosed after decades of silence, of a man who had been shaken and shocked by the direct impact of the evil he evokes here after a lifetime of brooding.

We need not concern ourselves now with the truth or otherwise, in whole or in part, of Conrad's vision of Russia. That is another story. My theme is the *effect* produced on him by Russia. The feelings here expressed by Conrad have been shared by many, including native

Russians, who have suffered, or simply viewed from close to, those manifestations of bleak inhumanity which seem to be a permanent feature of the land which also produced Solzhenitsyn and Sakharov – and who have sought as far as I know in vain, for a rational explanation in the history of Russia.

Many, many Russians have expressed their unease, their own horror and revulsion. One of the first of these wrote in terms so very close to Conrad's argument that it is permissable to wonder whether the Pole was not in fact paraphrasing the Russian. The Russian was Peter Chaadayev, aristocrat and cavalry officer turned philosopher, who deeply influenced the radical youth of Russia in the early days of Nicholas I and was the first Russian dissenter to be certified insane at the instance of the Tsar himself. Here is an extract from the first of Chaadayev's three celebrated *Philosophical Letters*, composed in 1830:

> Situated between the two great divisions of the world, between East and West, one elbow resting on China, the other on Germany, we should be able to unite in ourselves the two great principles of consciousness, imagination and reason. . . But this is not at all the role that Providence has assigned to us. On the contrary, she seems to take not the least interest in our destiny. Witholding from us her beneficent influence on the human spirit, she has left us completely to ourselves. She has not wished to involve herself in our affairs, she has not wished to teach us. The experience of the ages has meant nothing to us; we have profited not at all from all the epochs and the generations that have gone before. To look at us [now remember Conrad], one would say that the general law governing humanity has been suspended on our account. Alone among all the peoples of the world we have given nothing to the world, we have learned nothing from the world. We have contributed nothing to the development of the human mind, we have only disfigured it.

Russia was, of course, to give a great deal to the world in the years to come. Unofficial Russia, that is, and above all the writers and the musicians. But Russia as a society was to remain an arid void, offering no example, no ideas, until after the end of the dynasty – and what she has offered since then most of us would rather do without.

Obviously Conrad was not writing the whole truth about Russia in that astonishing essay, and he knew it. I think he was concerned about this, so concerned that in *Under Western Eyes* he sought to make amends. But to chase that hare would take us a long way. It would take us, for example, to Conrad's views on Dostoevsky! I resolutely

turn my face against it. Let us say then – and of this I am convinced –
that in *Under Western Eyes* he sought to exorcise his obsessional sense
of evil by examining its origins in the coolest and most neutral light:
through the eyes of the English language teacher.

'It is like a visitation, a curse from Heaven. . .' But what does it
mean, and how can one armour oneself against it? It is this sense of
an arbitrary, cruel, irresponsible, irrational, inexplicable fire which
could strike out of the blue and destroy at will the faithful work of
men's hands – and to do so by exploiting the least weakness in character
– which hangs over all Conrad's work. It is more than a sense of evil.
It is an acknowledgment of the omnipresence of evil and of the help-
lessness of ordinary, well-intentioned human decency in face of it.
Ordinary decency is not enough. What is enough?

Of course Poland provided a starting point for this long and
agonised exploration, the search for an answer to the unanswerable.
But it seems to me only a starting point. Dr Najder quotes from 'Prince
Roman' where Conrad writes about

> that country which demands to be loved as no other country has
> ever been loved, with the mournful affection one bears to the un-
> forgotten dead and with the inextinguishable power of a hopeless
> passion which only a living, breathing, warm ideal can kindle in our
> breasts for our pride, our weariness, for our exaltation, *for our
> undoing.* [my italics]

'Hopeless fidelity [to the memory of Poland], Dr Najder then observes,
'was the essence of Conrad's feeling for Poland, but that made him
not closer to but, on the contrary, more estranged from other Poles'.

Perhaps it did. Perhaps, again to quote Dr Najder, 'the dark,
desperate love, described in these sombre sentences, could not form a
bridge to the living and fighting people in Poland.'

Perhaps it could not. Perhaps Conrad himself never thought of it like
that. But I think it forms a bridge to us today and brings Conrad very
close. For the horrors of the past decades have brought us to recognise
the existence of evil as a force unimaginable to most citizens of the
Western world half a century ago. Conrad knew all about it when his
contemporaries did not. Of course the Russian autocracy was not the
only source of evil, but it was Russia which made him think about evil.
It seems to me that for Conrad Poland was only a starting point and a
symbol for lost innocence in face of evil, for which Russia was also in
fact no more than a starting point and a symbol.

As a young man Conrad escaped from Russia and could not write about it, any more than he could write about Poland. But by the hand of providence, or some inner compulsion, or both in conjunction, he escaped not to settle in a Western city cushioned against all elemental forces, but, rather, to the only other parts of the globe where individuals, like the people of Poland, found themselves pitted against precisely those immense, overwhelming powers – the sea and the jungle – which could strike and destroy for no reason at all and with no warning; which allowed the voyager to exist only on sufferance.

And with the material he gathered and the strange characters he encountered, he could, when he came to write, dramatise most plausibly the questions which obsessed him. Of course he was deeply concerned with the moral condition of his failed heroes; of course he sought to explore the weaknesses in their defences. No doubt, as I said much earlier, he asked himself searching questions about his own abandonment (might it not also be seen as a renunciation?) of Poland. But I believe the main stimulus came from his agonised preoccupation with the nature of a universe which drives imperfect men to almost inevitable failure while it impartially destroys the unheeding and the innocent. But who is innocent? In this scenario the apes grimacing in the universal jungle, the Browns, the Jones, the Donkins, the Travers and the rest, are only instruments of destiny. Far from being a particular confession, it seems to me that *Lord Jim*, like so many of Conrad's novels, should be seen as a warning, an urgent warning, to all dwellers in a fool's paradise, of the real nature of the universe and the infinite variety of the means whereby we may be crushed or led to our own undoing. It was, as he saw it, a universe for which the interplay between Poland and Russia was a perfect allegory. And an allegory of extreme, excruciating complexity – because, as he knew, there were good Russians and bad Poles.

8 Rhetoric and Ideology in Conrad's *Under Western Eyes*

ANDRZEJ BUSZA

Sit ergo nobis orator . . . is, qui a M. Catone finitur, vir bonus dicendi peritus. Quintilian, *Institutio Oratoria* XII, 1

. . . sic enim statuo, perfecti oratoris moderatione et sapientia non solum ipsius dignitatem, sed et privatorum plurimorum, et universae reipublicae salutem maxime contineri. Cicero, *De Oratore*, I, 34

Unlike many modern rhetoricians, though like Cicero and Quintilian, Conrad held a holistic view of the art of writing. He did not separate the author and the work, ethics and style. He believed that 'all writing worthy of the name is temperamental';[1] and while embracing the Flaubertian ideal that a work of fiction, like poetry, 'should carry its justification in every line', defined art itself in ethical terms, 'as a single-minded attempt to render the highest kind of justice to the visible universe.'[2]

Indeed, Conrad critics (the best ones) have found it difficult to treat his works as fully autonomous structures. Writing three years after the appearance of Wimsatt's *The Verbal Icon*, Albert J. Guerard said:

> The purest criticism attends only to the text, which it conceives as floating in a timeless vacuum: a text and meaning immutable, created by no flesh-and-blood writer and without flesh-and-blood readers in mind. This book [meaning his *Conrad the Novelist*] cannot hope to achieve such purity. For Joseph Conrad was one of the most subjective and most personal of English novelists . . . we cannot ignore the personality and temperament that pervade the best writings . . . and largely determine their form. For we are concerned with a style that is unmistakably a speaking voice.[3]

Resisting the pressures of theory, Guerard adapted his approach to the nature of the material he was studying, and produced one of the finest studies of Conrad that has been written. It is my conviction that it is this type of humanist approach to literature, based on respect for the work, openness to the problems posed by it, and sensitivity to the self-interpretative elements contained in it, that yields the most penetrating and worthwhile criticism. And I am rather sceptical of the ultimate value of criticism which, presumably for heuristic purposes, seeks to reconstruct a work in accordance with some pre-conceived system; but which all too often gives way to the temptation of cutting the crab's pincers in order to fit it into a box. Similarly, I have serious doubts about the feasibility and utility of certain recent attempts to arrive at the essence (whatever that may be) of a literary text and to describe it with quasi-scientific precision and objectivity. In another more sophisticated version of the same tendency, literary works are treated as autotelic systems of 'empty signifiers' devoid of truth value and moral significance.[4] Some works of literature, especially modern texts, which are products of the same artistic and philosophical climate as this kind of criticism, no doubt respond to it well enough;[5] but the richer and greater the work, the more intractable it becomes to such restrictive and reductionist methods. This to my mind is the case with Conrad's *Under Western Eyes*.

My particular approach in this paper results from the confluence of two trains of thought. One, ideological in substance, originates from a long-lasting interest in Conrad's complex attitude to Russia and things Russian; the other, rhetorical, derives from Frank Kermode's reflections on the use and usefulness of structuralist methods of analysis in the study of novels.[6] I do not intend to repeat here, nor hope to better, Kermode's diagnosis of the blindnesses and insights of the structuralist method, when dealing with complex narratives such as *Under Western Eyes*. In one sense, the thrust of my argument is wider, in that I question the adequacy of approaches that dogmatically refuse to go beyond the text; in another sense it is of course narrower, in that my main concern is Conrad, and primarily the problems of reading *Under Western Eyes*.

I shall consider first those extrinsic factors – intention, historical context, contemporary reference – which literary purists seek to exorcise by 'placing in brackets' *à la* Husserl. Then I shall turn to so-called intrinsic structures, and try to relate text and meta-text.

An irony of fate not unlike the one that takes Razumov to Geneva and his fateful meeting with Natalia Haldin, brought Conrad at the turn of the century into close personal and professional contact with a group of young English intellectuals who, having caught 'the Russian fever', were actively engaged in spreading it. Of course, in neither case was it really an accident. One of the things that aroused Edward Garnett's curiosity about the author of *Almayer's Folly* and led to their meeting was Conrad's Polish background: 'this increased my interest,' Garnett tells us, 'since my Nihilist friends, Stepniak and Volkhovsky, had always subtly decried the Poles when one sympathized with their position as "under dogs" '.[7]

Initially, Conrad found an area of enthusiasm that he could share with his English friends at 'Dostoevsky Corner', as Garnett called his home: the work of Ivan Sergeyevich Turgenev, a 'good' Russian, a liberal, ideologically as well as artistically sympathetic to the West.[8] But then – in Conrad's phrase – monsters came into fashion: Tolstoy, the purveyor of 'gratuitous atrocities'[9] and the anti-sensual apostle of 'the absurd oriental fable';[10] and Dostoevsky 'the grimacing haunted creature',[11] who wrote not about human beings but 'damned souls knocking themselves to pieces in the stuffy darkness of mystical contradictions'.[12] And so, Conrad felt, while artists such as James and himself struggled with their *'art trop difficile'*,[13] the crowd next door was fighting 'for a view of the Double-headed Nightingale' and 'the weak-kneed giant grinning through a horse collar'.[14]

The supplanting of Turgenev by Tolstoy and Dostoevsky, and the attendant vogue for the 'Russian Soul' were, of course, part of the general Idealist and Neo-Romantic reaction against nineteenth-century positivism. And we hardly need to be reminded that Conrad's own work, with its radical scepticism, anti-rationalist bias, pragmatic idealism, and gnostic tendencies, was equally symptomatic of the period. The accelerated tempo of political events – the Russo-Japanese War, the 1905 Revolution, and the Anglo-Russian Convention of 1907 – invested the enigma of the 'Russian Soul' with topical urgency. Finally, it received the supreme proof of public recognition by becoming a popular subject of sensational fiction.[15]

Conrad entered the Russian debate when interest in Russia was at its height: the Russo-Japanese War was coming to an end, and there had been a revolution in St Petersburg. In the spring of 1905 he wrote his long political essay, 'Autocracy and War', exposing Russia and predicting the effect of the Russian defeat on the balance of power in Europe.[16] His exposure of Russia, which is a kind of first sketch for the fuller and more incisive anatomy of things Russian in *Under Western Eyes*, is achieved not through rational argument but by rhetorical means. It consists of a sequence of mythopoeic and de-mythologising operations in which the reality of Russian might is alternately asserted and undercut.

X   First, the 'Russian Soul', which was idolised by Conrad's English contemporaries, becomes a synecdoche for the Russian autocratic state, which, in contrast, was viewed with misgivings and, in fact, feared. The resulting symbolic construct is presented in a very concrete, visual manner, as a grotesque phantom:

> This dreaded and strange apparition, bristling with bayonets, armed with chains, hung over with holy images; that something not of this world, partaking of a ravenous ghoul, of a blind Djinn grown up from a cloud, and of the Old Man of the Sea, still faces us with its old stupidity, with its strange mystical arrogance, stamping its shadowy feet upon the gravestone of autocracy . . .[17]

And then the Russian idol, which has already been undermined by the grim, satiric humour of the text, is toppled and annihilated by a touch of whimsy: 'The task of Japan is done, the mission accomplished; the ghost of Russia's might is laid . . . as if by a touch of that wonderful magic for which the East has always been famous. . .'[18] But this is not the end of the process. Having de-mythologised Russia and revealed its hollowness, which, in fact, he describes as *Le Néant* – nothingness – Conrad proceeds to create a new myth: the myth of a sinister and threatening void:

> There is an awe-inspiring idea of infinity conveyed in the word *Néant* – and in Russia there is no idea. She is not a *Néant*, she is and has been simply the negation of everything worth living for. She is not an empty void, she is a yawning chasm open between East and West; a bottomless abyss that has swallowed up every hope of mercy, every aspiration towards personal dignity, towards freedom, towards knowledge, every ennobling desire of the heart, every redeeming whisper of conscience.[19]

In this way the 'Russian Soul' which was associated with promises of spiritual wealth and regeneration, is transformed by Conrad into the embodiment of the spirit of negation. This hesitation between horror and ridicule is characteristic of the grotesque mode, which Wolfgang Kayser has described as 'an attempt to invoke and subdue the demonic aspects of the world'.[20] Conrad's attitude to Russia reminds one, as has been pointed out, of Marlow's feelings towards Kurtz. On the one hand, Conrad despises and is repelled by the monstrous 'Russian Soul', on the other, he is fascinated by it. The rhetoric of hesitation in

'Autocracy and War' also points to a duality in Conrad's intention: while he ridicules the English overvaluation of things Russian, he does not want England to underestimate Russia./

The intention of a political article is a relatively straightforward matter; one is, of course, on much more difficult ground when dealing with works of fiction. And yet it seems to me that in the case of a novel such as *Under Western Eyes*, it is an aspect that should not be ignored, if only because it can help us to see more clearly the rhetorical structure of the text.

In an often quoted letter to William Blackwood, Conrad said: 'My work shall not be an utter failure because it has the solid basis of a definite intention.'[21] That part of Conrad's intention in *Under Western Eyes* was ideological, is abundantly clear from comments scattered through his correspondence, as well as from the 'Author's Note' to the novel. Particularly interesting and revealing in this respect are some remarks in a letter to Garnett: '. . . in this book,' writes Conrad, 'I am concerned with nothing but ideas, to the exclusion of everything else, with no *arrière pensée* of any kind. Or are you like the Italians (and most women) incapable of conceiving that anybody ever should speak with perfect detachment, without some subtle hidden purpose, for the sake of what is said, with no desire of gratifying some small personal spite – or vanity?'[22] Clearly, Conrad protests too much; and one is led to suspect that there was an *arrière pensée* at the back of his mind – not some small 'personal spite', but something more fundamental. Just as Conrad's African fiction attacks the imperial myth, and *The Secret Agent* is an ironic thrust at the utopian illusions of a Cunninghame Graham and an H. G. Wells, so *Under Western Eyes* is conceived at one level as a polemic and a warning addressed to Garnett and other Western European enthusiasts of things Russian.

In the tradition of Mickiewicz, Krasiński, de Custine, and Marx, Conrad assumes the role of a Cassandra seeking to open Western eyes to the danger from Russia, especially on the ideological plane: 'In the book . . . I am exclusively concerned with ideas.'[23] He is not, it seems, as worried by the direct political threat posed by Russia, as by the subversive nature of the 'Russian Idea'.

Men like Garnett discriminated nicely between servants of the autocratic principle, like Councillor Mikulin, and apostles of utopian revolutionism, like Haldin; Conrad sees both as simultaneously products and victims of the moral anarchy – lawlessness, extremism, cynicism, and mysticism – at the heart of the 'Russian Idea'. The third and most tragic member of the vicious triangle of oppressors and oppressed is, of course, Razumov, the silent, reasonable, unattached young man, who wants to avoid 'taking definite sides'.[24] The metonymic relationship between autocracy and revolution stressed by Conrad, but obscure to many Western eyes, was nothing new to the Russians themselves. Herzen had written in 1851 that 'Communism is the Russian autocracy turned upside down.'[25] And Dostoevsky dramatised this Russian ideological paradox in *The Possessed*, where the strong man, Stavrogin, is adored both by the nationalist, Shatov, and the revolutionary, Verkhovensky.[26] Lacking any kind of moral refuge, and prompted by practical reason and the instinct of self-preservation, Razumov persuades himself to embrace the stern Russian truth:

> Of course he was far from being a moss-grown reactionary. Every-thing was not for the best. Despotic bureaucracy . . . abuses . . . corruption . . . and so on. Capable men were wanted. Enlightened intelligences. Devoted hearts. But absolute power should be preserved – the tool ready for the man – for the great autocrat of the future. Razumov believed in him. The logic of history made him unavoidable. The state of the people demanded him. 'What else?' he asked himself ardently, 'could move all that mass in one direction? Nothing could. Nothing but a single will.'[27]

Razumov's new faith frees him from the restraints of an ordinary formal conscience and allows him to betray Haldin at the dictate of a higher command: Russian patriotism. Similarly, Haldin, who 'wouldn't hurt a fly',[28] says, 'God's will be done'[29] and throws his 'engine'.

Neither Haldin nor Razumov 'are the product of the exceptional but of the general – of the normality of their place, and time, and race.'[30] Mikulin assures Razumov: 'You shall be coming back to us. Some of our greatest minds had to do that in the end.'[31] Conrad was no doubt thinking here, among others, of Dostoevsky.

If there is one dominant presence and adversary underlying the polemical structure of *Under Western Eyes*, it is Dostoevsky. The confrontation was virtually inevitable. In the years that Conrad wrote his Russian novel, interest in Dostoevsky was increasing rapidly, and Constance Garnett was actually in the process of translating *The Brothers Karamazov*: the book that launched the Dostoevsky cult in England. (Curiously enough the writing of *Nostromo* similarly coincided with Constance Garnett's work on *War and Peace*.) Be that as it may, Conrad could not afford to ignore Dostoevsky because of his usefulness as a source of information on Russian psychology and ideas; at the same time, however, he found him deeply disturbing and antipathetic.

Richard Curle, I think, came as close as anyone to capturing the essence of Conrad's attitude to Dostoevsky:

✗I have an idea [writes Curle] that his real hatred for Dostoievsky was due to an appreciation of his power. It is on record that he once told Galsworthy that Dostoievsky was 'as deep as the sea', and for Conrad it was the depth of an evil influence. Dostoievsky represented to him the ultimate forces of confusion and insanity arrayed against all that he valued in civilization. He did not despise him as one despises a nonentity, he hated him as one might hate Lucifer and the forces of darkness.[32]

In one of the most comprehensive comparative studies of Conrad's and Dostoevsky's political fiction, Ralph E. Matlaw claims that: 'The patent similarity of two great novels, *Crime and Punishment* and *Under Western Eyes*, is unique in literature.'[33] Although this may be an exaggeration, the parallels between Conrad's novel and Dostoevsky's fiction are sufficiently numerous and obvious to suggest that Conrad meant his readers to make the connection. Conrad writes Razumov's story into the imaginative space created by Dostoevsky's narratives in order to define as sharply as possible his ideological disagreement with Dostoevsky, as well as to subvert the latter's postulates. The relationship of Conrad's text to Dostoevsky's writing is thus partly dialectical and partly parodic.

The contrast between the moral fulcrum of *Crime and Punishment* and *Under Western Eyes* is clear and significant. At the heart of *Crime and Punishment* we have a murder: a gratuitous transgression of the traditional moral code. (The Russian word *prestuplenie*, which constitutes the first part of the title, is not as heavily charged with value-judgment as the English word *crime*.) Dostoevsky thus puts into question the very basis of traditional morality. Raskolnikov conducts an ethical experiment, the outcome of which is by no means clear at the outset. The moral complexion of Razumov's act is far more intricate. He does not create a moral problem: it is forced upon him. Faced by a multiplicity of conflicting moral imperatives: loyalty to the autocratic state, commitment to the revolution, the right to self-preservation, and the dictates of human solidarity, Razumov makes the wrong choice. And there is never any doubt in Conrad's, or the reader's, mind about the wrongness of Razumov's action, stigmatised with the unequivocally condemnatory word 'betrayal'. Razumov's tragedy resides in the fact that he is living in a society which imposes upon its members extremely difficult moral problems, while simultaneously confusing their moral bearings. Indeed, Razumov is as much a victim of the cynical autocracy and the fanatical revolutionaries, as of the ethical chaos of the tormented 'Russian Soul' which out of despair seeks refuge in mystical solutions. Hermann Hesse once characterised Dostoevsky's work as 'the rejection of every definite morality and code of ethics in favour of a novel, dangerous and horrible type of holiness which sympathises with everything and accepts everything'.[34] It is against this Russian holy nihilism (which was welcomed with enthusiasm by the contemporaries of Nietzsche) that Conrad defends and asserts traditional Western values.

Conrad also attacks and exposes the seemingly transcendental character of Russian thinking:

> Razumov stood on the point of conversion. He was fascinated by its approach, by its overpowering logic. For a train of thought is never false. The falsehood lies deep in the necessities of existence, in secret fears and half-formed ambitions, in the secret confidence combined with a secret mistrust of ourselves in the love of hope and the dread of uncertain days.
>
> In Russia, the land of spectral ideas and disembodied aspirations, many brave minds have turned away at last from the vain and endless conflict to the one great historical fact of the land. They turned to autocracy for the peace of their patriotic conscience as a weary unbeliever, touched by grace, turns to the faith of his fathers for the blessing of spiritual rest. Like other Russians before him, Razumov, in conflict with himself, felt that touch of grace upon his forehead.[35]

The irony is unmistakable: Razumov is merely rationalising his self-interest, and clothing it in the rhetoric of the 'Russian Idea'. Razumov's ironic conversion to the autocratic principle is a process whereby he becomes possessed by words, turning into a kind of 'wonderful parrot'.[36] 'Generally his phrases came to him slowly, after a conscious and painstaking wooing. Some superior power had inspired him with a flow of masterly argument. . .'[37] The discourse which he conducts with himself, in fact, reads like a parody of that quintessential exposition of Russian reactionary ideology: Konstantin P. Pobedonostsev's *Reflections of a Russian Statesman*, which appeared in English in 1898. Incidentally, Conrad's grotesque description of Mr de P— at the beginning of the novel – 'that fanatical, narrow-chested figure in gold-laced uniform, with a face of crumpled parchment, insipid, bespectacled eyes, and the cross of the Order of St Procopius hung under the skinny throat'[38] – sounds more like a caricature of Pobedonostsev, the High Procurator of the Holy Synod, who knew and influenced Dostoevsky, than of the Minister of the Interior, V. K. de Plehve, who was actually assassinated in 1904.

The turning point for Razumov is the moment when he feels the hard ground of Russia under his feet: 'inanimate, cold, inert, like a sullen and tragic mother hiding her face under a winding-sheet, his native soil! – his very own. . .'[39] We are reminded here of similar 'mystical' moments in Dostoevsky: Alyosha Karamazov rushing out under the open sky and embracing the earth, and Raskolnikov kneeling down in the middle of a city square, bowing to the earth, and kissing it ecstatically. For Dostoevsky's heroes, the gesture symbolises the renunciation of intellect and individuality in order to be integrated into the sacred communion of all life. Razumov, too, yields to the 'sacred inertia'[40] of the immense land; but the resulting sacrifice of 'personal longings of liberalism'[41] and the submission to the 'over-powering logic'[42] of Russian 'mystic phrases',[43] alienates him both from himself and from other men. And he does not achieve inner peace and integrity until he has recovered his authentic, individual self, by breaking out of the 'prison of lies'[44] built around him by the revolutionaries and the servants of the autocracy. For Conrad, though not for Dostoevsky, the goal of spiritual development is individuation, and not a mystical union with 'the all'. By inverting and re-interpreting Dostoevskian patterns Conrad contests their philosophical import and substance. At times the contestatory strategy becomes blatantly parodic. Thus Ivan Karamazov's encounter with the Devil is mocked in Ziemianitch's 'mystical' experience; and Tekla in her final role of nurse to the deaf and dying Razumov – a task in which there was nothing 'to become disillusioned about'[45] – is an ironic version of Raskolnikov's spiritual midwife, Sonia.

Dostoevsky's all-embracing sympathy and the corresponding openness to contradictory ideologies is related to what Mikhail Bakhtin calls the polyphonic structure of his novels, the essence of which is the coexistence within the text of a plurality of independent, distinct, and equally authoritative voices.[46] It is a parallel phenomenon to the conscious perspectivism that we associate with Conrad's fiction. However, in Conrad's political novels, and especially *The Secret Agent* and *Under Western Eyes*, the polyphonic character of the text is checked and modified by means of an ironic gloss that pervades the entire work, often including even the dialogue, as for instance in Sophia Antonovna's final declaration: 'Peter Ivanovitch is an inspired man.'[47] This ironic coding of the whole text seems to be a consequence of a combination of the Flaubertian imperative to render every detail of the structure functional and of the rhetorical orientation of the novel. In *Under Western Eyes*, however, we have a complication in that the old teacher of languages, who provides an ironic perspective on things Russian is himself a target of irony on account of his myopia. Thus Conrad's irony while directing the reading of the text on one level, creates ambiguities on another.

Something similar is true of the way in which imagery works in the novel. To a greater extent than in Dostoevsky's work, for instance, the ideological content of *Under Western Eyes* is embodied in imagistic structures. This is to be expected in view of the predominantly visual nature of Conrad's imagination. Earlier on we saw how even in a political essay Conrad presents his argument through visual images. The technique is natural to fiction, and can be used in a complex and effective way. Russia's lack of history and tradition is expressed by means of an image which conveys simultaneously the monstrous size of the country:

> Under the sumptuous immensity of the sky, the snow covered the endless forests, the frozen rivers, the plains of an immense country, obliterating the landmarks, the accidents of the ground, levelling everything under its uniform whiteness, like a monstrous blank page awaiting the record of an inconceivable history.[48]

Russia – Conrad is telling us – is an inhuman void, in the spatial as well as the temporal dimension. Its inhabitants have faces that are as featureless as the landscape: 'He had one of those bearded Russian faces without shape, a mere appearance of flesh and hair with not a single feature having any sort of character. His eyes being hidden by the dark glasses there was an utter absence of all expression.'[49] In fact, we suspect that there is absolutely nothing behind Peter Ivanovitch's glasses, just as his words are empty rhetoric. The veneer of civilised life is still very thin in Russia; below it lurks the dangerous vitality of primitive man. Walking through a fashionable quarter of the Russian capital Razumov notices 'a pretty woman – with a delicate head, and covered in the hairy skins of wild beasts down to her feet, like a frail and beautiful savage.'[50] The citizens of Geneva, on the other hand, are civilised, respectable, but extremely dull, like their tiny, ordered, enclosed world:

> . . . there was but little of spring-like glory in the rectangular railed space of grass and trees, framed visibly by the orderly roof-slopes of

that town, comely without grace, and hospitable without sympathy. In the very air . . . there was but little warmth; and the sky, the sky of a land without horizons, swept and washed clean by the April showers, extended a cold cruel blue, without elevation, narrowed suddenly by the ugly, dark wall of the Jura. . .[51]

The trouble with images is that their imaginative impact is as powerful as their semantic direction is difficult to control: they import associations, accumulate meaning, reverberate, or establish unexpected relations. Images that perform a topical metaphoric function generate complex metonymic chains which act in counterpoint, or even in opposition, to the explicit meaning. These are the latent formal relations and suggestions which, as Frank Kermode puts it, 'grow out of the writer's love for his material, his dislike of loveless sequence'.[52] The text of *Under Western Eyes* is thickly interwoven with a network of such 'inexplicit relations' that cut across narration, dialogue, description, and commentary. Thus we have a complex structure of spatial imagery; a sequence of supernatural metaphors with ghosts, phantoms, apparitions, and, of course, the ubiquitous 'soul'; related to it, but more melodramatic in character, is the gothic sequence that emanates from the Chateau Borel and the ghoulish Madame de S—; and there is also a rich constellation of images and metaphors dealing with eyes and vision.

Under Western Eyes is one of Conrad's most carefully written and elaborately structured texts. Indeed, André Gide felt that Conrad had overstructured the novel. 'A masterful book,' comments Gide in his *Journal*, 'but one that smells a bit too much of work and application; overconscientiousness (if I may say so) on Conrad's part, in the continuity of outline.'[53]

And yet, even this inward-looking, autotelic quality of the text seems to be related to extrinsic factors. Defending his novel against some criticism from Garnett, Conrad said: 'But it had to be a performance on one string. It had to be. You may think such self-imposed limitation a very stupid thing. But something of the kind must be done or else novel-writing becomes a mere debauch of the imagination.'[54] Isn't it likely that Conrad was thinking here of the lack of artistic discipline which he saw in the work of Dostoevsky, and that he conceived his novel, as a number of critics have argued, as an aesthetic as well as an ideological rebuttal to his Russian rival? Moreover, the formal *askesis* which he practised helped him to keep in check the potentially dangerous influence of Dostoevsky.[55]

Because of the multiplicity of typically Conradian tensions in the book's conception, execution, and effect – between ideological and formal concerns, between writing as *praxis* and writing as a reflexive (in Roland Barthes' metaphor 'intransitive') activity, between the Flaubertian and the Dostoevskian conceptions of the novel – *Under Western Eyes* invites, and in fact, demands a pluralistic approach. One finds that critics who do not take these fundamental dualities into full consideration either oversimplify the political stratum of the novel, or in an effort to cope with the ambiguities and complexities of the text, develop highly ingenious interpretations, which not only cry out for Ockham's razor, but are often incoherent with Conrad's thinking as a whole. A particularly interesting area of enquiry is precisely the complex and fruitful interrelationship between the ideological and aesthetic imperatives that underlie, and in many ways determine, the structure of the novel.

Conrad once told Henry Davray, the French translator of *The Secret Agent*, that a major concern of his work was the effect that it produced on his readers.[56] In *Under Western Eyes* Conrad wants to move his reader both aesthetically and ideologically; and the essence of his art is rhetorical in the best sense of that word.

NOTES

1. Letter to Kane, 12 November 1919, Joseph Conrad, *To My Brethren of the Pen* (Privately printed, 1927), p. 1.
2. *The Nigger of the 'Narcissus'* (London: Dent, 1950), p. vii. All references to Conrad's works are to Dent's Collected Edition in twenty-one volumes, published in London, 1946–54.
3. Albert J. Guerard, *Conrad the Novelist* (Cambridge, Mass., 1958), p. 1.
4. In *S/Z* (Paris, 1970) Roland Barthes describes the ideal text as 'une galaxie de signifiants, non une structure de signifiés' (p. 12); and presumably as in the Japanese *vides* there is 'point de dieu, de vérité, de morale *au fond* de ces signifiants' (Barthes' jacket note to *L'Empire des signes* [Geneva, 1970]).
5. For example some of the French *nouveaux romans*.
6. See, especially, 'The Structures of Fiction', *Modern Language Notes* 84 (1969), 891–915; and 'Novel and Narrative', in *The Theory of the Novel*, ed. John Halperin (New York, 1974), pp. 155–74.
7. *Letters from Joseph Conrad, 1895 to 1924*, edited with Introduction and Notes by Edward Garnett (New York, 1928), p. 2. In the early nineties Garnett came to know, through the Rossettis, a number of Russian political exiles living in London. They were mostly revolutionaries, who had belonged to the Populist Chaykovsky Circle, and included in addition to N. V. Chaykovsky himself, F. Volkhovsky, P. A. Kropotkin, A. A. Cherkesov, and S. M. Kravchinsky. Under the influence of, first, Volkhovsky and then Stepniak-Kravchinsky, Constance Garnett learned Russian and embarked on her long translating career, in the course of which she translated some seventy

volumes from the Russian. Edward also developed an interest in Russian literature and wrote books on Tolstoy and Turgenev, as well as many articles on other Russian authors.

8. Turgenev once proclaimed: 'I am a European, and I love the banner, I pin my faith to the banner which I have carried since my youth' (quoted by Gilbert Phelps in *The Russian Novel in English Fiction* [London, 1956], p. 54).

9. *Joseph Conrad; Life and Letters* by G. Jean-Aubry (London, 1927), II, 77.

10. *Letters from Conrad*, p. 245.

11. *Letters from Conrad*, p. 249.

12. 'Turgenev', *Notes on Life and Letters*, p. 47.

13. *Lettres françaises*, avec une introduction et des notes de G. Jean-Aubry (Paris, 1930), p. 62.

14. *Notes on Life and Letters*, p. 48.

15. The following are a few characteristic titles: Sinclair Ayden, *The Old Bureaucrat: A St Petersburg Story* (London, 1909); Anna Brodsky, *Natasha* (London, 1910); J. R. Carling, *By Neva's Waters* (London, 1908); Elinor Glyn, *Three Weeks* (London, 1907); Richard Henry Savage, *For Her Life: A Story of St Petersburg* (London, 1897); David Whitelaw, *The Man with the Red Beard* (London, 1911); and W. H. Williamson, *The Traitor's Wife* (London, 1908).

16. For a discussion of the political aspect of 'Autocracy and War' see Avrom Fleishman, *Conrad's Politics* (Baltimore, 1967), pp. 32–7.

17. *Notes on Life and Letters*, p. 89.

18. *Ibid.*, pp. 90, 94.

19. *Ibid.*, p. 100.

20. *The Grotesque in Art and Literature*, trans. Ulrich Weisstein (New York, 1963), p. 188.

21. *Joseph Conrad: Letters to William Blackwood and David S. Meldrum*, ed. William Blackburn (Durham, N. Carolina, 1958), pp. 155–6.

22. *Letters from Conrad*, p. 233.

23. *Ibid.*, p. 235.

24. *Under Western Eyes*, p. 11.

25. In his *Du développement des idées révolutionnaires en Russie* (1850); quoted by Hans Kohn in the Afterword to *Marx vs. Russia*, edited with an Introduction by J. A. Doering (New York, 1962), p. 193.

26. In his essay on *The Possessed* Ryszard Przybylski writes: 'Shatov and Verkhovensky represent the two major trends in Russian political thought in the nineteenth century: nationalism and the revolution. Both associate the realisation of their aims with the supernatural power of the Great Individual. . . In the West nationalism and the revolution constituted in the nineteenth century an absolute antinomy. In Russia the deep-rooted myth of the Tsar systematically transformed these two trends into two forms of one, and one only, Muscovite Caesaro-Papism.' ('Stawrogin', *Teksty* 4 [1972], p. 17.)

27. *Under Western Eyes*, p. 35.

28. *Ibid.*, p. 22.

29. *Ibid.*, p. 23.

30. *Ibid.*, p. x.

31. *Ibid.*, p. 295.

32. Richard Curle, *The Last Twelve Years of Joseph Conrad* (New York, 1928), p. 26.

33. 'Dostoevskij and Conrad's Political Novels', *American Contributions to the Fifth International Congress of Slavists* (The Hague, 1963), II, 218.

34. In 'Die Brüder Karamasow oder Der Untergang Europas' (1919); quoted in Karl Pfleger, *Wrestlers with Christ*, trans. E. I. Watkin (New York, 1936), p. 203.
35. *Under Western Eyes*, pp. 33–4.
36. *Ibid.*, p. 3.
37. *Ibid.*, p. 35.
38. *Ibid.*, p. 7. There was, of course, no 'Order of St Procopius' in Tsarist Russia; and Conrad is presumably alluding here with ironic intent to Procopius, the author of *The Secret History*, that brilliant *exposé* of Byzantine corruption at the time of Justinian and Theodora.
39. *Ibid.*, p. 33.
40. *Loc. cit.*
41. *Ibid.*, p. 36.
42. *Ibid.*, p. 33.
43. *Ibid.*, p. 104.
44. *Ibid.*, p. 363.
45. *Ibid.*, p. 379.
46. Mikhail Bakhtin, *Problemy poetiki Dostoevskogo* (Moscow, 1963), chap. 1.
47. *Under Western Eyes*, p. 382.
48. *Ibid.*, p. 33.
49. *Ibid.*, p. 120.
50. *Ibid.*, p. 40.
51. *Ibid.*, pp. 141–2.
52. 'The Structures of Fiction', *Modern Language Notes* 84 (1969), p. 914.
53. *The Journals of André Gide*, trans. Justin O'Brien (New York, 1949) III, 94.
54. *Letters from Conrad*, p. 234.
55. For a stimulating discussion of the problems of literary influence see Harold Bloom, *The Anxiety of Influence* (New York, 1973).
56. *Lettres françaises*, p. 87.

9 Speech and Writing in *Under Western Eyes*

AVROM FLEISHMAN

A long line of theoreticians of language, from Rousseau to Saussure and on into our own time, has maintained the myth that writing is a cursed labour inherited from the Fall, while speech, despite Babel, remains a vital and creative activity. For the living flow of spoken words and the organic change of popular language, writing substitutes the sterile forms of imposed conventions and fixes the dynamic immediacy of individual speech acts in an embalmed and lifeless hulk, the text. More sceptical writers on language, like Jacques Derrida, have called into question this preference for speech over writing, holding that spoken words cannot escape the taints (or what he calls the 'trace') of their origins as found in written words. Recent discussions of these and related matters by linguistics-oriented critics not only renew our questionings of the special nature of literary texts; they also show that literature itself regularly questions its privileged status as written language.

What does it mean to say that the object one holds in hand is a literary text? Quite apart from the contextual signals provided by publishers, merchandisers and reviewers, it would seem that there are linguistic indicators in the text itself that mark it as a writing of a certain kind. But if the signal is made, it is never made unambiguously; there is a standing opportunity for writers to express their anxieties about the nature of their act of writing. A prime virtue of the linguistic critics is their discovery that self-referentiality is not confined to the more modish contemporary novels but is apparently inherent in literary texts. From the Greeks onwards, writers have attested to the problematic assumptions in positing a fictional world – whether they do so in the form of authorial intrusions about the difficulties of executing the task in hand, or by using self-consciously certain conventions of narrative that always startle us when their peculiar locutions are singled out for attention.

Among these expressions, one of the strangest – and among the rarest, although presenting itself as perfectly conventional – is the epigraph of *Under Western Eyes*: 'I would take liberty from any hand as a hungry man would snatch a piece of bread – MISS HALDIN.'[1] Quite apart from the striking metaphor by which the revolutionary impulse is here expressed, the quotation might trouble an orderly mind. Assuming what may be called the *linearity* of a literary text – that is, that its elements exist in the order in which they are presented – the epigraph comes before the novel proper, and thus before the statement on page 135 (Part II, ch. iii) of the Dent edition that a Miss Haldin said, 'I would take liberty from any hand as a hungry man would snatch at a piece of bread.' Epigraphs conventionally quote statements made in historical time before the appearance of the text they decorate; what can we say of an inscription that adds a piece of the writing to itself – and not after but before that writing is presented? And what uneasiness must we feel when we observe that the epigraph, in common with so many literary and scholarly citations, is a *misquotation*, the word 'at' being omitted?

Some of our disturbance at a work that quotes itself, and does not even quote itself correctly, may be relieved when it is remembered that *Under Western Eyes* is one of those novels that presents itself as a text written by one of its characters. If we call the fiction written by Joseph Conrad the A-text and the document prepared by the narrator the B-text, we can associate the epigraph with the A-text as a quotation from the B-text. If it be objected that the two texts are identical, a short search will suffice to assemble the elements of the A-text that distinguish it from the B-text; in addition to the epigraph, these are the title, the author's name, the dedication, and the Author's Note. (The latter, added after the original publication, is admittedly of another order of existence in the A-text, and I would surrender it if pressed.) Here may lie a justification for that curious misquotation: the A and B texts are accepted as not identical, for in the transition from one citation of Miss Haldin's statement to the other a change of assumptions occurs, such that the reader accepts the disparity as an instance of the rule that misquotations *will* occur when one text quotes another.

The peculiar epigraph, then, must be counted among those linguistic devices by which the author of the novel establishes (or gives the appearance of establishing) that he is not an inventor but only the conveyor of an authoritative document written by another, the narrator. Conrad's apology for the narrator, in the Author's Note, is well known: 'He was useful to me and therefore I think that he must be useful to the reader both in the way of comment and by the part he plays in the development of the story. In my desire to produce the effect of actuality it seemed to me indispensable to have an eye-witness of the transactions in Geneva' (pp. viii–ix). These are the standard arguments of verisimilitude, which link Conrad's experimental technique to the aesthetics of realism; yet even while we register the 'effect of actuality' produced by the 'eye-witness', we register also the effects of the multiple narrative structure. Quite apart from the objections that have been raised about the characterisation, the usefulness and the consistency of the narrator, a number of statements ascribed to him call into question the authority claimed by his act of writing, and help to define Conrad's highly inventive language.

At two points in his narrative, the English, *émigré* language-teacher pauses to deliver an apparently heartfelt expression of sincerity. On both occasions he puts forward as a reason for believing his narrative its 'artlessness', in both the literal sense (without the traits pertaining to a work of art) and in the figurative sense (ingenuous, unfabricated, straightforward). Both statements reek of dissimulation on someone's part: 'In the conduct of an invented story there are, no doubt, certain proprieties to be observed for the sake of clearness and effect. . . But this is not a work of imagination; I have no talent; my excuse for this undertaking lies not in its art, but in its artlessness' (II, i, 100); 'A novelist says this and that of his personages, and if only he knows how to say it earnestly enough he may not be questioned upon the inventions of his brain in which his own belief is made sufficiently manifest by a telling phrase, a poetic image, the accent of emotion. Art is great! But I have no art . . .' (II, iv, 162). Now there is nothing here to shock the initiated; novelists, like rhetoricians, have always protested that they are to be believed because they are plain speakers, not artful deceivers – that they speak truth without adornment, although their conventional disclaimers are themselves striking instances of adornment. But the effect of these protestations in *Under Western Eyes* is very like that produced by Cervantes' elaborate explanation that the text of *Don Quixote* is not his own work but came into his hands in a Toledo marketplace. Both make the disclaimer in so playful a way that the artfulness of the authorial hand is thereby underscored. To put the matter in my somewhat awkward code, the language-teacher's insistence that his writing, the B-text, is not a work of fiction like the A-text has the contrary effect of reminding us that it, too, is a fictional construct (B-text-within-A-text), a 'useful' arrangement in an artist's effort to create an illusion – the illusion that his invention is true because it is reported by an eye-witness.

If so much artfulness can be ascribed to the devices of the B-text, even more may be discerned in the elaboration of the narrative structure by the positing, if not the complete presentation, of a C-text. For the scheme requires that the language-teacher's report be based on written documents, as well as on his direct observation of the action. Among these documents – which include the newspaper report of Haldin's arrest, Peter Ivanovitch's autobiography, and sources relating to Mr de P— which provide a background sufficient to place if not to understand events in Russia – there is a primary source, Razumov's notebook. Assigning this writing to a precise genre gives the language-teacher some difficulty: 'The document, of course, is something in the nature of a journal, a diary, yet not exactly that in its actual form. For instance, most of it was not written up from day to day, though all the entries are dated. Some of these entries cover months of time and extend over dozens of pages. All the earlier part is a retrospect, in a narrative form, relating to an event which took place about a year before' (I, 4). The language-teacher's awareness of aesthetic form is obviously sufficient to make him sensitive to the difference between a diary, written more or less daily, a journal, written more randomly but keeping some chronological order, and something else, which he calls a 'retrospect', characterised by its narrative form and covering events in the life of its author at some remove from the time of writing. The usual term for a writer's narrative of his life (or parts of his life) is *autobiography*, and we are given to understand that Razumov's text contains not only fragmentary memoranda of events as they occur but also large autobiographical reflections on the shape of his career and the tragic ironies of his destiny.

There is at least one other kind of writing included in the C-text: Razumov's letter to Natalie Haldin, which is quoted in the B-text and given in the novel on pages 358–62 (IV, iv) of the Dent edition. The language-teacher's artless method of presentation is inevitably disturbed by his elegant use of the words of his primary source, at the precise moment when the protagonist rises to a height of fervour and decision. The B-text introduces the quotation in this way: there comes 'a page and a half of incoherent writing where his expression is baffled by the novelty and the mysteriousness of that side of our emotional life to which his solitary existence had been a stranger. Then only he begins to address directly the reader he had in his mind, trying to express in broken sentences, full of wonder and awe, the sovereign (he uses that very word) power of her person over his imagination, in which lay the dormant seed of her brother's words' (IV, iv, 357–8).[2]

Despite the greater drama of Razumov's previous confession to Natalie and of his subsequent self-exposure to the revolutionists, this written declaration is the climactic moment in the novel, bringing to a crescendo the tragic theme of the hero's loneliness. Moreover, as an expression of Razumov's love for Natalie, the letter reveals a new dimension of the novel: it is, besides being a political novel, a love story, complicated by subtle but unmistakable hints of the narrator's competing love for the heroine and his suppressed jealousy of Razumov. If a quotation from the primary source, the C-text, has the power to endow the B-text with a tragic dimension, and further to elaborate the formal order of the A-text, it is because a 'sovereign power' *is* at work in all three texts. That this power is a linguistic one is made clear when the hero acknowledges that Natalie's sway over him takes its potency from 'the dormant seed of her brother's words'. (We may even find here the shadowy apparition of a fourth level of discourse, or D-text, composed of Haldin's written letters to Natalie [not quoted] and his spoken words to Razumov, some of which the latter quotes in the C-text.)

It would be too much to claim that Razumov falls in love because Natalie embodies Haldin's revolutionary spirit, as carried by his words. But it is evident that language exhibits here its character of *resonance*, flowing from Haldin into Razumov and Razumov's writing, on into the observer's record of their relationship, and finally into the language of art, becoming part of the fabric of Conrad's creation. Language has this peculiar ability to allow itself to be seen on one level of discourse or another, for a series of words can exist at one and the same time within a novel, within a quasi-historical report, within a personal notebook, and within a letter or direct address. Although as sensible men we know that there is only the one set of words, all of them written by Conrad and to be found only in the pages of a book called *Under Western Eyes*, as sympathetic readers we also assent to the varied modes of discourse in which those words are engaged.

Given the multiple resonances of language, it is not surprising that men discover that writing which they think to compose on one level of discourse exists simultaneously – sometimes primarily – on another. An absurd limit of such linguistic malleability is proposed in *Under Western Eyes* by the radical journalist, Laspara, who urges Razumov to 'write something for us': He could not understand how any one could refrain from writing on anything, social, economic, historical –

anything. Any subject could be treated in the right spirit, and for the ends of social revolution' (III, iv, 287). A more profound linguistic transformation occurs in the narrator's discovery that he is writing not simply a personal but a social history: 'The task is not in truth the writing in the narrative form a *precisé* of a strange human document, but the rendering – I perceive it now clearly – of the moral conditions ruling over a large portion of this earth's surface . . .' (I, iii, 67). But the most important shift in the nature of a writing occurs at the peak of Razumov's career as a writer. Beginning as the inscriber of school exercises, bursting out as the composer of his gnomic set of theses ('History not Theory' etc.), Razumov moves at last from merely instrumental writing, designed for attack or defence, to what we may consider the aesthetic manner, creating a verbal image of his own identity. As this process is essential to the dramatic action, yet complicated in its stages, it is worth tracing in some detail.

What Razumov writes, in response to Laspara's invitation, is his first spy report: 'Write. Must write! He! Write! A sudden light flashed upon him. To write was the very thing he had made up his mind to do that day' (III, iv, 288). But the hero finds that writing a spy report is not enough, and that he must go on to confessional writing; Razumov returns to his room and regains 'a certain measure of composure by writing in his secret diary'. The one kind of writing leads into the other, it seems, and the kinetic effects which the writer hopes to accomplish with the report give way to the aesthetic effects of the notebook. For it is an aesthetic evaluation of the notebook that emerges: 'Mr Razumov looked at it, I suppose, as a man looks at himself in a mirror, with wonder, perhaps with anguish, with anger or despair' (III, i, 214). The traditional metaphor of the mirror of art is deceptive, suggesting an already prepared reflecting surface to which the Narcissus-like figure approaches; whereas language-become-art is something not found but made. Razumov sees himself in his own language, not as something given, but as a composition created by his acts of writing. Insofar as the notebook provides the materials out of which the B-text and ultimately the A-text are composed, we can say that the writing of the notebook establishes the linguistic equivalent of Razumov's identity.

The hero, moreover, affirms his own creation by bequeathing it to his beloved. The power of writing to preserve the vital being of the writer is attested to when Natalie turns the notebook over to the language-teacher (by virtue of which action we are allowed to have the text): 'She walked to the writing-table, . . . a mere piece of dead furniture; but it contained something living, still, since she took from a recess a flat parcel which she brought to me. "It's a book," she said rather abruptly. "It was sent to me wrapped up in my veil"' (IV, v, 375). Thanks to the gift of this writing, we are enabled to project the living Razumov, for in it he achieves the aesthetic self-realisation at which autobiographical writers aim. How does it fulfil so august a role? These is no hint here of the traditional motif of immortality through art – 'So long as . . . eyes can see, So long lives this' – even though the notebook is considered 'something living' while wrapped in a veil within a piece of 'dead furniture'. To grasp the dynamics of self-embodiment in language may help us to fathom the complex structure of writings that is *Under Western Eyes*.

At first, the process seems simple: 'I want to be understood', says Razumov (I, ii, 39). If one can convey one's inner life to another there may be said to exist an image of the self outside one's own skin. But the narrator, in tune with Conrad's scepticism, immediately describes Razumov's wish as 'the universal aspiration with all its profound and melancholy meaning'. The language-teacher has already given us his views on the limits of communication by language: 'Words, as is well known, are the great foes of reality. . . To a teacher of languages there comes a time when the world is but a place of many words and man appears a mere talking animal not much more wonderful than a parrot' (I, 3). Not only language-teachers may find it so; many a creative and critical writer shares the view. If one and all wish only to be understood, it would seem that language, as here described, would be a last resort. Yet we are all more or less Russians, to judge by the succeeding account of 'the Russians' extraordinary love of words': 'There must be a wonderful soothing power in mere words since so many men have used them for self-communion. Being myself a quiet individual I take it that what all men are really after is some form or perhaps only some formula of peace' (I, 5).

This last may appear to be another of the language-teacher's self-indulgent puns, like his continuation of the thought: 'What sort of peace Kirylo Sidorovitch Razumov expected to find in the writing up of his record it passeth my understanding to guess' (I, 5). But the distinction he draws between a 'form' (or kind) and a 'formula' (or symbolic equivalent) provides a clue to the function of language envisaged here. If one can formulate a verbal equivalent of one's sense of oneself, or of life, or of the ideal, one has done something to fend off silence, which in *Under Western Eyes* is repeatedly seen as a kind of death. (A Derrida might claim that what language does is to propitiate the silence by building it into the fabric of the text.)

Although words grope for an understanding that is never reached, and for a peace not to be found in this world, the alternatives to language are disturbingly meagre. Silence may be golden but, as with other precious metals in Conrad's world, the possession of such a treasure may prove one's undoing. Indeed, the entire tale is generated by Razumov's taciturnity, for he is misjudged as a sympathiser with revolutionary action because of his very detachment and restraint.

After such a display of the dangers of keeping silent, we come back to language with renewed faith – or is it only with more urgent needs? Words may be impotent, but silence is empty; though language may fail in all its declared aims, at least it is not nothing, and it helps to fill the vast empty spaces in existence. As the language-teacher has suggested, if we can't have peace, at least we can content ourselves with a 'formula of peace'. Yet such faint praise may seem to damn language too thoroughly. I have been speaking as though language were all of a piece, but it may be possible to distinguish between relative and utter vanity in its operations.

One conclusion that might be drawn from Razumov's career is that writing is in vain, but that speech may not be so ineffectual after all. On completing his letter to Natalie and, with the same stroke, bringing his notebook to an end, Razumov 'stopped writing, shut the book . . . and then flung the pen away from him into a distant corner' (IV, iv, 362). At this point, the hero turns to oral language, most dramatically in his declaration to the revolutionaries, but also in his subsequent role: 'Some of *us* always go to see him when passing through,' Sophia Antonovna relates. 'He is intelligent. He has ideas. . . He talks well, too' (IV, v, 379). How does it come about that this, the most literate of Conrad's heroes (barring Heyst, perhaps), a man of books who spends much of his time making a book, turns at the end, without being able to hear them, to spoken words?

Let us consider Razumov's sequence of confessions as a means of interpreting his passage from the written to the spoken word. For the hero, we recall, makes three distinct confessions in the denouement. The first is a spoken one, made privately to Natalie (with the narrator present when he shouldn't be); in it, Razumov exposes only his guilt, naming – or rather, pointing to – himself as Haldin's betrayer: 'There is no more to tell! . . . [The story] ends here – on this very spot' (IV, iii, 354). The second confession is also person-to-person, but written, amending the spoken revelation: 'Listen – now comes the true confession. The other was nothing . . . do you know what I said to myself? I shall steal his sister's soul from her . . . [but] I felt that I must tell you that I had ended by loving you' (IV, iv, 359, 361). This is a confession not of guilt but of love and hate, not of the overt deed but of the inner life. Just as it looks back to the earlier confession, it anticipates the later one: 'And to tell you that [I love you] I must first confess. Confess, go out – and perish' (IV, iv, 361). (Here Razumov makes the avowal of love conditional on his avowal of guilt – in effect, makes the second confession [the emotional climax] follow from the third [the dramatic climax] by arranging that the delivery of the letter and notebook occur after he has spoken out.) The third confession is, unlike both the first and second, public: 'Haven't you all understood that I am that man?' (IV, iv, 366). The sequence, then, moves from impulsive speech through written preparations to dramatic oratory; and Razumov's subsequent discourses to the faithful suggest that he has taken on the role of a populist sage.

If we find this transformation from author to oracle a falling-off, we must nevertheless admit that writing has failed the hero. The pathos of his letter-writing is all too clear: 'In this queer pedantism of a man who had read, thought, lived, pen in hand, there is the sincerity of the attempt to grapple by the same means with another profounder know-ledge' (IV, iv, 357). Having tested, not to say exhausted, the potential-ities of writing – having achieved whatever self-definition and personal revelation is available to the writer – Razumov can never hope to bridge the gap between him and his beloved with words. He is still very much alone – has named his tragic loneliness but not overcome it. By public speech, however much hostility it rouses, he remarkably accom-plishes something which all his writing cannot: his rhetoric puts the speaker into permanent relationship with his audience. The alienated hero is suddenly transformed into a Russian orator, for better or worse; and Russians will continue to listen to him, as he indulges in the national trait of speech-for-its-own-sake. Luckily for him, he is deafened and doesn't have to listen to his own words.

It would be too much to claim, from this evidence alone, that Conrad's final twist of the denouement is a declaration of ultimate despair of written language, and of the art of fiction along with it. Yet the elaborate structure of writings which constitutes *Under Western Eyes* perhaps expresses no more than the anxiety of every conscientious writer about the efficacy of his writing. Certainly there must be some sympathy with the man who, when invited to contribute a paper, can say, 'I have written already all I shall ever write' (IV, iv, 364).

NOTES

1. All quotations are from the Collected Edition published by Dent (London), hereafter cited parenthetically by part, chapter and page numbers.
2. On the seminal power of language and the seed-like character of words, Jacques Derrida has written pregnantly in *La Dissémination* (Paris, 1972). For Derrida's general account of speech and writing, see *De la grammatologie* (Paris, 1967).

10 Narrative Form in Conrad and Lowry

M. C. BRADBROOK

I

The Man and the Myth have become part of the novels of both Conrad and Lowry – seamen, exiles, and perhaps the two most personal of English novelists. Both worked and reworked their own past, and in each case the transformation had become a matter of personal integrity, of integration, so that the novels and stories, whilst rooted in history, would 'transform it from particular to general, and appeal to universal emotions by the temperamental handling of personal experience', as Conrad observed, whilst 'Public mind fastens on externals, on mere facts, such for instance as ships and voyages, without paying attention to any deeper significance they may have.' (*Life and Letters*, II, 321, 320).

For Conrad, the 'interior journey' involved struggles of such intensity that his slightest work bears the impress, even though at times he might seem to be merely hamming his way into magazines. Taken as part of the whole work (Lowry termed his *oeuvre The Voyage that never Ends*), the attentive reader may discern even in the second rate an adumbration of the greater works. Not an artistic triumph perhaps but

> a psychological triumph of the first order . . . a matter of life or death, or rebirth as it were, for its author, not to say sanity or otherwise . . . not Dante's personal spiritual position when he wrote *The Inferno* was worse . . . the bloody agony of the writer writing it is so patently extreme that it creates a kind of power in itself that, together with what humour or lyricism it may possess, takes your mind off the faults of the story itself, which, incidentally, are of every kind (Lowry, *Selected Letters*, p. 339)

This is not Joseph Conrad but Malcolm Lowry on his latest work, *October Ferry to Gabriola*.

Why, you may ask, am I preparing to link these two? Is it just 'so and so and sea-water'? An idle game of influences or parallel passages or source materials? This is not my object. My object is rather to trace configurations, or structures – including structural absences – in the subjectively based work of Lowry, by which I hope also to direct new emphasis upon the last works of both; in particular upon Conrad's *Victory* and *The Shadow Line*.

Albert Guerard long ago suggested that the achievement of Conrad came closer to Faulkner, Graham Greene or Malcolm Lowry than to his contemporaries (*Conrad the Novelist*, 1958, p. 300). On Eliot's assumptions that 'comparisons and analysis are the chief tools of the critic', and that 'the past should be altered by the present as much as the present is directed by the past',[1] the reader of today who has to accommodate Henry James' 'new novel'[2] with Barthes' *nouveau roman*, may find in Conrad and Lowry a bridge between the two. Moreover, the development of each of these men in relation to his chosen roles interacts with his development as an artist. If Lowry's *Ultramarine* (published in 1933, nine years after Conrad's death) may be compared with *Youth*, and *Under the Volcano* with *Nostromo*, my main object is to correlate the works of what is often termed Conrad's decline with those of Lowry's latest phase, which have also been dismissed by many, including his biographer, as the end products of alcoholic degeneration. In particular, *October Ferry to Gabriola*, 'Through the Panama' and 'The Forest Path to the Spring' may offer a configuration relating to *Victory* and *The Shadow-Line*.

Both depicted in the end haunted men, yet men who exorcised the dark powers. And here perhaps is the place to quote a sonnet entitled *Joseph Conrad* written by Lowry:

> This wrestling, as of seamen with a storm
> Which flies to leeward – while they, united
> In that chaos, turn, each on his nighted
> Bunk, to dream of chaos again, or home –
> The poet himself, struggling with the form
> Of his coiled work, knows; having requited
> Sea weariness with purpose, invited
> What derricks of the soul plunge in his room.
> Yet some mariner's ferment in his blood
> – Though truant heart will hear the iron travail
> And song of ships that ride their easting down –
> Sustains him to subdue or be subdued.
> In sleep all night he grapples with a sail!
> But words beyond the life of ships, dream on.
>
> (*Selected Poems*, p. 74)*

And Conrad wrote: 'In the year 1874 I got into the train (Vienna Express) as a man gets into a dream – and here is the dream going on still' (*Life and Letters*, II, 155). His guardian and uncle had preached at him the importance of 'facts, facts, facts'[3] and *his* motto '*usque ad finem*' was the pursuit of duty – 'the love of duty which circumstances define', which he opposed to 'grandiose ideals'. Conrad took the phrase and turned it round:

> I tell you, my friend, it is not good for you to find you cannot make your dream come true. . . A man that is born falls into a dream like a man who falls into the sea. If he tries to climb out into the air . . . he drowns . . .
>
> For that, too, there is only one way. . . . In the destructive element immerse. . . . To follow the dream, and again to follow the dream – and so – *ewig – usque ad finem*.

II

The chameleon quality of Conrad's whole writing may be seen by the variety of stress that at various times have been laid on different parts of it. Variety of interpretation, as we shall see, was built into his writing by Lowry, who developed very special writing techniques to this end. The element of *performance* is suggested by various devices, of which the first and simplest is that of the seaman's tale. The most sophisticated form comes near that of the French structuralist, Jean Thibaudeau, in *Tel Quel, Théorie d'ensemble* (1968): 'Le roman ne sera entendu comme une forme, proposé par l'institution littéraire . . . mais debuté par hazard par des mots, des phrases, des morceaux de texte apparemment quelconque . . . ce texte indefensible, exclusif, sans retour.'

Such a form was not open to Conrad; his particular insulating force lay in the use of the English language – a language learned only in manhood, which sometimes betrayed him into magniloquence, at other times into a painful jocularity (as in his descriptions of that supreme outsider, Mr Verloc). This accent of jaunty assurance can be heard from time to time in *A Personal Record*; it is that of a foreigner trying desperately to be at home. It can be heard in Lowry the schoolboy, and is caught dramatically in his last novel, where the undergraduate taunting his despairing friend into suicide is recalled: 'All right, Mr Peter Bloody Cordwainer. . . Go ahead and do it. Grandmother won't let you down, I'm sure. . . She's got a lot of friends in high office. And besides, the Tibetans say you can be comfortable even in hell, just so long as you're clever. As you are, if not so damn clever as you used to be.' (*October Ferry*, p. 68)

At the age of seventeen Lowry left his public school to take a voyage as a deck-hand to Yokohama via Port Said and Penang; he had told newspaper reporters 'No silk cushion youth for me. I want to see the world and rub shoulders with its oddities and get some experience.' This voyage gave the basis of his first novel *Ultramarine*, heavily laced with borrowings from a young Norwegian novelist who had also gone to sea 'for experience'. The artless testimony of one of the crew shows Lowry a minor variant of Lord Jim.

> What a man he was! I remember on one occasion, one of our un-bidden passengers was a dove, 'Lobs' was fond of it, as indeed were all the sailors, but in Port Swettenham the dove fell overboard, and could not rise from the water. Lobs decided he had lost the chance to prove himself a hero, by not diving in after it, even although as he watched its struggles, there was a sudden skirmish in the water and the dove had become a meal for a hungry inhabitant. Yes, Lobs wanted very much to shine, but at the vital moment or moment of truth, he just could not make it. (Liverpool City Library, Local History Dept. No. 1069)

This tale went into *Ultramarine*.

The hero's chance comes later when he is sent down below to act as a coaltrimmer (Lowry had won *The Hairy Ape* as a school prize):

> Yes, but shall I be able to do it? . . . that's great, Nicholai, that's great!
> My God, that's wonderful! Well; will you come and take a turn on deck?
> – Sure. But don't be saying it's great till you've tried it.

The simple narrative is interrupted by random yarns of the seamen – tall tales, 'old salts' lies' – and by a sophisticated drunken sequence in the manner of James Joyce's 'Nightown'. Here there is a boast Conrad also used, swathed in the comic however, for these are mad vaunts of a boy: 'I have lived. I have bathed in blood at Saigon and Singapore. I have like Masefield worn my jack-knife in my cap to catch lightning at Cape Horn . . . once for a week adrift in an open boat, I kept up the spirits of the crew by playing the taropatch. In the end we had to eat the strings.'[4] Such fantasy even wins over the seamen, as the boy hero spins a fantastic yarn about a cargo of animals who break away, take over the ship and run it.

Fo'castle yarns perhaps deserve a little more consideration. The short story which gets spun out into a novel later is highly character-istic of Conrad and Lowry (and for both a story is apt to begin slowly and work up to sharp short action).[5]

Two of Conrad's most deeply personal stories are based on seaman's yarns – the tale of the *Jeddah*, which became the root of *Lord Jim*, and a tale of the *Cutty Sark*, which became *The Secret Sharer*. *Youth*, *The Shadow-Line* and *The Nigger of the 'Narcissus'* are based on Conrad's own voyages in *Palestine*, *Otago*, and *Narcissus*.

Conrad set out his views on yarns in a letter to John Livingstone Lowes apropos of *The Ancient Mariner*. It begins

You ask me whether the tale the summary of which you sent me is one of the usual sailors' yarns. That it certainly is not. The so-called sailors' yarn proper is never concerned with the supernatural. A sailors' folk lore is to me an inconceivable thing.

The only legend that is authentic of which I have heard and which is often referred to in sailors' talk (or at any rate before the sailors became mere deckhands of mechanically propelled vessels) is the tale of the Flying Dutchman...

After commenting on the yarn Lowes offers him, Conrad decides it is 'a shore fabrication' current on some northern coast. In a postscript he declared that Coleridge invented this albatross, whose habits are quite otherwise; he also praises Edgar Allen Poe's 'Manuscript found in a Bottle' as a fine piece of work and authentic in detail.

Conrad himself radically changed the character of the tales he told. *Typhoon* grew out of a tale of Chinese coolies shipped in a heavy sea, but MacWhirr grew out of twenty years' experience of the sea. In 'The Secret Sharer' he radically altered the characters of the mate and the captain (who in real life committed suicide) and he emphasised, apparently without recognising it, the element of the supernatural in *The Shadow-Line*, both tales being partly based on the voyage of his first and only command, *Otago*.

Conrad believed in rendering the truth, but this requires mediation and skill, not enslavement to what Eliot termed 'the historical fact'.

Conrad observed of his chief-narrator, Marlow:

The yarns of seamen have a direct simplicity, the whole meaning of which lies within the shell of a nut [as in the seaman's letter about Lowry]. But Marlow was not typical (if his propensity to spin yarns be excepted) and to him the meaning of an episode was not inside like a kernel but outside, enveloping the tale which brought it out only as a glow brings out a haze, in the likeness of one of these misty halos that sometimes are made visible by the spectral illumination of moonshine (*Heart of Darkness*, ed. Sherry, p. 4).

The narrator enables the novelist to introduce those dislocations of time, those elaborate shifts and breaks in narration, which give depth to the action, set up a rival sequence – 'the tick of real death, not the tick of time' and 'do a thing in the way that shall make it undergo most doing'.[6] In the final sequence of *The Heart of Darkness* Marlow is living under two time-clocks: in a 'grave' or 'tomb' in Brussels and in the last hour of Kurtz. At the end of *Under the Volcano*, in Chapter XI, the horse that the Consul loosed is encountered running free and the shot that kills him is heard before the events themselves are told in Chapter XII.

III

In the opening chapter, Lowry describes his hero, ex-naval officer, ex-consul, ex-husband, alcoholic, as 'a kind of more lachrymose pseudo Lord Jim, living in self-imposed exile' but eventually boasting of his misdeed and 'unlike Lord Jim, grown rather careless of his honour' (p. 38). Yet the four chief characters, the Consul, his younger brother, his wife and his friend, Laruelle, the film director, whose recollections of the distanced story of the Consul's last day provide the prologue, all reflect aspects of one invisible protagonist.[7]

The novel may be seen as Laruelle's film, with its zooming close-ups, panning, 'dollies', tracing shots (perhaps Lowry's command of alternate media may be held to offset Conrad's trilingual competence). The break-up of the relationship between husband and wife is at the centre, but the story spreads out to political, and cosmological and religious levels. The twelve chapters which chronicle the pitiable and relentless progress of the Consul's Faustian last day, to the moment when he is shot and flung, still alive, into the ravine, are each complete as a unit, and Lowry explained this in the long letter to his publisher which is his chief statement of intent. Written 'with provision made for every reader' this post-Joycean novel (in distinction to Joyce) simplifies the originally complex process. Begun in Mexico in 1937, it was worked and reworked for years and finished only on Christmas Eve, 1944. Built in are Lowry's responses to the war years, which he spent in his beach shack on the shores of Vancouver Bay, in temporary reprieve

from drink, living as it were in Patusan or Samburan, in the first years
of his happy second marriage.

What this many-layered story, thickened with all sorts of literary
allusions, offers to each reader is the chance to play it in his own way,
to emphasise whatever his own psychic configuration finds sympathetic.
To quote Lowry again, 'It can be regarded as a kind of symphony, or
in another way, as a kind of opera – or even a horse opera. It is hot
music, a poem, a song, a comedy, a farce, and so forth. . . It can even
be regarded as a sort of machine; it works too, believe me, as I have
found out.' (*Selected Letters*, p. 66)

Conrad's nearest approach to this is in a letter to Barrett Clark on
Victory.

> I . . . put before you a general proposition, that a work of art is very
> seldom limited to one exclusive meaning and not necessarily tending
> to a definite conclusion. And this for the reason that the nearer it
> approaches art, the more it acquires a symbolic character . . . all the
> great creations of literature have been symbolic, and in that way have
> gained in complexity, in power, in depth and in beauty. (*Life and
> Letters*, II, 204)

Both Lowry and Conrad are given to using Baudelaire to define this
approach to their work, but the effect of having completed his book
was to precipitate Lowry into an identity crisis. In the most dream-like
of the later tales, 'Through the Panama', the writer, Sigbjørn Wilderness, holds dialogues between his rival selves and with characters in the
book he is writing. Mrs Conrad records the same of Conrad during the
breakdown that followed the completion of *Under Western Eyes*.[8]
Lowry uses quotations from other works as 'blocks' in his communication
(among them a dull history of the Panama Canal itself) to force the
reader to question himself. *The Rime of the Ancient Mariner* counters
with the highest symbolic level of this inner voyage, told in diary form.
It follows an actual voyage by Lowry and his wife from Vancouver to
Le Havre in November–December 1947. In another story of this
collection, Sigbjørn finds consolation as a writer among writers of the
past. The craft of writing imposed the idea of duty on Lowry and 'the
inheritance of a great dynasty'.

> Their sheer guts – which commentators so obligingly forgot! –
> Character in a high sense of that word, the sense in which Conrad
> sometimes understood it, for were they not in their souls like hapless
> shipmasters, determined to drive their leaky commands, full of

valuable treasure, at all costs, somehow, into port, always against time, yet through all but interminable tempest, typhoons that so rarely abated? (*Hear Us O Lord*, p. 108)

These later short stories 'complete in themselves, with the same characters interrelated . . . full of effects and dissonances that are impossible in a short story'[9] nevertheless harmonise in 'a novel of an odd Aeolian kind'.[10] Implicit unity had also been adumbrated by Conrad in the preface to his shorter tales; though his statement is naturally in the more formal manner of an earlier day.[11]

Even if the deep complex feelings and contradictory attitudes of an author to his creation are built on illusion (says Conrad), they are real enough; each volume of his short stories had a unity of outlook in this way 'covering the mingled subjects of civilisation and wilderness, of land life and life on the sea'; so each story has to stay in the position where it originally appeared. This position, however, was not the result of a preconceived plan. 'It just happened by drawing from sources profounder than the logic of a deliberate theory suggested by acquired learning . . . or by lessons drawn from analysed practice. . .' Therefore he carefully rearranged the volume of collected shorter tales to bring out the pattern. Conrad knew the 'Aeolian' method of construction, the open form of symbolic construction to provide something for every reader; Lowry, in his latest works – where his wife contributed much to the writing and rewriting, so that there is a form of collaboration built in, and an editor has termed them 'corrupt texts' – could work with different cosmic clocks, could re-shape his own past and his own work. 'The Forest Path to the Spring' is placed by its opening sequences in the period 1940–1, when the Lowrys found their waterside home, and the tragic novel *Under the Volcano* was being rewritten here. 'On one level we go back in time, in another sense we are working through the war years'. In the latter idyll, the nameless hero is composing an opera to be called 'The Forest Path to the Spring' – his daily walk, in which a mystic expansion and contraction of time brings him through inner storms to a recovered peace. This tale is the most triumphant celebration of 'a condition of complete simplicity costing not less than everything', In *October Ferry*, driven to leave 'this place that I love or loved more than my life', the anguished choice of exile again awakes a buried remorse – the memory of that suicide which I have already cited.

IV

In *Joseph Conrad and the Fiction of Autobiography* (Harvard, 1966), Edward Said has probed most sensitively the writer's 'immense struggle with himself' (p. 4), his 'repeated encounters with what caused pain and required effort' so that 'the dramatic spirit of partnership between himself and the external world' constitutes the appeal of his life. (p. 9) Henry James declared that the elaborate plot manoeuvrings of *Chance* were justified as self revelations. 'What Mr Conrad's left hand gives back then is simply Mr Conrad himself' (*Notes on Novelists*, p. 277).

Constantly Conrad remade his own life for himself; like Lowry's his past was symbolic, but in 'winning a sense of truth, of necessity, above all of conduct' for the characters of his fiction, he rescued these struggling forms from deep within himself.

Remorse, detachment and involvement, catastrophe reoccur through Conrad's work, but in the later ones (like a theme played *da capo*) develop with each repetition. The breaking of human ties, the collapse of political idealisms, the vulnerability of even the most detached observer, are worked out in structures that instead of loosening (as did Lowry's) become tighter and tighter. This is the paradox of Conrad's latest work. Powerfully symbolic as *The Rime of the Ancient Mariner*, their efforts at honesty and self-explanation meet the resistant structures of novels based on society and its habits. He invited 'derricks of the soul' to plunge in his 'room', but had learnt his trade from Balzac, de Maupassant, Flaubert and Henry James, impersonal artists.

He reworked early unfinished tales; *Chance* (1912) is based on a short story 'Explosives', on the perils of collision for a ship carrying dynamite – a symbolism which hardly needs comment. The theme of violence just under the surface is continued in *Victory* (1914), which opens in the voice of an anonymous narrator – who soon disappears; like Marlow he is 'one of us' (and at the end is revealed as Davidson, master of the *Sissie*). The tale begins at a distance from the island paradise, the retreat where we see Baron Heyst, the hero sitting:

An island is but the top of a mountain . . . his most frequent visitors were shadows, the shadows of clouds, relieving the monotony of the inanimate, brooding sunshine of the tropics. His nearest neighbour – I am speaking now of things showing some signs of animation – was an indolent volcano which smoked faintly all day with its head just above the northern horizon . . . (p. 4.)

Under the volcano! At night its red glow expanded and collapsed in time with Heyst's cigar, like some cosmic signalling system. It is the volcano which guides to Heyst's retreat the infernal trio of card-sharper, murderous sailor and human ape ('Satan, Jack-the-Ripper and Caliban'), all of whom are aspects of the one invisible protagonist. Paradise becomes a trap for Heyst, the Pygmalion who has brought his Lena to life yet hates and mistrusts life himself. Plain Mr Jones, the spectral Shadow of Shadows, is the one who kills, after all three have been dredged from the sea by Heyst, dying of thirst. The fable in this Eastern myth gives Victory to the damsel, who rescues her knight but is killed by 'the monster Polypheme'.[12]

All the characters at first exist in a fragmentary fashion, drawn with a few obsessional traits; Schomberg, garrulous teller of vile tales, compulsive trader in the fears and miseries of mankind, had first appeared in *Lord Jim*, then in 'Falk', so he is himself a kind of spectre from earlier tales; and his famous *table d'hôte* might be taken as an illustration of Schopenhauer's theory that to eat is the first and most primitive form of absorbing the world into the self. It is no coincidence that he reappears from a tale of an ordeal that culminated in cannibalism. In this story there are expurgations: Ricardo's fo'castle language is represented by 'Je-minny', and the sexual tie between Ricardo and Jones, hater of women, is never brought into the open. Most of the characters in *Victory* have alternative or patently false names; the girl is also known as Alma and Magdalen (of which Lena is presumably a diminutive).[13] She does indeed represent soul and body but her death scene is copied word for word from a Polish novel of 1908, Stefan Zeromski's *History of a Sin*.[14] Axel Heyst, also known as Hard Facts Heyst, Enchanted Heyst, as a Hermit and a Utopian, is named from the blighted hero of Villiers de l'isle Adam, *Axel's Castle*. The plot is re-shaped from Conrad's own story 'Because of the Dollars', whose hero is Davidson, the English captain; he suddenly materialises at the end, the sole witness, to recount it all to some nameless 'Excellency'. The volcano is blazing on the island where beside the dead coal of the old enterprise, Heyst is 'ashes'.

Lena, Heyst, the trio of villainy are all disposed of with the nonchalance of puppets being thrust back into a box. Male puppets differ first chiefly by huge beards (for Schomberg and the villainous Zangiacomo) and a pair of military bronze moustaches for Heyst. The evil Mrs Zangiacomo is balanced by Mrs Schomberg, whose relations with her husband are very much like those of Mrs Quilp and Quilp in Dickens. Heyst's remote sanctuary is absurdly parodied by the fiercely enfenced compound where his Chinese servant grows vegetables and keeps a native woman; but when Heyst tries to get shelter for Lena after the trio have revealed their menace, he is confronted by his own stolen revolver poking out from a jungle of leaves with Wang's face 'no suggestion of a body belonging to it, like those cardboard faces' in toy shops. The psychologist has but to murmur 'Melanie Klein', for its sentimental story of damsel in distress and rescuing knight to lie open to reductive treatment; but I would maintain that if it is seen as an attempt to reach 'sources profounder than the logic of a deliberate theory', to anticipate Joyce and Lowry, this melodramatic tale with its extreme simplification, its cinematic techniques may also be recognised as 'a sort of mighty preposterous deed of some obscure sort, testifying to an underlying toughness of staying power in his character.'

Heyst is a man who has learnt to use language itself 'playfully' as a barrier between himself and others; his 'delicate playfulness' is often covertly insulting, tolerable only because it so plainly covers pain and fear. 'There are no voices here to remind us ... nothing can break in on us here', he tells Lena (p. 223) yet he – and she – remain conscious of different origins. He ends cursing his own 'fastidiousness' which puts a taboo on tenderness even at the moment when Lena is dying. Conrad himself declared 'It is a book in which I have tried to grasp at more "life-stuff" than perhaps in any other of my works' (*Life and Letters*, II, 342).

Heyst, paralysed by his stoic creed ('Look on. Make no sound.') in his reflective habits – 'the most pernicious of all habits found in civilized man' – is explicit, even verbose, philosophically; but Lena conceals her depths in her illiterate, inarticulate voice whose warmth and 'enchantment' is insisted on (like Heyst's 'delicacy'); from a frightened victim she blossoms out into a girl who is physically able to grapple with Ricardo. The epitaph suggests ghostly menace from subliminal levels:

Calling shapes and beckoning shadows dire
And airy tongues that syllable men's names
On sands and shores and desert wildernesses.

When the story gradually sinks into the depths of the mind away from reality, the structure, because it is so strictly formal, forces the reader either to leave it, or to enter into his *own* struggle with this resistant material. This is the technique of the *nouveau roman* of our day. Gaps, reticences are part of the thrust design.

When Virginia Woolf ventured to disagree with the general verdict and find *Victory* below the author's best level, she noted an uneasy shift of opinion – 'perhaps Conrad was going out, perhaps the moment had come to disparage him'.[15] I am suggesting that, on the contrary, this work, in spite of the fact that it is not a 'good' novel, may offer to modern readers, in Lowry's words, 'a machine that works'. It is a story one doesn't forget. 'We are in his case allowed to contemplate the foundation of all the emotions – the one joy which is to live' ('Falk', p. 246 of *Typhoon*). The contest of life – Lena – and death – Mr Jones – is so basic, so primitive as to be at once glaring and elusive; designated by Freud in his later work as the contest of Eros and Thanatos,, it cannot be developed. 'Not an artistic triumph perhaps, but a psychological triumph of the first order.'

IV

The Shadow-Line (1917) reverts to the story of Conrad's first command, already recalled in 'The Secret Sharer' and 'Falk'. England was now at war and 'to sit down and invent fairy tales was impossible', but Norman Sherry, in *Conrad's Eastern World* has shown how much Conrad added to the original event. The author declares that he has left some gaps – the last exchanges of the captain with the faithful seaman cannot be loosed to the public's incomprehension; yet '*J'ai vécu tout cela* . . . that experience is transposed into spiritual terms – in art a perfectly legitimate thing to do, as long as one preserves the exact truth enshrined therein (*Life and Letters*, II, 182–3). The young captain begins by suffering from something of the ennui which had seized the diabolic Mr Jones. Given his first command he goes aboard and confronts his own image in a mirror – 'this latest representative of what for all intents and purposes was a dynasty' – perceiving he had his place in a line of men whom he did not know. At sea, becalmed, with a sick crew and robbed of remedies by the treachery of his predecessor, he takes to a diary; this represents another kind of committal, to what

> the poet himself, struggling with the form
> Of his coiled work, knows

'I suppose that I did exist on food in the usual way; but the memory is now that in those days life was sustained on an invincible anguish, a sort of infernal stimulant, exciting and consuming at the same time' (p. 179).[16] The epigraph to this story is from Baudelaire, *La Musique*:

> D'autre fois, calme plat, grand miroir
> De mon desespoir.

A haunted voyage – haunted by the spectre of the dead evil captain – is presented for its effect on the young man. Conrad did not succeed any such sinister being when he took over the *Otago* in 1888 at Bangkok; not all his crew, but three members only, went down with cholera (the disease that in 1880 had killed Lowry's grandfather in the Indian Ocean, incidentally). The work must therefore be compared with something as inward as 'Through the Panama'. Otherwise its transformation of the past is too radical for Conrad's claims of 'exact truth'. It is the truth of 'confession' (the sub-title) not of the court-room.

Another dream haunted Conrad, but was never so successfully transposed. Although in recent years *The Rescue* has had its defenders, this work had from its beginnings in 1896 (the season of his honeymoon) represented something like a mirage. In November 1898 he wrote

> I get on dreamily with *The Rescue*, dreamily dreaming how fine it could be if the thought did not escape – if the expression did not hide underground, if the idea had a substance and words a magic power, if the invisible could be snared into a shape. And it is sad to think that even if all this came to pass – even then it could never be so fine to anybody as it is to me now, lurking in the blank pages in an intensity of existence without voice, without form – but without blemish.[17]

Later he wrote 'That story I can't write weaves itself into all I see, into all I speak, into all I think. . . My story is there in a fluid, in an evading shape. I can't get hold of it' (Garnett, *Letters from Joseph Conrad*, p. 135). It was not finished, merely given an ending, twenty years later; then only because 'I am settling my affairs in this world and I should not have liked to leave behind me this evidence of having bitten off more than I could chew.'[18]

The Rescue acted as catalyst for other works: in 1898 it was interrupted by *Heart of Darkness*; later, 'The Planter of Malata' and even the autobiographical *Arrow of Gold* point forward to this last invasion of an island paradise. In the regrouping of the symbolic figures, however, the woman has joined Mr Jones's party.[19] Here may be discerned the outline of one work which remained in the full sense unwritten.

Postscript

In the South Sea Islands, all monsters come from the sea. Returning to these islands, Conrad presents the conflict of Eastern mythology with Heyst's Western philosophy: Lena's charm becomes that of a Balinese or Javanese girl, and she seems on the Island to undergo a sort of metamorphosis into an embodiment of that eternal struggle of light and darkness, the subject of the Javanese or Balinese dance, the conflict between Goodness unarmed and the Sea Demon with his followers. The Bandong Dance symbolises this, as the Balinese Kriis dance symbolises the struggle enacted in Lena's contest for Ricardo's knife. The ironic victory of Eastern mysticism over deathly Nihilism culminates in the Brahmin funeral rite of purification by fire.

Thus at the mythological level *Victory* draws, in ways that have not been recognised, upon the deeper faiths and rites of the region where it is set.

NOTES

1. T. S. Eliot, 'The Function of Criticism', 1923 in *Selected Essays*, 1932. 'Tradition and the Individual Talent' in *The Sacred Wood*, 1920.
2. 'The New Novel' appeared in *Notes on Novelists*, 1914.
3. c.f. Eloise Knapp Hay, *Political Novels of Joseph Conrad*, p. 53.
4. 'J'ai vecu tout cela.' Conrad's boast about *The Shadow Line* (see below).
5. Ford Madox Ford termed it 'progression d'effet' (*Joseph Conrad*, 1924, p. 210).
6. Henry James, *Notes on Novelists*, p. 274 – speaking of *Chance*.
7. *Selected Letters*, p. 60. Especially the two brothers. The younger who is a journalist and a seaman, had taken a voyage as a boy and deliberately sought ordeals but had 'nothing in his mind of Lord Jim about to pick up pilgrims going to Mecca' (p. 170). He is about to ship a cargo of arms to Spain for the Loyalists.
8. Jocelyn Baines, *Joseph Conrad: A Critical Biography*, p. 372.
9. *Selected Letters*, p. 28.
10. *Letters*, p. 320.
11. Preface to the Shorter Tales. c.f. T. E. Eliot on the poetic method of 'doing things separately, and then seeing the possibility of fusing them together, altering them and making a whole of them' (*Paris Review*, Spring–Summer 1959, vol. 21, p. 58); he is speaking of his own poetic sequences.
12. See Postscript.
13. Falk's nameless young woman is nurse to an infant Lena.
14. See Andrzej Busza, 'Conrad's Polish Literary Background', in *Institutum Historicum Polonicum*, Rome (Rome and London, 1966).
15. Quentin Bell, *Virginia Woolf, a Biography* (1972) vol. 2, p. 50.
16. c.f. *A Personal Record*, pp. 98–100. The passage in which Conrad describes the dream-state of anguish in which he worked at *Nostromo* is the nearest reflection of the captain's mood.
17. Letter to Heffer (Jocelyn Baines, *Joseph Conrad*, p. 223).
18. Garnett, *Letters from Joseph Conrad*, p. 263. The date is 7 July 1919.
19. Virginia Woolf's review, interesting in its perceptions and its misunderstandings, alike, is reprinted in Norman Sherry, *Joseph Conrad: the Critical Heritage*, 1973.

11 On Editing Conrad

KENNETH W. DAVIS, DAVID LEON HIGDON and DONALD W. RUDE

In a letter to John Galsworthy, dated 17 April 1899, Joseph Conrad observed '*every* word is an object to be considered anxiously with heart searchings and in a spirit of severe resolution. . .'[1] These words, expressing the author's attitude towards the craft of fiction, provide a motto for all textual scholars editing Conrad texts. Indeed, from his very uniqueness as stylist and as fastidious craftsman stem many of the most challenging problems facing those who would give his works the careful attention they need and so richly deserve. Our observations are based upon three years of work with the texts of *The Nigger of the 'Narcissus'*[2] and *Almayer's Folly*.[3] The Textual Studies Institute of Texas Tech University, which sponsored the work, plans to produce a complete scholarly edition of Conrad. We believe that many of our observations will apply to problems which will arise in editing any of Conrad's works.

I: *The Nigger of the 'Narcissus'*

Had Conrad been less the painstaking craftsman, seemingly compelled to revise his novels constantly to achieve the effects he desired, editing his work would be an easier task. In his pioneering study, *Joseph Conrad: The Making of a Novelist*, John D. Gordan demonstrated that Conrad time after time reworked his texts. Our work with the holograph manuscript of *The Nigger*, and the fragmentary typescript of the novel prepared by Mrs Jessie Conrad, confirms Gordan's observations, while suggesting that the author's revisions were more extensive than Gordan demonstrated, a view confirmed by a collation of the printed editions and the copies Conrad marked for revision. Indeed, the text of the novel frequently poses the problem not of whether to admit an emendation, but which emendations should finally be included. In the case of *The Nigger*, collation of the printed texts reveals that the early copyright edition (London: William Heinemann, 1897) most closely reflects the state of the holograph and typescript. The serial version in

The New Review contains abundant evidence that Conrad revised Chapters III–V of that text, while the first British and American editions contain evidence proving that the author made another, separate revision prior to their publication; later Conrad grudgingly bowdlerised proofs of the Heinemann text. Conrad soon revised two of the early printed texts. Marking a copy of the copyright edition for presentation to Edward Garnett's mother, he entered changes from the serial version and the book text as well as one new change. A little later, he marked grammatical corrections in his copy of the Heinemann edition at W. H. Chesson's suggestion. Both of these revisions must have been forgotten nineteen years later when Conrad prepared corrected copy for the Sun-Dial edition of the novel, for he apparently consulted neither. Letters in print confirm that the author made another revision when Heinemann prepared its collected edition; some of these revisions appear in Doubleday editions printed in and after 1923.

The whole process of composition and transmission, spanning twenty years illustrates what Fredson Bowers has called the 'radial' transmission of a text. None of the printed versions of the novel derives directly from the holograph. Only the copyright edition of the novel seems directly descended from the fragmentary typescript. In the absence of marked proofs for the serial edition and the setting-copy and proofs of the two book editions, one must conjecture which of the intervening changes represent authorial intervention.

It would be tempting in the case of *The Nigger of the 'Narcissus'* to use the hand-marked 1910 Heinemann edition as our copy-text. However, the fact that Conrad overlooked his earlier substantive revisions, coupled with abundant evidence of compositorial and/or editorial intervention in the accidentals of that edition, complicates the matter. For our copy-text, we have selected the 1897 copyright edition, which best preserves the author's accidentals. This choice gives us a base upon which to reconstruct a valid text for the novel, but provides no final solution to the problem of determining what Conrad really wanted.

The following readings indicate the types of problems one encounters. In the holograph manuscript, when the cook approached James Wait's cabin, Conrad had written:

> He was delighted, frightened, exalted – like on that evening when (the only time in his life – thirty-seven years ago; he loved to recall the number of years) when as a young man he had through keeping bad company – become intoxicated in an East-end music hall.[4]

The passage occurs in this form on page 95 of the fragmentary type-script. However, all of the printed editions appearing in 1897 differ. The copyright edition preserves the passage with slight alteration, eliminating the conjunction 'when' near the beginning of the sentence. Since this alteration occurs in all the printed texts, we regard the change as authorial. When the same passage appeared in *The New Review*, we note additional alterations:

> He was delighted, frightened, exalted – as on that evening (the only time in his life – thirty-seven years ago; he loved to recall the number of years) when, as a young man, he had – through keeping bad company – become intoxicated in an East-end music hall.[5]

The substitution of 'as' for 'like' in the sentence may indicate the hand of an editor at work; similarly, the introduction of commas, setting off the phrase 'as a young man' typifies the variant punctuation that sets the serial edition off from other editions. The editorial complexity increases when one considers that Conrad, whose use of 'like' and 'as' was criticised by W. H. Chesson, posted this change in his copy of the Heinemann edition, indicating that he wished to make a change that may have been introduced earlier by an editor, compositor, or proof-reader.

In the text of the novel in book form, the passage is again altered:

> He was delighted, frightened, exalted – like on that evening (the only time in his life – twenty-seven years ago; he loved to recall the number of years) when as a young man he had – through keeping bad company – become intoxicated in an East-end music-hall.[6]

The common agreement of the Heinemann edition with *The Children of the Sea*, an edition in which Conrad had no hand, argues that this reading reflects the author's wishes. When, in 1916, Conrad marked his copy of a Heinemann reprint for revision in the Sun-Dial edition, he again turned his attention to this passage, cancelling the preposition 'like' and substituting 'as'. Then he cancelled the change. The final hand-written revision of the sentence reinstates the word 'like', placing it within commas. Curiously, all the collected editions contain the word 'as', a change Conrad approved when it was called to his attention earlier, but one which cannot be demonstrated to have ever been introduced by the author. Thus, in one sentence, we can see all of the numerous complexities posed by a Conrad text. The substantive variation found in the book editions probably should be admitted; even though the grammatical correction can be traced only to his

personal copy corrected at Chesson's behest, that change should probably be admitted to the text, for the author was concerned with the
grammatical accuracy.

In so far as it is possible, we are restoring readings from the holograph, which we can reasonably assume Conrad wanted. We have
frequently based our judgments upon the content of the fragmentary
typescript, a draft of the novel which accounts for the striking variations that set the manuscript and printed texts apart. This is an 'ur-
text', in all probability used only by the compositors who set type for
the copyright edition. Numerous readings occur *only* in the typescript
and this edition of seven copies. We plan to incorporate all of the
hand-written changes of a substantive nature which Conrad introduced
in his copy of the 1910 Heinemann edition of *The Nigger*. Not all of
these changes were included in the collected editions. We also plan to
introduce those few substantive changes that derive from the Heinemann collected edition and appear in later Doubleday editions.

As we work with the various texts of the novel – especially with the
holograph and typescript – we often wish that Conrad could have had
the benefits of a careful study of some system of punctuation. Conrad
had a fine disregard for, or ignorance of, the subtle and ordinary
distinctions between purposes or functions served by commas and
semicolons. The holograph contains numerous examples of these two
marks used interchangeably – if used at all. In still other instances,
Conrad will employ the dash as a substitute for the comma, or the
colon, or the semicolon, or the full stop, or the exclamation mark, or
even the question mark. His unique punctuation with its at best only
sporadic consistency has complicated our efforts to provide an accurate
text.

Compounding the problem are the efforts of many compositors who
set type for the various editions of the novel, and perhaps more
importantly, Mrs Conrad's role in the preparation of the initial typescript of the novel. A clear illustration of the sort of problem posed by
the typescript occurs in the treatment of this passage found in the
manuscript:

> He went on 'Ba! ba! ba! brrr..br ba! ba!' – 'Stop that!' cried Mr.
> Baker groping in the dark. 'Stop it!' He went on shaking the leg he
> found under his hand. 'What is it Sir!' called out Belfast with the
> tone of a man awakened suddenly. 'We are looking after that 'ere
> Jimmy!'[7]

In the typescript, the passage reads:

He went on 'Ba..ba.ba.brrr.brr. ba. ba.' – 'Stop that!' cried Mr.
Baker groping in the dark. 'Stop it!' He went on shaking the leg he
found under his hand. 'What is it Sir?' called out Belfast *in* the tone
of a man awakened suddenly. 'We are looking after that 'ere Jimmy.'[8]

The most obvious variation separating the two passages is the absence
of the exclamation marks in the initial speech. Their absence reflects
the general state of the typescript where Conrad or his wife usually
added superscript punctuation in longhand. When the speech was set
in type, the curious punctuation was transformed into a series of ellipses
in the serial typesetting and replaced with dashes in the first editions in
book form. In both cases, the series of exclamations is transformed into
a sort of elongated stutter.

This same passage provides other comparable illustrations. In the
serial and Heinemann editions, the first sentence is repunctuated to
read: "He went on:— '. . .' ", whereas in the Dodd, Mead edition,
the dash does not appear. However, the Dodd, Mead edition contains
a dash separating Mr Baker's speech from the seaman's utterance.
While this usage reflects the usage of the manuscript and typescript, it
also reflects the common practice of Dodd, Mead compositors, who
regularly inserted dashes separating adjacent lines of dialogue, and
just as regularly eliminated them elsewhere. The variants suggest the
extent to which compositors imposed house style on the text, perhaps
in an effort to perfect and regularise the many confusions of the typescript. However, the two editions in book form share one change of a
semi-substantive nature; the final two sentences are combined in both
texts. This change, one of approximately 200 variants occurring in
both editions, argues for Conrad's having revised his text after the
British serial edition had been prepared. Such variants should be
admitted to a definitive edition.

We believe that the holograph manuscript, *where it is adequately
punctuated*, provides the best accidentals. In other cases, where the
printed texts share a common pattern of punctuation and the holograph was unpunctuated we have accepted the punctuation of the
printed text. Where the texts disagree, we are inclined toward the
earliest reading, particularly when the variant accidental can be traced
to a pattern of compositorial intervention. In the matter of substantive
variants, we are fortunate that there are few instances in which Conrad
made more than one revision of the same passage. With the exception
of bowdlerisations urged on the author by William Heinemann, and
grammatical corrections in the serial text, we believe that all the early

substantive variants should be introduced. Those variants uniting the
two editions in book form have a clear stamp of authority.

There are other instances when a collation of the texts and manuscript reveals variants more difficult to account for. During the burial
scene, we find this reading in the holograph:

> . . . the gray package started reluctantly to all at once whizz off the
> tilted planks with the suddenness of a flash of lightning . . .[9]

In the copyright edition, the Heinemann edition and *The Children of
the Sea*, the passage reads:

> . . . the gray package started reluctantly to, all at once, whizz off the
> lifted planks with the suddenness of a flash of lightning . . .[10]

One notes that the reading is altered both in substance and in accidentals. The substantive change, the substitution of 'lifted' for 'tilted'
is probably authorial. The holograph manuscript is, at this point quite
legible, and nothing suggests that the change resulted from a typist's
misreading the word. Furthermore, the change reflects the great
emphasis placed on the extreme exertion expended by the seamen in
their efforts to release their heavy burden.[11]

The substitution of the latter reading seems appropriate, for it reflects
the kinetic effort of the men more accurately than the less forceful
'tilted'. But should the added commas be retained? While the holograph reading has a vitality in its rhythm, suggesting both the reluctance and suddenness of the motion described, the punctuation added
in the copyright edition and retained in the two editions in book form
emphasises the words 'all at once', reflecting the surprise of the body's
sudden departure from the planks, and probably reflects Conrad's
final wishes.

But there are other choices; the passage appears in altered form in
The New Review and in the collected editions. At this point the serial
reads:

> . . . the gray package started reluctantly – all at once to whizz off the
> lifted planks with the suddenness of a flash of lightning . . .[12]

And all editions printed after the Sun-Dial edition read:

> . . . the gray package started reluctantly to whizz off the lifted planks
> all at once, with the suddenness of a flash of lightning . . .[13]

The editors of *The Nigger* then confront a group of puzzling variants.
There is always the possibility that *all* of these changes may reflect

Conrad's intervention, or that *none* do. Internal evidence supports the argument that Conrad did revise proofs of Chapters III–V of the novel for *The New Review*. He also prepared copy for the collected editions of the novel, read proofs for Doubleday, and was closely engaged in the editing of the Heinemann Collected Edition. However, neither of the latter changes adds appreciably to the sense of the passage: the reading in *The New Review* breaks the sentence into two sections fracturing its kinetic tension, and the collected editions are similarly marred, for without the split infinitive the internal tension of the sentence disappears. In such a passage, we favour retaining the reading found in the copy-text, for the later changes suggest the interference of an editor, more concerned with the grammatical problem of the split infinitive than the rhythms of the sentence. Such a judgment is inferential and aesthetic, but, in the absence of marked proofs or typescripts for the later editions, or correspondence indicating that the author wished to make such changes, inference and taste must play their parts in the editorial judgment.

II: *Almayer's Folly*

After study of the typescript and manuscript and collation of the various editions and issues of *Almayer's Folly*, one generalisation emerges: Joseph Conrad did not write *Almayer's Folly*. Instead, at least six individuals had a hand in the creation of this novel: the Conrad of 1889–94, a seaman writing 'with the serene audacity of an unsophisticated fool';[14] the Conrad of 1894–95, suddenly become a man of letters to whom '*every* word was an object to be considered anxiously with heart searchings and in a spirit of severe resolution';[15] the Conrad of 1916, a confident, mature artist with considerable reputation behind him; the Conrad of 1920, a confessed 'mentally tired' writer;[16] and at least two unnamed compositors, the Macmillan grammarian and the Heinemann punctuater. If we wish to discover the 'true' early Conrad of this novel, do we select the first American edition, which contains the earliest state of printed text but which has been corrupted by frequent compositorial intervention, or do we select the first English edition, which was revised in proof and thus contains a far more sophisticated state of artistry and text? If we wish the 'definitive' Conrad, do we select the collected editions incorporating the 1916 revisions, or the collected editions adopting the 1920 revisions Conrad made while reading the proofs so carefully for Heinemann?

The choice is crucial because there are 306 variants, 95 of them substantive, between the first editions, and 440 variants, 105 of them substantive, between the first English edition and the collected editions.[17] The American reader of 1895 could praise Conrad's psychological perception and subtlety in having the unarmed Dain, after facing the armed Almayer, admit ' "I was much afraid" ' (M233.22).[18] The English reader, on the other hand, encountered the more conventional bravado and heroism of ' "I was not afraid" ' (U232.2).[19] In the English edition, the corpse pulled from the river by Mahmat is a 'formless mass' (U131.22); the American edition uses the almost archaic word 'inform' (M129.7) to describe the 'mass'. The American edition contains melodramatic 'violent' flames (M266.18), an 'unmoved' Nina (M133.1), and a 'sound of' wild pigs (M220.14); the English edition has impressionistic 'violet' flames (U262.21), and 'attentive' Nina (U135.11), and a 'sounder' of wild pigs (U219.12). In the first editions, Mrs Almayer equips herself with 'theological luggage' (U57.12) and is given to 'floods of savage invective' (U36.29); in the collected editions, she has a 'theological outfit' (SD41.31, H49.3)[20] and is given to 'outbursts' (SD25.35, H29.10) rather than 'floods'. In the first editions, Dain makes his 'way stealthily through' (U88.23) the banana plantation; in the collected editions, he only makes his 'way through' with no hint of stealth or duplicity. Finally, in the first editions, 'Great red stains on the floor and walls testified to frequent and indiscriminate betel-nut chewing' (U24.8–11); in the collected editions, both the betel-nuts and the 'great red stains' have been expunged even though the sentence extended and substantiated the picture of 'squalid neglect'.

There are two major periods in the history of *Almayer's Folly*, the first lasting from 1889 to 1895, the second from 1913 to 1923. One of the most obvious differences between the editions of the early period is Conrad's restoration of a five-line sentence (U69.20–24) missing in both the typescript and the Macmillan edition, but present in the manuscript. In Chapter IV, Nina Almayer returns home and unexpectedly finds a prosperous looking brig anchored in the Pantai near her father's house. She lands her canoe and silently makes her way into the house. The restored sentence, 'Stopping her course by a rapid motion of her paddle, with another swift stroke she sent it whirling away from the wharf and steered for a little rivulet which gave access to the back courtyard of the house,' precisely describes her handling of the craft. Restoration of the sentence bespeaks a master mariner's attention to the step-by-step process in handling any kind of boat. Not all the substantive variants which so markedly distinguish the Unwin edition from the Macmillan edition involve lengthy additions. Conrad's revisions, however, are astonishingly diverse and numerous, and demonstrate his preoccupation with the problems of repetition and redundancy, idiomatic rephrasing, precision of image, and grammatical consistency. For example, in the description of Nina's contemplation of a storm, the American edition has her standing 'motionless there in the still and oppressing calm of the tropical night' (M23.4). To avoid the redundancy of 'motionless', 'still', and 'calm', the phrase 'still and oppressing' was condensed to the single adjective 'oppressive' (U28.17).

Because of the Chace Act of 1891, which stipulated that foreign works could secure American copyright only if they were set and printed in the United States and only if they were published simultaneously abroad and in the United States, no British and American editions could be expected to be identical.[21] However, consider several compositorial interventions which occurred because of the Chace Act's 'manufacturing clause'. In at least ten instances the Macmillan compositor undertook to 'correct' the text when no correction was necessary. A few moments with any dictionary would have demonstrated that 'sounder' is the correct collective noun for a herd of wild pig and not an error for 'sound of'. And his substitution of 'violent gleams' (M266.18) for 'violet gleams' (U262.21) to describe the flames of Almayer's burning house as they appeared flashing in 'the strong sunshine' renders the description obtrusively melodramatic and destroys the colour progression from 'brick-red' to 'violet' to 'clear blue' – an important detail considering Conrad's relationship to impressionistic style. The noun 'gleams' and the adjective 'violent' are incompatible in that one suggests brief glints of subdued light, while the other connotes fury and intensity.

Perhaps the most significant substantive emendation calls into question Dain's bravery by changing his response to Almayer following a brief scuffle with him for a revolver from ' "Your hand shook much; for myself I was not afraid" ' (U232.3) to ' "Your hand shook much; for myself I was much afraid" ' (M233.22). The Macmillan version presents a strikingly modern hero willing to admit fear, and thus unlike Conrad's later protagonists who cling to illusions of their self-sufficiency. Unwin's Dain is a more conventional protagonist whose adventure-story ancestry shows clearly through his boast.

The second major period, 1913–23, is best heralded by the Sotheby, Wilkinson, and Hodges' description of the marked copy of *Almayer's Folly*, the copy containing the revisions for the Collected Editions. This copy, which sold in 1924 for £64 and promptly disappeared, was advertised as containing revisions 'all in the author's handwriting, [which] are of great interest as showing the critical spirit in which Conrad re-read his earliest work. Adjectives, redundant phrases and whole passages are ruthlessly deleted, and here and there a fastidious change of word bears witness to his continued striving after perfect expression.'[22] The revisions are interesting, but neither as extensive nor as significant as the catalogue claims.

Conrad's ability to redefine the essence of an action or a character still clearly evidences itself in the revisions. Early in the novel, Lingard several times begins to sound out Almayer on marriage to a native girl. Conrad first described the scene thus: 'More than once he would astonish Almayer by walking up to him rapidly, clearing his throat with a powerful "Hem!" as if he was going to say something, and then turning abruptly away to lean over the bulwark in silence, and watch, motionless, for hours, the gleam and sparkle of the phosphorescent sea along the ship's side' (U16.23–25). By changing 'as if he was going to say' to 'as if he intended to say', Conrad refocused the quality of Lingard's action. 'Was going' implies a less planned, less intense, more spontaneous action. 'Intended' implies more design or thought, as if Lingard wished to manipulate and use Almayer, and suggests a veiled purposefulness of which Almayer knows nothing. Similarly, the revision of 'Will come to-morrow, he said' (U26.8) to 'Promised to come to-morrow' (SD17.28, H19.20) provides a keen glimpse of Almayer placing his own favourable interpretation on action. He is reporting Dain's visit to Nina and in his desire to avoid simple futurity, he asserts that Dain 'promised'. He does not know that Dain fully intends to return, but for Nina, not for him.

But Conrad's revisions are not always so felicitous. Just how powerful and unprincipled are Almayer's antagonists? The first editions allow us to say that Lakamba is capable of murder. After all, the text clearly states 'He [Almayer] had built for her a riverside hut in the compound where she dwelt in perfect seclusion. Lakamba's visits had ceased when, by a convenient decree of Providence and the help of a little scientific manipulation the old ruler of Sambir departed this life' (U39.3–4). In the Collected Edition, the ruler of Sambir simply dies. There is no hint of 'scientific manipulation' – read poisoning – on the part of Lakamba or his factotum, Babalatchi.

Elsewhere, the entire history of Nina and her mother disappears. The passage referring to Nina's education originally read:

She had tasted the whole bitterness of it and remembered distinctly that the virtuous Mrs. Vinck's indignation was not so much directed against the young man from the bank as against the innocent cause of that young man's infatuation. And there was also no doubt in her mind that the principal cause of Mrs. Vinck's indignation was the thought that such a thing should happen in a white nest, where her snow-white doves, the two Misses Vinck, had just returned from Europe, to find shelter under the maternal wing, and there await the coming of irreproachable men of their destiny. Not even the thought of the money so painfully scraped together by Almayer and so punctually sent for Nina's expenses could dissuade Mrs. Vinck from her virtuous resolve. Nina was sent away, and in truth the girl herself wanted to go, although a little frightened by the impending change. (U58.8–26)

Here, with one stroke of his pen, Conrad dispatched a most ironical passage which supplied much of Nina's motivation in her distrust of and eventual rejection of white civilisation. Gone are the vivid imagery, the arch tone, and the incisive history of Nina's years in Singapore. Gone too is the adolescent sexual appeal of Nina. By removing an almost identical passage detailing Mrs Almayer's encounter with the same white civilisation in the convent school, Conrad destroyed the basic similarities between mother and daughter and crippled our understanding of the two characters.

Is a critical edition of *Almayer's Folly* needed? By now, we hope the question is merely rhetorical. It may be objected that in novels, which are by definition so vast, variants in a word here and there, punctuation added or deleted, an occasional misprint, or a slightly revised passage cannot affect the totality of our response to the work. If authors never revised a page, if compositors never deviated from their copy-text, and if plates never suffered damage, we would agree. But first show us such a text. Graham Greene's *It's a Battlefield*? Virginia Woolf's *To the Lighthouse*? Anthony Burgess's *A Clockwork Orange*? The first of these was systematically rewritten and restructured. The second exists in two quite different versions. And the third has totally different concluding chapters in its English and American editions.[28] If these major variant states exist in the days of standardised printing practices, what must be the condition of Conrad's texts? Unless we know the history and condition of the text before us, we always run the danger that the very sentence which cinches our interpretation of *Almayer's Folly* or *Nostromo* or *Victory* was written not when we think it was or even by whom we thought it was.

When we have completed our projects with *The Nigger of the 'Narcissus'*, and with *Almayer's Folly*, our editions will include the following:

(1) critical introductions to the novels which will include discussion of the techniques we used to derive the text;

(2) tables listing all editorial emendations with annotations offering as much justification as possible in those instances in which we are compelled to make arbitrary choices;

(3) tables of historical collations listing all instances of variants either substantive or accidental;

(4) tables of hyphens.

For each of the tables we will provide head-notes.

The long and tedious process of editing two Conrad novels has been worthwhile. Conrad deserves the time and effort we have expended and continue to expend. We recommend to all who would edit Conrad that they exercise the same painstaking care which we believe we have employed.

NOTES

1. Georges Jean-Aubry, *Joseph Conrad: Life and Letters* (Garden City: Doubleday, Doran, 1927), I, 276.
2. Edited by Kenneth W. Davis and Donald W. Rude.
3. Edited by David Leon Higdon and Floyd Eugene Eddleman.
4. *The Nigger of the 'Narcissus'*, Holograph Manuscript, p. 124; subsequent references to this text will be cited as MS. We are indebted to the trustees of the Rosenbach Foundation Museum, Philadelphia, Pennsylvania, for making the manuscript available to us, and we wish to acknowledge the Trustees of the Joseph Conrad Estate for granting us permission to quote from the holograph and typescript of the novel.
5. Joseph Conrad, *The Nigger of the 'Narcissus'*, *The New Review*, XVII (November, 1897), 493; all subsequent references to this text will be cited as *NR*.
6. Compare Joseph Conrad, *The Nigger of the 'Narcissus'* (London: William Heinemann, 1897 [date 1898]), p. 170, and Joseph Conrad, *The Children of the Sea* (New York: Dodd, Mead, 1897), p. 143. In all subsequent references, the Heinemann edition will be cited as H, the Dodd, Mead as DM, and the copyright edition as CR.
7. MS, p. 82.
8. Joseph Conrad, *The Nigger of the 'Narcissus'*, Typescript with manuscript corrections, p. 67. We are indebted to Professor Bruce Brown, librarian at Colgate University, for making a copy of this typescript available for our use.
9. MS, p. 179.
10. CR, p. 111; H, p. 238; and DM, p. 200.

11. See CR, p. 110; the punctuation of the passage is altered slightly in both H and DM, with only the copyright edition retaining the reading of the holograph.

12. *NR* (November, 1897), p. 619.

13. Compare Joseph Conrad, *The Nigger of the 'Narcissus'* (The Sun-Dial Edition, Garden City: Doubleday, 1920), p. 160, and Joseph Conrad, *The Nigger of the 'Narcissus'* (The Collected Edition, London: William Heinemann Ltd., 1921), pp. 181–2. Other American collected editions are separate issues of the Sun-Dial Edition and share its pagination; frequently, they contain altered substantives.

14. Jean-Aubry, I, 196; letter to E. L. Sanderson, 21 November 1896.

15. Jean-Aubry, I, 276; letter to John Galsworthy, 17 April 1899.

16. Jocelyn Baines, *Joseph Conrad: A Critical Biography* (New York: McGraw-Hill, 1960), p. 422; letter to John Galsworthy, 4 April 1920.

17. For full discussion of the many variants see, Floyd Eugene Eddleman, David Leon Higdon, and Robert W. Hobson, 'A Comparison of the First Editions of Conrad's *Almayer's Folly*', *Conradiana*, 4 (1974), 83–108, and Floyd Eugene Eddleman and David Leon Higdon, 'Collected Edition Variants in *Almayer's Folly* ', *Conradiana*, 9 (1977).

18. *Almayer's Folly* (New York: Macmillan, 1895). All subsequent references to this text will be abbreviated M, followed by page and line numbers.

19. *Almayer's Folly* (London: T. Fisher Unwin, 1895). All subsequent references to this text will be abbreviated U, followed by page and line numbers.

20. *Almayer's Folly* (Sun-Dial Edition, Garden City: Doubleday, Page, 1920) and *Almayer's Folly* (Collected Edition, London: William Heinemann, 1921). All subsequent references to these texts will be abbreviated SD and H, followed by page and line numbers.

21. Hellmut Lehmann-Haupt, in collaboration with Laurence C. Wroth and Rollo G. Silver, *The Book in America: A History of the Making and Selling of Books In the United States*, 2nd ed. (New York: R. R. Bowker Company, 1951), p. 203. Also see Simon Nowell-Smith, *International Copyright Law and the Publisher in the Reign of Queen Victoria* (London: Oxford University Press, 1968), p. 65.

22. *Catalogue of Valuable Printed Books* (London: Sotheby, Wilkinson and Hodge, 1924), p. 75, Item 621.

23. See Gordon N. Ray, 'The Importance of Original Editions', in *Nineteenth Century English Books* (Urbana: University of Illinois Press, 1952), p. 11, and J. A. Lavin, 'The First Editions of Virginia Woolf's *To the Lighthouse*', *Proof*, 2 (1972), 185–211.

12 Conrad and Pinker*

FREDERICK R. KARL

Joseph Conrad's lengthy series of letters with James Brand Pinker, his literary agent from 1899 to 1922, is his true autobiography. Except for his sea career, this correspondence of over 1200 items touches on virtually every aspect of Conrad's professional and private life, but is especially compelling in two major areas: first, his day-to-day personal life as he wrote his novels and stories; and, second, the development of the fiction itself, the details of the slow, tortuous manner in which his literary work passed through his mind and pen. As we know, none of his major works came easily, and particularly in his middle years, when he wrote *Nostromo, The Secret Agent, Under Western Eyes, Chance,* and *Victory,* he was intensely pressed, to the extent that one could claim that Conrad functioned most successfully in literary matters when he was most panicked personally.

Focusing on the highly detailed correspondence with Pinker, we can see how these two forces interact, personal pressures on one hand, literary achievement on the other; so that we enter, as closely as we can ever hope to, into the particular chemistry of an important writer. There is, as far as I know, no comparable sequence of letters from a major novelist to someone as intimately associated as Pinker was with Conrad. If we think of other prolific contemporary letter writers – Lawrence, Huxley, Mann, Gide, Yeats – there is no single sequence that contains the intimacy and details of craft found in the Conrad–Pinker correspondence.

When Conrad and Pinker first became associated (the initial letter is dated 23 August 1899), the agent was thirty-six and Conrad was forty-one; and their meeting coincided with a critical period in the latter's professional life. It followed shortly after he had met Hueffer and had decided to collaborate with the much younger man, at a time when his

* For permission to quote from unpublished material, the author is indebted to J. M. Dent & Sons Ltd., acting for the Trustees of the Joseph Conrad Estate; to the Henry W. and Albert A. Berg Collection of the New York Public Library, Astor, Lenox and Tilden Foundations; to Yale University Library (Beinecke Rare Book and Manuscript Library).

literary circle was broadening out to include Wells, Crane, Galsworthy, Cunninghame Graham, James, Garnett, Gosse, and Hudson. More importantly, the correspondence with Pinker was a form of decision for Conrad. He had, figuratively, entered the valley of the shadow of death, making personal decisions which allowed no retreat. Just as when still short of seventeen he had embarked on a twenty-year sea career from which there was no immediate redress, so now, at over forty and a family man, he was entering a new phase. In his own work, he had received fairly generous support from publishers and critics (especially Wells and Henley), and his Preface to *The Nigger of the 'Narcissus'* as well as his letters to Edward Noble indicated he had found sufficient theoretical underpinning to continue. His movement into the world of the publisher Blackwood and the prestigious *Blackwood's Magazine* reflected a seriousness of purpose and dedication to literature far beyond simply a desire to be published. All these aspects of his career, taken together with his comments to Marguerite Poradowska, reflected a man setting forth to carry out an intense inner mission.

The personal aspects, however, were far more complicated. If we can judge by the two works he was then alternately engaged in, *Lord Jim* and *Heart of Darkness*, Conrad was grappling with terrifying ideas and severe nightmares. A persistent image of himself as shards and fragments, as mad, pokes through in Conrad's letters. To Galsworthy, for example, he wrote 'my memory is good and sane even if my mind is diseased and on the verge of craziness' (17 April 1899). The yawning chasm or sense of engulfment, the oceanic feeling he sensed, was belied by his social position: married, the father of a small boy, the friend and companion of respectable writers and editors, the author of three novels and several short stories. All that was on the surface, however; within, the opposite beckoned, his own Congo with its strange rites. Like Aschenbach setting out for Venice, Conrad was moving into the destructive element of a new art and a new aesthetics.

In this grey, ambiguous, undefined area, the relationship with Pinker commenced and was established for many years. Although Pinker would not recognise himself in Conrad's image, the author saw this ultimately very generous and loyal man as the enemy; for Pinker demanded that Conrad should not lose sight of his obligation to his craft and his profession for a moment. In this respect, Pinker, while making Conrad's continuing career financially more stable, at the same time caused Conrad to appear, in his own eyes, a slave to the demands of his agent. Each stage of Pinker's generosity only intensified

Conrad's indebtedness, and each new project of Conrad's put increased strain on Pinker's generosity and tolerance. Both moved uneasily toward the limits of the other's endurance. Although we lack Pinker's responses to Conrad's letters, we can tell from the latter's correspondence that Pinker bridled at unexpected requests for money and at delayed instalments of manuscript, especially when Conrad's indebtedness climbed into hundreds of pounds (as high as £1600 in 1908, about £12–14,000 in current purchasing power).

The early years of the relationship, as we shall see, were the most difficult, for neither understood what the other really wanted or what the terms of the arrangement actually were. In addition, Conrad had already entangled himself in prior commitments, which meant he had to bypass Pinker even as he was asking the latter to negotiate for him and to support his efforts financially. Further, Conrad had accumulated publishers (Fisher Unwin, for one) who insisted on retaining copyright, which created numerous difficulties in his dealings with Pinker concerning reprint and foreign rights, all sources of potential income for the agent.

In discussing this vast correspondence (perhaps one million words from Conrad), one must select, and I have decided to focus on a few matters: firstly, the personal side of the exchange, noted above, as it touches on Conrad the writer, including some of the intimate financial arrangements; and secondly, the progress and development of Conrad's long fiction as he expressed his concern to Pinker, with special attention to *Under Western Eyes* and some lesser notice of *Nostromo, The Secret Agent*, and *Victory*.

Since the exchange began at the time Conrad was writing *Heart of Darkness* and *Lord Jim* and these works were already consigned (to Blackwood), his early letters to Pinker were often inconsequential, more matters of fencing than of substance. Once past these novels, however, Conrad began to use Pinker for the sale of his collaborative work with Hueffer, 'Seraphina' (*Romance*), and his own *Typhoon*, while lamenting the impossibility of completing *The Rescue*(r). Very soon in the tentative relationship the entire enterprise almost foundered, seemingly over 'Seraphina'. Conrad's letter of 8 January 1902, the first substantial letter after fifteen or so cursory exchanges, indicates some of the pressure under which he was writing. The subject, ostensibly, was 'Seraphina'. Pinker, apparently, had asked for more prompt work in order to justify his considerable outlay of money, and Conrad responded:

I fail to apprehend what inspired the extraordinary contents of your letter which I received this morning. All you had to do was to say yes or no. Mine was written fully not to get the easier at your pocket but from another motive – not worth explaining now. But it was never intended to give you an opening for a lecture. It will take more than the delay in delivering *S* to make *me* a failure; neither do I believe it will put you into the B'cy Court. And I am not just now in the right frame of mind for the proper appreciation of a lecture. I am working twelve hours in the twenty-four with the full knowledge of my ideal and of my risk.

After detailing some of the problems with Hueffer – illness, his contracting for another work – Conrad moves into the area that is to dominate his side of the correspondence: his own sense of literary worth, the process he has devoted his middle years to.

Pray do not write to me as if I were a fool blundering in the dark. There are other virtues than punctuality. Have you the slightest idea of what I am trying for? Of what is my guiding principle which I follow in anxiety and poverty, and daily and unremitting toll of my very heart. Come, my dear fellow, I am not one of your 25-year-old genuines [geniuses?] you have in your pocket, or one of your saleable people who drive three serials abreast . . . don't address me as if I were a man lost in sloth, ignorance or folly. Were you as rich as Croesus and as omnipotent as all the editors rolled into one I would not let such a tone pass without resenting it in the most outspoken manner. And don't write me of failure, confound it, because you and I have very different notions of failure.

Conrad closes the letter:

Am I a confounded boy? I have had to look death in the eye once or twice. It was nothing. I had not then a wife and child. It was nothing to what I have to go through now pen in hand before what to *me* spells failure. I am no sort of airy R. L. Stevenson who considered his art a prostitute and the artist as no better than one. I dare say he was punctual – but I don't envy him. (Berg ALS [Autograph Letter Signed])

Particularly trying for Conrad at this time (January 1902) was the fact that he was between major projects. His most immediate work, such as *Typhoon* and 'Tomorrow', as well as other short fiction, must have seemed to him second drawer, or else Pinker's comments could not have touched such a nerve or brought forth such a bravura display

of self-assertion. Whatever the precise reason, Conrad was now in a
literary limbo, stalled on 'Seraphina' and not yet immersed in a
definitive project. The shaky nerves, the wounded ego, the nervous
sensibility – all these are indicative of a man anxious to take combat
but uncertain who or where the enemy is. In a letter dated two days
before the above, on 6 January, Conrad by his rather high evaluation
of *Romance* indicated his ambivalence toward the enterprise, an inner
conflict that would partially explain his volatility with Pinker:

> You may take my word for it that it ['Seraphina'] is a piece of
> literature of which we are neither of us at all ashamed. It is rather
> the old thing (if you like) done in a way that is new only through the
> artistic care of the execution. The aim being to present the scenes
> and events and people strictly realistically in a glamour of *Romance*.
> The hero goes (accidentally so to speak) to seek Romance and finds
> it – a thing rather hard and difficult to live through. The time about
> 1823 is just far enough to bear the glamour of the past and near
> enough to enable us to dispense with elaborate explanations. In fact
> it is a serious attempt at *interesting, animated Romance*, with no
> more psychology than comes naturally into the action. (Berg ALS)

Two months later, on 16 March, Conrad indicated he was ready to
transmit a 'considerable batch of *Nostromo*', a 'first rate story' which
he felt would eventually run to 75–80,000 words. Conrad apparently
expected a good deal financially from *Nostromo*, for the theme of
'recuperation' as a consequence of the book runs through his exchanges
with Pinker. On 3 May, however, even as he writes that '*Nostromo*
ought to put me right', he has thoroughly misjudged his progress. For
in the same passage, he indicates that the end of the novel is near. This
may have been a way of comforting Pinker, whose outlays were
increasing, or, more likely, Conrad's own misjudgment of the length of
his work. Like *Lord Jim*, *Nostromo* was to begin as an idea for a long
story and then expand relentlessly, a weakness in construction not lost
upon his early reviewers. Even while he was filled with his new project,
Conrad could not rest easy with *The Rescue* only eight months later.
He mentions (on 5 January 1903) that he has been re-reading the
manuscript so as 'to do away with retrospect', at the same time promis-
ing a story provisionally called *Nostromo*, which will run in all about
35,000 words. Mixed in with this is continued worry that Pinker has
not placed *Romance* serially and his nervous reaction to the accidental
incineration of 'End of the Tether' and the pressures of rewriting it.
In addition to these literary worries during the early composition of

Nostromo were financial anxieties and Conrad's growing dependence on Pinker for expense money. The pattern now appears set.

Conrad would be engaged in several parallel or even contradictory activities, all going rather badly, so that when he began a new novel, usually misconceived as a long story or novella, he would be in a state of near panic. In addition to his literary anxieties, he would apparently be somewhat careless about money, which was never abundant, and thus increase his apprehension about supporting his wife and children. Evidently, this accumulation of anxieties, worries, and fears about the future was connected to his way of working and to the functioning of his literary imagination. Evidently, he could not work effectively unless he was close to breakdown, on the edge of psychic disorders, ill in body and mind. Conrad's physical disorders were legion – recurring gout, arthritis, delirious fevers, neuralgia, influenza. These, however, were symptoms. The inner disorder was far greater, and when it was at its greatest and most intense, he functioned most effectively artistically. While we cannot pinpoint precisely his most productive days or weeks, we can cite his most effective creative periods. As we traced in the letters to Pinker, these periods often coincided with his most trying times, when financial, personal, mental, and literary burdens appeared to be unbearable.

During *Nostromo* alone, we can cite the following letters: 'I am so muddled in everything but my work that I imagined the dinner to you was for the 28th. I seem to live in a sort of dream till something of that sort wakes me up to the sense of my absurdity. . . I am not fit to live in the world' (23 March 1902; Berg ALS). Or: 'I can't shake stuff out of a bag – as I've said. Life with, as one may say, the halter round one's neck is a well nigh intolerable trial. I am tired of it' (4 February 1903). Yet he could also write:

> I have never worked so hard before – with so much anxiety. But the result is good. You know I take no credit to myself for what I do – and so I may judge my own performance. There is no mistake about this. You may take up a strong position when you offer it here. It is very genuine Conrad. At the same time it is more of a novel pure and simple than anything I've done since Almayer's Folly. (17 March 1903; Berg ALS)

Conrad recognised that financially Pinker stood in some danger of losing his investment if his unsuccessful writer died suddenly, and he indicates that Pinker could recover with *Nostromo*. After requesting a subsidy of £20 'for the next three consecutive months', while he

completes *Nostromo*, Conrad mentions that Hueffer, 'who is in possession of my innermost mind', is confident of his ability to finish it 'should
something unforeseen occur'. And in a letter of 29 March 1904, Conrad
indicates Galsworthy 'has been here to see me on Sunday and I have
arranged with him to correct for me the MS of Nostromo should I
have no time myself.' In this same letter, Conrad's mind is already
churning up new material, new plans: 'I've a Meditt [Mediterranean]:
story (of another kind) up my sleeve', the eventual *Suspense*. He closes
the letter with: 'For goodness sake don't drop me now I am just hang-
ing on by my teeth.' (Berg ALS)

As Conrad notified Pinker of these developments and implored
patience, he was writing Paper V of *The Mirror of the Sea*, while still
desperately trying to complete *Nostromo*, which was now well over
100,000 words above his original estimate. We recognise his state of
mind when we read in a 'Saturday' (May 1904) letter that he is sending
the 'first batch of Pt III' to Pinker. Such desperation has its literary
overtones as well, since Conrad evidently saw *Nostromo* as holding up
his entire assembly line of fiction and non-fiction, and he was, therefore, particularly anxious to dispose of it. Yet, at the same time, he
writes: 'I verily believe that N. has elements of success in book form.
I've never written anything with so much *action* in it. The thing is not
half bad upon my word.' (Berg ALS)

After the completion of *Nostromo* in late August 1904, as early as
20 September 1905, Conrad speaks of *Chance* as simmering 'slowly on
to be ready by the end of the year'. Such an early beginning for the
novel, well before *The Secret Agent*, moves us back from 1906 as the
assumed starting date. We also note an intricate literary dimension, in
that *Chance*, *The Secret Agent*, and *Under Western Eyes* overlapped,
with *Chance* reaching back virtually to the period of *Nostromo*. This
interweaving indicates a tightness of conception and creativity far
more intense than we had previously believed, with four long novels in
various stages (manuscript, typescript, corrected galleys, serial) moving
in and out of Conrad's mind during this six-to-seven-year period in a
kind of mosaic pattern. Conrad's letters to Pinker detailing the progress
of *The Secret Agent* also pick up fragments of *Chance*, with the letter
of 25 January 1907 indicating he has 'done a lot to it'. He adds: 'I
won't say a big lot but just fair. Neither will I say I am very pleased
with what I've done. It's just tolerable. However I plod on with that
and shall see my way better presently. I've been doing the story because
I may just as well be doing it as worrying about the other stuff.' (Berg
ALS) He also mentions the idea of *Suspense*: 'I think I've got a theme

for the Mediterranean novel with historical interest, intrigue and adventure. There may be even a success – who knows. All I want now is to discover the moral pivot – and the thing will be done.' Perhaps even more compelling is the fact that Conrad, after he had apparently completed *The Secret Agent* and moved on to *Chance*, expanded the *Agent* to the tune of 26–28,000 words, almost a quarter of the novel's final length.

Such furious activity right up to the threshhold of the writing of *Under Western Eyes*, was accompanied, as we might suspect, by desperate personal affairs, financial, physical, and familial. Beginning in the letter of 26 February 1907, written from Montpellier, Conrad speaks of his older son's illnesses, a sequence of plaints extending through the spring and part of the summer. These letters are the anguished cries of a man at breaking point, citing problems that finally precipitated a nervous collapse in 1910. Mixed in with his son's measles and other complications, followed by the possibility of incipient tuberculosis, are both Conrad's requests for money to subsidise treatment in Switzerland and his frantic rush to turn in pages of *Chance* in order to justify the loans.

Two important letters bring together all the Conradian threads: familial chaos, personal depression, an attack of gout, desultory work on a long-term project (*Chance*), financial pressures, the need to correct galleys, and, through it all, the brain readying itself to churn up a new novel. On 6 May, Conrad writes (on the eve of departing from Montpellier for Geneva):

> I was not in a fit state to write you fully last time. I am getting better rapidly tho' I can't use my hand as yet. It's extremely bothersome. But the hand is getting better and that's the main thing. The weather is horribly wet here and poor Borys has started coughing again. I can hear him now; it's a sound that robs me of my composure in a great measure. . . Do not doubt for a moment that I will do all I can to get the S. A. ready for the printer soon. If there is hurry I will leave off Chance completely for a fortnight or so. I suppose it will be just as well. My only anxiety was to get Chance forward – you understand. The S. A. however has its importance as a distinctly new departure in my work. And I am anxious to put at much 'quality' as I can in that book which will be criticised with some severity no doubt – or *scrutinised* rather I should say. Preconceived notions of Conrad as sea writer will stand in the way of its acceptance. (Berg ALS)

The 18 May letter is the full cry of anguish: unforeseen expenses, the baby with whooping cough, misconceived plans, inability to work on *Chance*, galleys of *The Secret Agent*.

> I have miscalculated my expenses in Montpellier and must ask you to send me frcs *1100* . . . in the course of the week. I left that much in his [the hotel manager's] debt. And please don't scold me because I have just now as much as I can bear. Here I am stranded again with baby at its last gasp with whooping cough. . . Really I haven't got my share of the commonest sort of luck. I suppose Chance will have to pay for all this. (Berg ALS)

A new theme, not unusually, pokes persistently through: the need to increase sales, the desire to be popular. 'The *S. A.* approached with a fresh eye does not strike me as bad at all. There is an element of popularity in it. By this I don't mean to say that the thing is likely to be popular. I merely think that it shows traces of capacity for that sort of treatment which may make a novel popular.' (18 May 1907; Berg ALS). Conrad nevertheless guaranteed a lack of readership with his next project, 'Razumov' (*Under Western Eyes*), first mentioned in a letter marked only Thursday, which we can ascribe to December 1907, thus noting the book's inception as being some time before 1908. In that December 1907 letter, he indicates to Pinker he has in hand '*10* pp. of *Razumov* the first of the two short stories'. Even on 7 January 1908, he is still speaking of it as a tale. He says he is 'anxious to throw that story off my chest'. With that, we enter a familiar Conrad drama: fiction that begins as a short story or novella and then takes on its own shape. He adds, possibly to sweeten what awaits Pinker: 'Here is given the very essence of things Russian. Not the more outward manners and customs but the Russian feeling and thought. You may safely say that. And, I think, the story is effective. Nothing of the sort had been done in English. The subject has long haunted me. Now it must come out.' (Berg ALS)

The reader who scrutinises the first five or ten thousand words of *Under Western Eyes* finds no breaking off point: there are no apparent seams short of 25–30,000 words. And we may recall Conrad's description of the novel to Galsworthy, on 6 January 1908 – one day *before* he wrote to Pinker – to the effect that at first he planned a psychological novel. In this early version, Razumov was to marry Miss Haldin and then, when their child resembles Haldin, he confesses to her his role in her brother's death. Conrad is quite clear about the St Petersburg and Geneva locales of the story, all of which indicates something considerably more than the 'short story' he was outlining to Pinker. Making his comment even more inexplicable is that he speaks of the possibility of including 'Strong Man' ('Gaspar Ruiz'), 'The Duel', and 'Razumov' in the same volume, only to conclude that the latter, because of 'its sustained intensity', would be more suitable for another volume, presumably of stories. Quite rightly, he saw it as 'altogether on another plane'.

Intermixed with the January letters about *Under Western Eyes* are some of Conrad's most compelling words about his financial hardships and his refusal to cheapen himself, sometimes in response to what he feels about Pinker's prodding:

> It is extraordinary that people who understand that a carpenter can't make a box if someone keeps on jogging his elbow will say that no jog of any sort shall matter to a mind. I have no charm, no flow of wit or of facetiousness or mere patter to fill in chinks with. I have only a mind a quite different gift from the gift of the gab. I have no literary tradition even which will help to spin phrases – the chewed up silly phrases. I am not a 'sedulous Ape'. I wish sometimes I were. Why none of the business men would *sit* as I do with nothing but an inkstand and a pen to make things of. They couldn't. Their health would give way. Mine, rotten as it is, has got to stand it. I have no amusement, no relaxation of any kind – none whatever. (14 January 1908; Berg ALS)

These words strengthen our contention that romantic martyrdom, intense commitment in the face of adversity, a view of himself as Sisyphus struggling behind the boulder fired Conrad's imagination, not unlike the sea captain moving into the eye of the storm ready to test his ability to neutralise Nature itself.

The next few letters, written in February and March 1908, at a time when Conrad was professionally involved in Hueffer's *English Review*, run the gamut in almost equal amounts of 'Razumov', illness (mainly gout and nerves), monetary troubles, worry about professional standing, pride of accomplishment, feelings of extraordinary achievement and inadequacy. It is difficult to pinpoint how much of Conrad's anxiety resulted from his growing involvement in the *Review*, how much from his own lack of popular recognition, or how much from a sense of futility as he saw everything slipping away. He had, after all, turned the corner of fifty and he was little better off than he had been at forty, with *The Nigger of the 'Narcissus'*. We do know that his letters take on a biting, querulous edge, not only to Ford, but also to Galsworthy and Wells.

In the 12 February letter to Pinker, he speaks of needing a 'freer hand with that story ["Razumov"]. If I can't have a free hand – time – for elaborating my work and freedom from interference I would just as soon stop writing entirely.' He says this apparently to keep Pinker from prodding him about a short story for *London Magazine*, which Conrad feels will mangle 'Razumov'. Possibly, he knows no 'story length' is there. He then defends himself against any charges of indolence, citing thirteen volumes since 1895 and indicating one-third of his time was lost in illness. In the same letter, he moves to a new tack, mentioning for the first time he may try his hand at writing in French. 'I have also proposals [presumably from the *Mercure de France*] for working in French and I don't feel too old to make a fresh start. In the general uncertainty of what is to happen to me the idea doesn't seem so very bizarre. Rather interesting in fact.' (Berg ALS) In another letter in February, Conrad says 'the end is in sight' for 'Razumov', at a time when he was more than 100,000 words from completion. The letter is itself mainly full of Conrad's diatribes against Methuen, who were insisting on the letter of a contract calling for four novels of over 75,000 words each.

> I am not a sausage machine that takes rotten scraps on at one end and turns out a marketable sausage at the other. Morally I feel bound to let M. have another novel after *Chance*, and that's all – and morally he has no right to expect more. There is the legal aspect of the case I know. But if I am to go to the devil I'll go in my own way – where he certainly will find neither profit nor honours. When one has got an unique autor [sic] one had better treat him in a special way. (Monday; Berg ALS)

In a March letter on 'Razumov', he states categorically that Chapter IV will be the last and the story will be precisely 43,000 words, which is a little longer than *Heart of Darkness*. This leads us to believe that Conrad possibly intended to terminate the story with Part I, when Mikulin asks Razumov where he can go – the theme of 'Where to?' which runs throughout the completed novel. Yet if this is indeed so – and the Yale manuscript of the novel gives us no further clues – then what happened to Conrad's former plan, outlined to Galsworthy less than three months before, to have Razumov marry Miss Haldin in Geneva and then confess his role to her?

In an undated letter, which we can place as having been written in

May 1908, we have the first firm note of the novel's length. Conrad writes: 'I can't let you have "Razumov" yet. That story must be worked out as it is worth it.' And in still another undated letter, probably July of the same year, Conrad has got himself trapped between the demands of the novel, which is apparently growing, and what he feels to be undue prodding from Pinker for a completed project.

> Hall Caine takes two years to write his books. J. C. may be allowed some time. If your idea is that my stuff is unsaleable, then all I can say is that I haven't made it so. If I must starve or beg I won't do it *here*. That's all I have to say really. Consider whether it would be a good policy (from a practical point of view) to drive me away. This is nothing but a *statement of the case*. Don't take it in another spirit. I have no vice to prevent me working and I am willing as soon as practicable to get away into a most economical hole imaginable and write there night and day. I can't believe that my reputation has gone to pieces suddenly. (Berg ALS)

In October, 'Razumov' appears to be going well enough, so that Conrad is full of *Reminiscences*, which he sees as a way of making 'Polish life enter English literature'. He is evidently feeling renewed confidence: 'Everyone thinks well of it, the latest favourable opinion coming to me in your letter this morning. My literary reputation, which seems more clearly defined with every published vol. (I am struck by the general tone of the reviews of the *Set*), has already enough substance to weigh favourably in the scale for the success of a personal book.' (Berg ALS) Toward the end of the letter, he recognises that when 'Razumov' is completed, he must push on with *Chance*, although he hopes to guarantee 1500 to 2000 words a week of *Reminiscences*.

With this letter, 'Razumov' begins to recede, dovetailing with Conrad's other activities in what is an intricate pattern of literary and personal detail. Conrad was increasingly caught up in the *English Review*, to the extent he was offered an active 'participation', a transaction whereby he would be a business partner in the magazine. While nothing came of this, his interest in the publication and his growing disenchantment with Hueffer, ostensibly on grounds of questionable taste in personal and literary matters, created a diversion in his correspondence from purely novelistic considerations.

With the completion and publication of *Under Western Eyes*, the correspondence with Pinker enters thickets of problems, little of which is indicated by the few letters published by Jean-Aubry for this period.

Conrad had now entered into several worlds: as noted, the *English Review* and his growing rift with its editor, Hueffer; the enormous problems with *Chance*, which would not get done; a Mediterranean novel, the eventual *Suspense* of more than a decade later, which Conrad envisaged as the culmination of his career; the incredibly complicated beginnings of *Victory*, cited in a letter of April 1912, which Conrad intended first as a short story and then as a short novel of about 30,000 words, all the while he was rewriting *Chance*; the planning of a volume of short stories, *'Twixt Land and Water*, which appeared in 1912 as *'Twixt Land and Sea*. Added to the above was the pressing factor of breaking physical and mental health, with a major collapse in 1910 that made work and even thought impossible. The series of letters to Pinker demonstrates nearly every aspect of these furious years, which reveal a Conrad so hard pressed that his sole form of escape was his work, into which he apparently poured all his resources.

Conrad's misjudgment of *Victory*, as we learn from the Pinker sequence, was prototypical of his entire career. First conceived, as noted above, as a short story or short novel with the name of 'Dollars' (not to be confused with the short story 'Because of the Dollars') and variously called 'Mr G. Berg', *Victory* expanded in Conrad's imagination even as he planned to focus completely on his Mediterranean novel. That novel, not *Victory* in any of its forms, was to be the major effort of his later career, the keystone, something he had contemplated for over a decade; and yet *Victory* was to dominate for the next two years.

As we follow Conrad's remarks on 'Dollars', we see that he lacked the clear-cut working patterns he had developed with his other major efforts, *Nostromo, The Secret Agent, Under Western Eyes*. His development of 'Dollars' was becoming increasingly involved with several other strands of his career, such as his growing reputation in England and America, contractual complications, the sale of his manuscripts and typescripts, courtship by a wider circle of friends and admirers. All of this activity was different from his earlier periods when writing was relatively unencumbered by complex external affairs, and Conrad was engaged mainly in a battle between his creative imagination and his various illnesses.

With 'Dollars', Conrad entered into an agreement with Pinker for the latter to pay him £10 against each 3000 words of copy submitted, an arrangement that would not have made sense unless Conrad suspected that he had more than a short story or novella within him. In any event, in his letter of 13 May 1912, he speaks of 12,000 words while warning that the piece may grow to 30,000 and need serialising.

He mentions the *English Review* for such a serial, although his split with Hueffer made the *Review* seem unlikely. In the same letter, he also indicates that he is reading seriously for the Mediterranean novel, 'to be done round Napoleon in Elba', and he cautions 'it may turn out to be a biggish thing', even though he is still in doubt whether to make it a first person narrative or 'a tale in the third'.

Conrad's world was full of uncertainties, all of which made him work at his best. Not for another six months did he view 'Dollars' as a novel, or realise that he would have to postpone the Mediterranean novel – which, like the still incomplete 'Rescue', seemed to be a constant hedge against the future, heralding a time when he would consider his career complete. On 3 September 1912, he says he has 'begun formally the novel', by which he means *Suspense*. He hopes to begin work on it steadily, he states, by March or April 1913. At this time, he saw 'Dollars' as a 250-page novel, still only half of the completed book. Next month, he wrote that since he expected 'Dollars' to fall under 75,000 words, he did not think he could use it to complete his Methuen agreement, which still called for three novels each of over 75,000 words. He continued:

> When you return [from the United States] you will find something of mine to negotiate about and I rather think fairly manageable. Meantime should you be asked over there with a view to serialisation you could perhaps tell them something. As, for instance that it has a tropical Malay setting – an unconventional man and a girl on an island under peculiar circumstances to whom enters a gang of three ruffians also of a rather unconventional sort – this intrusion producing certain psychological developments and effects. There is philosophy in it and also drama – lightly treated – meant for cultured people – a piece of literature before everything – and of course fit for general reading. Strictly proper. Nothing to shock the magazine public. (7 October, 1912; Berg ALS)

On 9 October, he returns to the idea of Napoleon and *Suspense*, as if that were the important development while the novel at hand were an unwelcome intrusion. He tells Pinker that the next year, 1913, will be given over to the 'Elba novel and perhaps 3 stories'. He says Harpers will then be able to publish the novel just one hundred years after Napoleon's exile to Elba. He expects 'Dollars' to be completed by Christmas of 1913. Discrepancies between what Conrad was telling Pinker and what the novel was telling him are clear: for even when he finally indicated 50,000 words as the expected length of the manuscript, an examination of the latter (at the University of Texas Humanities Center) indicates Conrad would have needed at least another 40–50,000 words to complete the work. We must also keep in mind that the manuscript indicates one-fifth greater development of the novel than the published version demonstrates, so that the manuscript would have run an additional 60–70 pages if printed out as written before revision. Thus, when Conrad outlined a 40–50,000 word novel or novella, he was deep into Part II, with Heyst and Lena on the island, Schomberg irate and vengeful, and Jones and Co. seeking loot. The development toward any resolution involved so many sub-elements Conrad could not possibly have gotten out without as many words again as he had already written. He was himself to tell Pinker several months later: 'That tale is the very devil to manage. It has too many possibilities. It won't be so with the next novel . . .' (19 February 1914; Berg ALS) [p. 30]

To return to the previous year: he continues to speak of an ending, first on 26 January 1913, and then on 20 February. In the latter, in fact, he notes an imminent conclusion, within that month. Sixteen months were to pass, however, and an additional 70–80,000 words, before Conrad saw the end of 'Dollars'; and yet once again he could speak, on 13 April, of the novel 'drawing to an end'. The length in April is crucial, since the most he could have written then was between 65–75,000 words, about 600–625 pages of a total of 1199 manuscript pages. The only conclusions we can reach are, tentatively, as follows:

1. Conrad was simply feeling his way into the book, still unsure of development and pacing – although the manuscript does indicate considerable control and certainty; and/or:

2. He had to assure Pinker, so as not to let his agent know of the morass into which he had fallen; such assurances would be Conrad's way of surviving as a writer, on his own terms, insisting on the kind of book he wanted to write, regardless of consequence; and/or:

3. He was so badly off financially that he was thinking primarily of the weekly quota and payment; that is, writing 3000 words in order to receive the £10 a week stipend; and/or:

4. He was so personally harassed with internal and external affairs that he honestly did not know where he was – his creative imagination had taken over from his conscious mind; and/or:

5. That while none of the above are precisely true, all of the above are partially feasible, and that they added up to Conrad's subconscious way of driving himself into a corner so that he could function best creatively; his plan involved facing symbolic death – words against

money, pen against bread – and this sense of the ultimate, of final things, fed his imagination and allowed him to work effectively.

An additional factor was the arrival in the spring of 1913 of the galleys of *Chance*, which meant time lost in anguished alterations and revisions. On 12 September 1913, he wrote: 'I am gone so stale all over that I can't trust myself to do what I most desperately mean to do. It's the beastly fact. Re your letter of this morning. You know how I am situated with this long novel. It has got to be finished soon – and I've been jammed for six weeks with it, all worry and no work. I think I had better stick to what I have in hand now.' (Berg ALS) Having held off Pinker through the summer and autumn, by 10 December 1913, he indicates that he is prepared to sell 'Dollars', a work of 100,000 words, still 40,000 short of the complete book. So Conrad continued, hesitant and encouraged by turns, until on 1 July 1914, he stated that he had completed the novel on about 20 June. Well into 1915 Conrad's letters discuss *Victory*, even as he mentions that he is preparing to complete 'The Rescue(r)'.

Victory fades, and 'The Rescue(r)' now becomes insistent, along with progress on the Collected Edition and the French translation of his works under the general editorship of André Gide, and particularly Gide's translation of *Typhoon*. In a 1917 letter to Pinker (dated only 'Thursday'), Conrad found *Typhoon* 'wonderfully done – in parts. In others utterly wrong. And the worst is that with all my knowledge of the two languages I can't do much either in the way of suggestion . . . there are passages that simply cannot be rendered into French – they depend so much for their meaning upon the very genius of the language.' (Berg ALS) He adds: 'I was not fully aware how thoroughly *English* the Typhoon is. I am immensely proud of this, of course.'

Even *Typhoon* and the other French translations, however, could not relieve the pressure of 'The Rescue' on his creative imagination. Now in the twilight of his career, Conrad found this novel taking on para-literary dimensions, possibly because of its connection with the days of *Heart of Darkness* and *Lord Jim* and its return to the Malay period of his relative youth. Two letters (for 31 December 1918, and 15 February 1919) indicate his high evaluation of the work in progress, too high in the light of the completed novel. In the first of the letters, he tells Pinker that 'the interest of that romance is all in the shades of the psychology of the people engaged – as is obvious from the four parts already completed.' He continues:

It is sustained by the presentation alone. You may, however, assure

the representative of the Cosmopolitan Magazine that the story will
end as romantically as it began, and that no one of any particular
consequences will have to die. Hassim and Immada will be sacrificed,
as in any case they were bound to be, but their fate is not the subject
of the tale. All those yacht people will go on their way leaving
Lingard alone with the wreck of the greatest adventure of his life.
For indeed what else could have happened? Any tragedy there is in
this 'denouement' will be all in the man's feelings; and whatever
value there may be in that must depend on the success of the
romantic presentation. This statement, I have the right to hope, will
be enough for the mature mind which directs the editorial department of the Cosmopolitan Magazine. There are many kinds of
romance and this one is not fit for juvenile readers, not because it
raises any sort of problem but on account of the depth and complexity of the feelings involved in the action. . . (Berg TLS [Type-
script Letter Signed])

In the second letter, for 15 February 1919, we find Conrad trying to
finish 'The Rescue' with one eye on the Nobel Prize Committee. He
writes to Pinker:

There is however another distinction which has been mooted (by the
R. S. L.) and that is the Nobel Prize. That was in the air last year;
and as it is an international thing and less in the nature of an honour
than of mere reward, we needn't have any scruples about acceptance
if it ever comes in our way. And as it is not at all an impossible
development I must tell you of the thought which had occurred to
me as to the policy to follow.

I think sincerely that 'Rescue' has a particular quality. Novels of
adventure will, I suppose, be always written; but it may well be that
'Rescue' in its concentrated colouring and tone will remain the swan
song of Romance as a literary art . . . (Berg TLS)

The remainder of the letter is concerned with publication strategies
devised to catch the deliberations of the Nobel Committee.

Eventually completed in May 1919, 'The Rescue' was generally
well received, with the exception of Virginia Woolf in the TLS, who
while appreciative of nuances perceptively noted Conrad's failure to
work out his theme effectively. After this, the correspondence with
Pinker, until the latter's death in 1922, details the working down of
Conrad's creative career. All the familiar ingredients remain, but without his sense of great work in progress. By now Conrad was arranging

his career – monetary considerations, the Heinemann Collected
Edition, foreign rights, the French translations, film versions of his
novels and stories – as though he had to settle matters before disaster
struck. On this note, the correspondence of over 1200 items concludes,
although until his own death in 1924 Conrad retained Pinker's son,
Eric, as his business agent.

This outline of the Conrad–Pinker correspondence can only suggest
the intricate detail of the great volume of the letters themselves. What
they demonstrate repeatedly is Conrad's view of himself as a martyr
to his literary talents, a romantic stance he struck and evidently believed
in which apparently sustained him when financial and psychological
collapse seemed imminent. Such was the intensity of this belief in himself that he obviously convinced the business-like Pinker, whose
journalistic background had not prepared him to equate literature and
martyrdom. We have skimped on Pinker's side here, and have allowed
Conrad to record the better of every argument and disagreement; but
we lack Pinker's replies. In their absence, we can only remark that if
Conrad was a conscious martyr, Pinker was a saint. The full range of
Conrad's letters indicates a volatility and irritability so extreme, a
role-playing so dramatic – all connected to the nature of the work at
hand – that Pinker was forced to walk along the edge of a precipice;
one slip or unusual demand and Conrad felt threatened. Yet it is hard
to think of Conrad's career going forward in those crucial years between 1900 and 1915 without Pinker's aid, which Conrad relied on in
this period with as much insistence as he had depended on his Uncle
Bobrowski during those devastatingly difficult days of his earlier career
following upon his father's death; as much as he had relied on his
'Aunt' Marguerite's belief in him in the 1890s. A man compulsively
intent upon doing his work apparently can find the people who will
sustain him.

13 Conrad and *The Good Soldier**

THOMAS MOSER

Despite his reputation for telling tall tales, Ford Madox Ford's contributions to the achievement of Joseph Conrad now prove to be pretty much what he said they were.[1] Not only did he provide the stories for all three collaborations, he elicited Conrad's two memoirs, supplied material for 'Amy Foster' and *The Secret Agent*, backed up Conrad while he was writing *Nostromo*, and even wrote a few pages himself for the last. Especially, as Conrad's 'large, blond, phlegmatic' friend, Ford gave Conrad the 'moral support' he 'passionately needed'. As for exerting direct literary influence, Ford says modestly: 'I don't really imagine that I really influenced Conrad at all.'

But what, if anything, did Conrad contribute to Ford's masterpiece *The Good Soldier*, the book that Ford called, long after Conrad's death and shortly before his own, 'the only novel of my own that I considered – and indeed consider – at all to count'? Ford did not write *The Good Soldier* until five years after the memorable decade (September 1898 to March 1909) of his real intimacy with Conrad. Ford's 'place as general cook and bottle-washer in Conrad's literary establishment' had long been taken by their mutual friend Arthur Pierson Marwood, who was also 'large, blond, outwardly placid, and deliberate'.[2] Nevertheless, Conrad probably exerted two powerful influences upon *The Good Soldier* – the one literary and technical, the other biographical and deeply personal.

Graham Greene rightly finds the greatness of the novel in its 'sense of Ford's involvement'. The source of that involvement must be biographical: 'A novelist is not a vegetable absorbing nourishment mechanically from soil and air: material is not easily or painlessly gained, and one cannot help wondering what agonies of frustration and error lay behind *The Saddest Story*.'[3] Such agonies could have

* Portions of this essay originally appeared in *Mosaic: A Journal for the Comparative Study of Literature and Ideas*, published by the University of Manitoba Press, 8:1 (October 1974), 217–27, to whom acknowledgment is herewith made.

come only out of drastically altered relations with the people he was closest to: Elsie Martindale Hueffer, his wife of fifteen years whom he left in 1909 and who would not give him a divorce; Violet Hunt, who became his mistress in 1909; Conrad, his dearest and most distinguished friend, who had broken with Ford in March, 1909, but did respond in 1911 and 1912 to Ford's friendly overtures; and Marwood, the second-best friend of both Conrad and Ford, who also quarrelled with Ford in 1909 but who, along with his wife Caroline, appears very soon to have become temporarily reconciled with Ford and fond of Violet.[4]

And yet, when, on his fortieth birthday, on 7 December 1913, Ford sat down to write *The Good Soldier* 'to show what I could do', to put into that novel '*all* that I knew about writing',[5] he must have felt that his personal life was, once again and more so than ever before, in ruins. By then, Violet Hunt tells us, she was feeling distinctly un-sympathetic to Ford.[6] On 7 February 1913, in a highly publicised libel suit, Elsie had received £300 damages from a magazine that had applied the name Mrs Hueffer to Violet. Far more important, Marwood at this time ceased all communication with Ford, and Conrad, probably in sympathy for Marwood, apparently re-rejected Ford. At least, no letters from Conrad to Ford, datable between March 1913 and March 1915, have as yet appeared.[7] I believe, in short, that, by 1913, Ford must have realised at last that neither his artist-friend, who was like a father to him, nor his country gentleman-friend, who embodied the generous traditions of his beloved grandfather, Ford Madox Brown, that neither of these boon companions truly loved him anymore.

Yet, even granted that Ford in 1913 realised that those two English gentlemen could no longer bear him, why connect this with *The Good Soldier*? After all, Ford had been writing on its subject, marital compli-cations, for over twenty years and had been suffering from them almost as long. There are, however, some interesting coincidences of dates and of characters between *The Good Soldier* and the Hueffers, the Mar-woods and the Conrads. In the manuscript version of the novel, the crucial first meeting at Nauheim between the Ashburnhams and Dowells occurs in July 1906. Ford's first recorded mention of the Marwoods is February 1906. In May and June of that year, Ford and Conrad collaborated on *The Nature of a Crime*, that strange prefiguration of *The Good Soldier*. And, according to Jessie Conrad, Ford first brought Marwood to the Conrads in July 1906, just before Ford's departure for Germany.[8] In the book version of *The Good Soldier* Ford changed the date of the fatal meeting between the Ashburnhams and Dowells to 4 August 1904, another momentous occasion in Ford's psychic life. The winter of 1904 had marked the height of Ford's intimacy with Conrad, when he was helping with both *Nostromo* and *The Mirror of the Sea*. In the spring and summer of 1904, Ford suffered a severe mental breakdown. July found him weeping and staggering with agoraphobia under the hot sun of the Salisbury Plain. In response to Ford's cries for help, Conrad was unable to supply any financial, and very little moral, support. About 4 August 1904, under doctor's orders, Ford went off alone to seek psychiatric help in various German spas.[9]

The Good Soldier tells of an adulterous affair connecting two couples whose members are all, apparently, dear friends. The masculine Captain Edward Ashburnham, estranged from his wife Leonora, becomes the lover of Florence, wife of the epicene John Dowell, the only member of the quartet ignorant of the affair. Nine years of intimacy end with the suicides of Florence and Edward, the enlightenment of Dowell, and his estrangement from Leonora. Dowell writes down his tale of passion in order to get it out of his head. Both male characters, obviously and unsurprisingly, owe a great deal to physical and psychological aspects of Ford. Similarly, both female characters partake of various aspects of Ford's two women, Elsie and Violet. My own view, which differs from Arthur Mizener's, is that Florence principally reflects Elsie, and Leonora Violet. But Edward and Leonora, the model Tory couple, also owe something to the Marwoods.[10] Moreover, Ford sporadically believed that Marwood had, in 1909, made advances to Elsie; Ford himself, perhaps about 1913, may have thought himself in love with Caroline Marwood.[11]

If, as I believe, Marwood was the chief model beyond Ford himself for Edward Ashburnham, where in *The Good Soldier* is Conrad to be found? In John Dowell, of course. Dowell's small stature and non-English origin place him among recurrent caricatures of Conrad in Ford's novels. But far more important, Ford gives us in Dowell an impressionistic narrator like Marlow. If the publication of Conrad's *Chance* at the end of 1913 pained Ford with its portrait of de Barral, it would also have provided technically the resurrection of the complex impressionism of *Lord Jim* with its time-shift, its personal narrator Marlow and its plethora of sub-narrators, including the naive Powell (ur-Dowell?).[12]

Dowell, as narrator, owes much to the four manifestations of Marlow. Dowell's life with Florence and the Ashburnhams proves ultimately as devastatingly enlightening to him as Marlow's trip to the Congo to him. Before Marlow embarked on his voyage of discovery, he was like 'a silly little bird'.[13] Dowell says that he himself was simply a fool. However, the contrast between the narrator's pre- and post-enlighten- ment phases is endemic to *The Good Soldier* as it is not to *Heart of Darkness*. In the recurrent juxtaposition of an older, wiser Dowell with a young, naive one, we can see a trace of the relationship between old and young Marlow in 'Youth'. Old Marlow recounts in amaze- ment how his younger self foolishly leapt into a smoking hold, promptly fainted, and was fished out with a boat-hook. Dowell's tone is similar as he recalls how, on the night he eloped with Florence, he went up and down the ladder to her bedroom window 'like a tranquil jumping- jack' (p. 84). Dowell's choice of a hero is Marlovian as well. Like Jim, Edward is a big, blond, handsome, likeable, inarticulate Englishman with considerable skill in the service-profession he espouses, and with a subtle unsoundness not at all apparent to strangers. But whereas Jim's plague spot relates, tragically, to his professional performance, Edward's does not. On the other hand, Edward's overwhelming need to comfort a mournful female recalls Marlow's last subject, Captain Anthony of *Chance*, and his Flora.

It surely goes without saying that Dowell especially resembles Marlow as a master (for the first time in Ford's career) of what Ford considered Conrad's greatest literary forte, the 'architectonics' of the impressionistic novel. And so Dowell, in true Conradian style, gets in his strong first impression of Edward in the hotel dining-room, includ- ing the significant expression in the eyes, and then works backwards and forwards in time. 'When one discusses an affair,' Dowell says, 'a long sad affair – one goes back, one goes forward' (p. 183). Both narrators handle the reader's feelings with such consummate skill that the main, titular character, who has acted in some respects like a villain, proves ultimately sympathetic, even heroic, if ambiguously, suicidally so. Dowell, again like Marlow, handles masterfully the meaningful, illustrative digression and manages beautifully the Con- radian flexible chapter-unit. He uses apparently digressive, somewhat philosophical paragraphs to provide transitions between episodes of very different tonal qualities. Finally, Dowell recalls Marlow in his propensity to talk about how difficult it is to fulfil their common purpose to make the reader see and about how hard the impressionistic method really is. 'I am, at any rate, trying to get you to see what sort of life it was I led with Florence,' says Dowell early in the novel (p. 14). He admits elsewhere: 'I don't know how to put this thing down' (p. 12). He uses Conrad's pathfinder metaphor from *Chance*: 'I have, I am aware, told this story in a very rambling way so that it may be difficult for anyone to find his path through what may be a sort of maze. I cannot help it' (p. 183). Nevertheless, Dowell, like Marlow, insists upon the unquestionable, literal truth of his tale: 'I console myself with thinking that this is a real story and that, after all, real stories are probably told best in the way a person telling a story would tell them. They will then seem most real' (p. 183).

One fundamental, technical difference between Dowell's tale and the tales told by Marlow forcibly reminds us how Fordian a narrator Dowell is. Although Dowell asks the reader to pretend that they are spending a fortnight together in a cottage by the sea and that Dowell is talking, in a low voice, to his sympathetic auditor, all this is emphatically pretense. Dowell is not talking; he is 'really' writing down this sad story and over a period of two years. The closest Marlow comes to written narration is the packet containing the account of Jim's last days that he mails to his privileged listener. The difference is crucial because it allows Ford to give full rein to his solipsistic beliefs (Dowell is really writing only to himself) and to his devastating tendency to change his mind. Although Marlow's attitude always includes bewilderment, although *Heart of Darkness* and *Chance* are unique narratives inspired by special circumstances rather than frequently told yarns, and although Marlow's narratives are characteristically 'inconclusive', one never has the sense that Marlow would change events or his attitude. But as Dowell writes, he comes to dislike Leonora, for whom he earlier would lay down his life. Again, as Dowell writes, he suddenly sees events very differently from his earlier recollection of them. His impression at one time is that during their married years Florence was never out of his sight. But later he decides that she was almost always out of his sight. The method is congenial to Ford and provides excuses for apparent errors and inconsistencies. On the other hand, it is a common experience suddenly to remember correctly something one has misremembered; it is not unknown to change one's attitude toward a friend and to harden one's heart even more against an enemy.

Marlow's auditors in *Heart of Darkness* exist as real presences who may, if they wish, talk back; Dowell's auditor is imaginary and therefore mute: 'listener . . . you are so silent' (p. 14). Interestingly enough, whereas Marlow can recount long, complicated conversations, Dowell sticks to Ford's dictum that since one cannot, in reality, precisely remember long speeches, one should never quote more than a couple of lines.[14] Most significantly, Dowell gives us virtually nothing from his all-night-long conversation with Edward. Yet, since Dowell supposedly loves Edward more than anyone in the world, that night must have been a great event in his life.

Dowell differs from Marlow in one last, important, but rather indefinable way. Ford had said that it was all right for a novelist to use himself as a character if he was careful to make that character unsound, even villainous.[15] Clearly Ford has in mind a character very different from Marlow, who is not only Conrad (albeit anglicised) but also, despite his many claims to self-doubt, as perfect (in Conrad's terms) as anyone could hope to be. Dowell would seem to fit Ford's prescription of the author's self with many imperfections. In choosing Dowell to be his eyes and voice, Ford chose a man who would try to tell what he saw but who, like Ford, saw badly; who on rare occasions was involved in passionate scenes but was basically like the Ford of *The Soul of London* 'not made for strong impressions';[16] who admired passionate creatures as Ford admired 'the passion of Conrad'[17] and yet himself feared passion; who nevertheless was human and thus inevitably involved in suffering. To the extent that he can, Dowell suffers: 'my mind going round and round in a weary, baffled space of pain' (p. 233). Blind as he has been and perhaps still is, he has seen suffering great enough to drive people he loves to madness and suicide. Dowell's conviction of the meaninglessness of existence is even more desperate than Marlow's. For the latter, Jim's dilemma has fascinating ethical and metaphysical implications for all men that make his story worth telling again and again. But characteristically of Ford, Dowell is unsure whether other people's lives are at all like the lives of those good people the Ashburnhams and the Dowells. Dowell's chief purpose in telling the tale is not to understand it but to get it out of his head.

If then we grant that, as Graham Greene suggested, Ford wrote *The Good Soldier* out of personal, agonised involvement, we might still speculate a little on what Ford's feelings were as he created his masterpiece. How did he dare to do it, to write the first great work that follows Conrad's impressionistic manner, one in which Ford destroys or dismisses those formerly nearest and dearest to him? Ford's journalism of this period makes clear that he enjoys the role of ferocious critic. He acknowledges that it 'is an exhilarating thing to do' to chuck his 'cap into the face of quite estimable people . . . we need the saeva indignatio . . . one wants to be reckless nowadays . . . one wants it desperately . . . I should respect myself more if I could . . . just for once, say what I really think of a few people. But I have not the courage.'[18] Except that he did have the courage – in the guise of fiction – to admit his dislike for Violet, give Elsie prussic acid, cut Marwood's

throat and consider spitting on his grave. He had the courage to defy
Conrad, to write his own masterpiece of impressionistic fiction.

Ford had the courage because he had decided he was going to die
soon. We can only speculate why that should be. Perhaps the *crise de
quarante* was upon him. He was also getting toward the age at which
his father died. In a 1914 essay on impressionism, Ford says that he is
'tired out' and 'determined to drop creative writing for good and all.'[19]
In an article of 4 July 1914 he gives his *morituri salutamus*: 'I who am,
relatively speaking, about to die . . .'[20] Thus, half-persuaded of his
imminent demise, he who was so tender of skin could safely express
his savage indignation.

And yet *The Good Soldier* is great not so much for its bitter tone as
for the almost filial love that Dowell feels for Edward (analogous
presumably to Ford's deepest feelings for Marwood). If Edward's
flaws of stupidity, self-indulgence, and sentimentality lie exposed, they
are simply aspects of the great, living human being Ford was determined to create once in his life. Even if we do not believe that Edward
quite belongs, by virtue of his passion, among the 'Beati Immaculati',
he is appallingly human in his suffering.

Love of the father who had called him a 'stupid donkey'[21] and
guilt for having enjoyed his death perhaps won out after all and helped
Ford make *The Good Soldier* the great novel that it is. We do not need
merely to infer – from Ford's age, his death-thoughts, the misunderstandings with those two father-figures, Marwood and Conrad, and
Marwood's mortal illness – that Ford would also have been thinking
about his father at this time. We know it from the journalism. In
September 1914, when he had just completed *The Good Soldier,* the
image of his father and Swinburne talking together became for Ford
the symbol of the good life lost:

> some days ago . . . there suddenly jumped into my mind a dim
> recollection: . . . my father's high excited tones and Mr. Swinburne's
> mellow, exhortative, and beautiful organ . . . I like to think of my
> father and Algernon Swinburne discussing with heat the identity of
> Petronius Arbiter, or whoever he was. For that . . . is a picture of
> manners that I would very willingly see revived . . .[22]

Thus, at the very time Ford has apparently outraged Marwood and
again dismayed Conrad, he is thinking of how as a child he just loved
listening to his father talk. Ford's purpose in founding, with Marwood,
The English Review was to promote discussion. In *Mr Fleight* (1913),
the Fordian Fleight's happiest moments are spent talking to the Mar-

woodian Mr Blood. But it was, after all, with Conrad – according to Violet Hunt – that 'At Someries and The Pent they sat up all night helping each other to "find the word".'[23] Or, as Ford put it, precisely fifty years ago: 'For the writer [i.e., Ford himself] the pleasure of eternal technical discussion with Conrad was a sufficient motive for continuing our labours. . . And it is to be remembered that, during all those years, the writer wrote every word that he wrote, with the idea of reading it aloud to Conrad.'[24]

As a paean to both Conrad and Marwood,[25] *The Good Soldier* succeeded only with the artist-friend. Although Marwood apparently never again communicated with Ford, Conrad wrote a warm letter (undated but presumably of March 1915, or shortly thereafter) in praise of *The Good Soldier*.

> The women are extraordinary – in the laudatory sense – and the whole vision of the subject perfectly amazing. And talking of cadences, one hears all through them a tone of fretful melancholy, extremely effective. Something new, this, in your work, my dear Ford – c'est très, très curieux. Et c'est très bien, très juste.[26]

Perhaps Conrad realised, too, that Ford was throwing himself into the war effort by writing propaganda, would soon enlist (making Conrad his literary executor) and would suffer sorely while trying to be a good soldier.

NOTES

1. Thanks, in particular, to the following: Bernard C. Meyer, *Joseph Conrad: A Psychoanalytic Biography* (Princeton: Princeton University Press, 1967); Arthur Mizener, *The Saddest Story: A Biography of Ford Madox Ford* (New York and Cleveland: World, 1971); Norman Sherry, *Conrad's Western World* (Cambridge: Cambridge University Press, 1971).
2. Ford Madox Ford, *Return to Yesterday* (London: Gollancz, 1931), pp. 191, 198; and *Mightier Than the Sword* (London: Allen and Unwin, 1938), pp. 278, 280.
3. Graham Greene, ed., *The Bodley Head Ford Madox Ford*, Vol. I (London: The Bodley Head, 1962), p. 12.
4. See Mizener for a full and authoritative account.
5. Ford Madox Ford, *The Good Soldier: A Tale of Passion* (New York: Vintage, 1957), p. xviii. All further references are to this edition.
6. Violent Hunt, *I Have This to Say* (New York: Boni and Liveright, 1926), pp. 152, 200, *et passim*.
7. I am indebted to Professor Frederick R. Karl for confirming my own census of Conrad's letters to Ford.
8. Mizener, pp. 115, 118 ff., 544. Jessie Conrad, *Joseph Conrad and his Circle*

(New York: Dutton, 1935), p. 116. Charles G. Hoffmann, 'Ford's Manuscript Revisions of *The Good Soldier*', *English Literature in Transition*, 9: 3 (1966), 151.

9. Thomas C. Moser, 'From Olive Garnett's Diary: Impressions of Ford Madox Ford and His Friends, 1890–1906', *Texas Studies in Literature and Language*, 16:4 (Fall 1974), 511–33.

10. See Mizener, p. 183. Details on the Marwoods were supplied by Borys Conrad at the Conrad Conference in Poland, September, 1972. See the following magazine articles for resemblances between the Marwoods (who appear as Ford's anonymous Tory friends) and the Ashburnhams: *The Bystander* (London), 15 November 1911, p. 298; 29 November 1911, p. 438; 31 January 1912, p. 244; *The Outlook* (London), 28 February 1914, pp. 278 f.

11. Conversation with Richard Curle, July 1963. Other possible causes of Marwood's anger at Ford: Ford's large unpaid debt to Marwood; Ford's portrayal of Marwood in his novel *The New Humpty-Dumpty* (1912); Marwood's belief, based on unjust allegations in the libel suit, that Ford had neglected his children financially.

12. Thomas C. Moser, 'Conrad, Ford and the Sources of *Chance*', *Conradiana*, 7:3 (Fall 1975). The first issue of the first edition of *Chance* appeared 18 September 1913, the second (trade) issue 15 January 1914. See Theodore G. Ersham, *A Bibliography of Joseph Conrad* (Metuchen, N.J.: Scarecrow, 1969), p. 264.

13. Joseph Conrad, *Youth and Two Other Stories* (London: Blackwood, 1902), p. 60.

14. Ford Madox Ford, *Joseph Conrad: A Personal Remembrance* (London: Duckworth, 1924), pp. 184 ff.

15. Ford Madox Ford, *The Critical Attitude* (London: Duckworth, 1911), p. 34.

16. Ford Madox Ford, *The Soul of London* (London: Alston Rivers, 1905), p. 58.

17. *Joseph Conrad*, p. 20.

18. *The Outlook*, 7 February 1914, p. 174; 2 May 1914, pp. 599 f.; 9 May 1914, p. 636.

19. *Critical Writings of Ford Madox Ford*, ed. Frank MacShane (Lincoln: University of Nebraska Press, 1964), pp. 46 f.

20. *The Outlook*, 4 July 1914, p. 16.

21. Ford Madox Ford, *Ancient Lights* (London: Chapman and Hall, 1911), p. ix.

22. *The Outlook*, 26 September 1914, p. 399.

23. Hunt, p. 23.

24. *Joseph Conrad*, pp. 49, 203.

25. And a love letter to Brigit Patmore, as well. See Hunt, *passim*, who calls her 'Maleine' and equates her with Nancy Rufford of *The Good Soldier*; see also Brigit Patmore, *My Friends When Young* (London: Heinemann, 1968), pp. 52–6. Dame Rebecca West, in a conversation on 21 February 1975, not only confirmed the story of Ford's unsuccessful love for Brigit but also called his relations with Conrad at this time 'very strained' and remembered hearing Violet say that Marwood was so painful a subject one did not dare mention his name in Ford's presence.

26. From Violet Hunt's transcription of an undated letter in the Cornell University Library. Quoted by permission of the Cornell University Library and the Trustees of the Joseph Conrad Estate.

14 Ford's Interpretation of Conrad's Technique

IVO VIDAN

The fiftieth anniversary year of *Joseph Conrad, A Personal Remembrance* might be the occasion for a reappraisal of Ford Madox Ford's stimulating and tantalising book, a book full of information, insight, and misleading hints.

By now we know so much about Conrad that we can read Ford's *Remembrance* not for such factual illumination as it can give us about Conrad's life and even thinking, but for what Ford explicitly offers: he describes the book as a novel. Nowadays nonfiction so often employs the traditional forms of fiction that we should allow Ford's original contribution to the genre to exist in its own right. For a novelist, creating an object of a fictional kind, is like Sidney's poet in that he 'nothing affirmeth and therefore never lyeth'. Ford himself allows that his 'memory' may be 'at fault over a detail',[1] but claims that 'the truth of the impression as a whole' cannot be impugned.[2] Details and the whole belong, then, to two different levels of knowledge: the detail corresponds to a model outside itself, yet it contributes to the formation of an authotelic whole, and the whole obviously carries its own principle of justification. These Fordian implications are unlikely to have had their direct philosophical foundations in Kant or Aristotle, but they are in tune with responsible neocritical assumptions which do.

Ford claims that he and Conrad believed that 'a novel should be the biography of a man or of an affair, and a biography . . . should be a novel.'[3] The distinguishing feature of Ford's particular book is that in it we have 'a projection of Joseph Conrad as, little by little, he revealed himself to a human being during many years of close intimacy. It is so that, by degrees, Lord Jim appeared to Marlowe[4] or that every human soul by degrees appears to every other human soul.'[5] Ford tries to illustrate the growth of his acquaintance with Conrad and, by doing so, to make Conrad more graphically present to the reader. But he does not do so by means of a 'narration'[6] – by which, I take it, Ford means a sequential account of surface events. His starting point and his fictional unit is an impression, and he describes his book as 'the writer's impression of a writer who avowed himself impressionist.'[7] The inter-action between Marlow and protagonist could not be more symmetri-cally conceived.

A novel, a 'whole', a biography, a projection, a revelation, an impression. The intention is fairly clear. The work under discussion, like analogous ones, is designed to explore one particular situation, namely to render 'one embroilment, one set of embarrassments, one human coil, one psychological progression'.[8] This is an important critical notion which Ford attributes to Conrad and himself in *Thus to Revisit*, written several years before his Conrad book. In the light of this notion, a work like *Lord Jim* is no longer an intricate narrative web, but becomes the presentation of one single situation.

The organisation of Ford's *Joseph Conrad* seems to have been conceived along the lines of Conrad's own *A Personal Record*. This work deals consistently with two analogous themes, namely Conrad's initiation to sea-life and the writing of his first novel. Ford similarly interlinks the theme of Conrad's life with that of his work and his craftsmanship. Thus the method of the book corresponds to its own substance, because the book is both a memoir, in other words a record of lived reality, and, as we have seen Ford insist, a fiction.[9]

Ford's choice of *A Personal Record*'s 'rambling discourse'[10] for his model finds support in Conrad's own conviction that he was not 'a personage for an orderly biography'.[11] Using time shifts freely, Ford is able to drift among various concerns, occasionally returning to some earlier observation and reinforcing it by repetition. The way in which different aspects of Conrad's life and interests – at various points in his career – begin to take shape can be compared to the way in which he meted out information about his past adventures to listeners like Ford; he was a veritable Marlow, if one is to believe Ford's account of this oral procedure. 'Who knows? from the rambling discourse a person-ality of sorts will yet emerge,'[12] wrote Conrad on starting his own reminiscences, and in fact this turned out to be much more true of Ford's book.

Through his presentation of their contacts against the background of rural life on the Kentish downs, freely interchanging, as in a novel, scenic and panoramic methods of presentation, Ford brought to life the dour integrity of Conrad, his characteristic gestures, moods and attitudes. What emerges is a memorable picture, moving in its friendly respectfulness, yet not sentimental. The comedy of certain situations scrupulously avoids any possible over-emphasis on their mutual closeness or on the author's own importance, despite the use of the inherent potential of humorous exaggeration. To mark the genre, there are many purely literary suggestions throughout the book, such as – in the title of Part I – the use of Victor Hugo's rhetorical closing verse from 'Tristesse d'Olympio' to add aesthetic distance to the subdued pathos of Ford's memory of his friend: '*C'est toi qui dors dans l'ombre* . . .' Or again, there are Conradian references, like the opening of the book – a deliberate imitation of the beginning of Lord Jim: 'He was small rather than large in height; very broad in the shoulder and long in the arm; dark in complexion with black hair and a clipped black beard. He had the gestures of a Frenchman . . .'

Even devices of this sort enhance the effect of Ford's minor but genuine work of art. However, it is not my intention to point out these qualities, but to use statements from Ford's book in order to air some relevant critical concepts. To do so, it is not necessary to change the terms in which we began to discuss Ford's book. An account of abstract ideas which is thematically significant to the structure of a book, is now recognised as a legitimate feature of a novel. It need not be incorporated into dramatised interrelationships, but can be openly formulated in discussion or even in abstract summaries. No closer example need come to mind than Stephen's aesthetic theory in Joyce's *A Portrait of the Artist as a Young Man.* We will not attempt here to sum up Ford's presentation of what he calls his and Conrad's attitude, but rather sift out those points which seem to be most illuminating.

Ford maintains that his book is 'a novel exactly on the lines of the formula that Conrad and the writer [i.e. Ford] evolved.'[13] If you are writing about a character (and Ford cunningly suggests a seemingly invented person, the facts about whom are strongly reminiscent of Ford himself) 'you must first get him in with a strong impression, and then work backwards and forwards over his past'.[14] One thinks again of Conrad's Jim, presented in terms of his total situation, rather than of a story line. Ford himself illustrates this rather humorously by expanding on the fictitious example of a Mr Slack and the problem of his greenhouse, thereby demonstrating that 'life does not narrate, but makes impressions on our brains.'[15]

Whether the word impression is well chosen remains doubtful, though Ford maintains that Conrad himself accepted it. In the thirties he refers to a whole group of writers, including James, Crane and Hudson, as impressionists,[16] without justifying the use of a term clearly taken from music and painting: he does not seem to be aware of the way in which it applies to these non-literary arts. Conrad is much closer to applying the word in its usual sense – not to himself, but to a writer from whose work he is clearly at pains to distinguish his own, namely Stephen Crane.[17] In a letter to Graham he speaks of 'mere Cranelike impressionism',[18] and at that time he seems to have held that it produced only a momentary and superficial impact.

It is not our present aim to discuss fully the appropriateness of the word impressionist to an art which deals with meanings rather than presenting purely plastic and formal values. In any case, if there is some justification for applying the term to Crane, who himself conceived a novel as 'a succession of sharply outlined pictures, which pass before the reader as a panorama',[19] this is certainly not the case with Conrad, nor for that matter with Ford.

Indeed Ford never specifically tries to draw parallels between his own and Conrad's writings and impressionist art, and yet Conrad's descriptions of scene and landscape are often analogous to impressionist painting. The beginning of 'The End of the Tether' may serve as an example:

> For a long time after the course of the steamer *Sofala* had been altered for the land, the low swampy coast had retained its appearance of a mere smudge of darkness beyond a belt of glitter. The sunrays fell violently upon the calm sea – seemed to shatter themselves upon an adamantine surface into sparkling dust, into a dazzling vapour of light that blinded the eye and wearied the brain with its unsteady brightness.[20]

The difference between a text of this sort and an impressionist seascape painting is that such passages do not stand by themselves, but contribute to a larger thematic whole: their functional role implies symbolic connotations. In the passage from the beginning of 'The End of the Tether', the fact of Captain Whalley's blindness and its ambiguous significance within the context of the story is obliquely suggested by a long sequence of parallel presentations of the interplay of light and shadow, of reflected radiance and darkness. The atmosphere created is momentary and suggests evanescence, and in that respect it shares something with impressionist painting. A pointillist like Signac can produce a tree with pigments which contain almost no green at all;[21] we are told that Conrad and Ford try to convey an emotion, such as love, without naming it.[22] In another important respect Conrad is definitely *not* an impressionist. His fictional writing incorporates impressionist description, but does not lack precise outlines or design.

To Ford, apparently, impressionism hardly means more than a

subjective, personal creative approach to the materials from life which will be absorbed into one's writing.[23] It stresses art, the use of devices, as against mere copying and the use of trite conventions.

When he writes about what he calls the New Form, Ford is usually either vague, especially in the systematic section in which he describes his own and Conrad's thoughts on the novel, or again too precise, too insistent about specific details taken from random examples remembered haphazardly throughout the book. In a text published six years later he claims that 'the conception of novel-writing as an art began for Anglo-Saxondom with Joseph Conrad.'[24] In discussing Ford's observations, it would perhaps be appropriate to follow Roman Ingarden's analysis of a literary *Kunstwerk*[25] and consider the several distinct layers in such a work of art. Firstly that of vocabulary, conversation and cadence – what one calls style in the narrower sense of the word and what corresponds to the interplay of layers 1 and 2 in Ingarden; then the concept of rendering, which may be taken most profitably to correspond to Ingarden's stratum of 'represented objects'; and thirdly, fictional devices, shaping techniques of larger sequential units (Ingarden's layer of 'schematised views').

Among Ford's observations on technique, the most amusing and most frequent are his scattered remarks on Conrad's vocabulary and on their mutual efforts to create style; but there is no room here to remind ourselves of details of that kind.

Such remarks as 'by the use of indirect locutions, together with the rendering of the effects of other portions of speech, you can get a great deal more into a given space' have a wider purport, and it is to practical solutions of this kind that one would like to apply Ford's expression 'to render', a word singularly unspecific when one sees how often Ford introduces it into discussions of literary method. In terms of presentation or showing, definition no. 14 in *Webster's New International Dictionary* applies best; namely, 'to apply a medium, as ink or crayon, to (a drawing) as to bring out form and modelling.' Similarly, the *Shorter Oxford Dictionary*, under definition 4, defines 'render' as 'to reproduce or represent, esp. by artistic means, to depict'. But to Ford it often seems to mean what Henry James calls to 'dramatise', and it makes him aware of the Jamesian belief that 'the object of the novelist is to keep the reader entirely oblivious of the fact that the author exists – even of the fact that he is reading a book.'[26] However, if rendering were to take up too much room, 'you must . . . boldly and remorselessly relate and *risk* the introduction of yourself as an author.'[27] After all, Ford is not a dogmatist, and in the book he repeats twice – in italics – that he and Conrad were aware that theirs was not the only method.[28]

On the highest level of the organisation and movement of a literary work, Conrad's superiority both in awareness of problems and in actual performance is undeniable. Ford himself pointed out that his own search was for a non-literary vocabulary, while Conrad's was for a new form for the novel.[29] 'The writer [i.e. Ford] probably knew more about words, but Conrad had certainly an infinitely greater hold over the architectonics of the novel, over the way a story should be built up so that its interest progresses and grows up to the last word.'[30] Several years before writing his Conrad book, Ford – in *Thus to Revisit* – describes his and Conrad's idea of a novel. He stresses the unity of the work, as opposed to the Victorian practice of presenting a sequence of strong situations. One might add here, by way of comment, that the latter was also the principle on which Flaubert's novels were organised, though in certain scenes they are less melodramatic. For Ford and Conrad on the other hand, 'a Novel was the rendering of an Affair . . . the whole novel was to be an exhaustion of aspects, was to proceed to one culmination, to reveal once and for all, in the last sentence, or the penultimate; in the last phrase, or the one before it – the psychological significance of the whole. (Of course, you might have what is called in music your Coda.)'[31]

One feels that this statement should be modified in so far as the psychological significance is not merely summed up in a single sentence charged with meaning, but is instead conveyed by the situation described at the climax of the action. On the other hand, the coda is not a mere appendix, but an organic part of the whole structure: almost every one of Conrad's novels includes a scene or even a whole episode which, since it follows after the culminating point of the drama, loses in intensity. It usually serves as an indirect retrospective – perhaps through minor narrators – of events which follow the climax of the action but are directly described. By its very nature as an anti-climax the coda serves to reveal the meaning of the relationship which dominates the novel.

But the main principle of growth for a Conradian novel seems to be that of 'justification'. It is described in Ford's Conrad book as consisting of mannerisms, vocabulary and voice, and also ancestry and hereditary characteristics, or at least home surroundings. Its purpose is to convince the reader and to account for the character's effect upon his environment.[32]

It could be said that what justification presents on the level of the story, rendering achieves in terms of details, and the right word in terms of vocabulary. Implicit on all these levels is the principle of *mimesis*. A narrative procedure which may superficially appear as an arbitrary *tour de force*, is seen by Ford to be the very way in which life presents itself to an observer. This is how he explains the rambling manner in which a Marlow builds up a situation. The invention of such a procedure, however, is seen by Ford as an act of consciously artistic interference, a break with the inherited and superficial conventions of moral writing. Thus the principles of imitation of life and of the work as an independent entity which implies its own standards are both present in Ford's evaluative criteria. These are evident in his Conrad book, but can also be discerned in his other works on the art of writing, from *The Critical Attitude* (1911) to *The March of Literature From Confucius To the Present Day* (1939).

According to Ford, a writer has to start from a strong impression and work around it by means of a time shift. This indeed is the manner in which Conrad develops even his tidiest compositions. In *Almayer's Folly*, 'The End of the Tether' and *Victory*, for instance, he starts with a characteristic picture of the protagonist thinking or reminiscing, and works his way back to account for the hero's present position (i.e. achieves 'justification'!), often returning for a short while to the present, and then back again to a stage in his earlier history. Then, the circumstantial framework having been exhausted, the second, more rapid movement of the story begins, replete with action for which one has been prepared by the reminiscence stage.[33]

Ford's Conrad book appeared in the same year as *Some Do Not*, and the principles developed in the memoir can be related as much to Ford's recent work as to Conrad's fiction. But compared to Conrad's more radical indirections and temporal dislocations, Ford's structures, apart from the thoroughly *durchkomponiert*[34] *Good Soldier*, are fairly conservative, except for one basic feature – the consistent interplay of *leit-motifs* in the form of key-words, phrases and situations which recur in the reminiscing minds of characters. Ford does not mention this technique, which is effective for emphasising continuities and for reconcentrating thematic focal points throughout a novel. Yet when he is aware of this kind of procedure, as when he writes on *Nostromo* to Ernest Bendz,[35] Conrad seems to owe the idea to Ford. Characteristically, Conrad's *leit-motifs* are less static and do not occur in the character's mind alone. As M. D. Zabel put it, 'the recurring incident (Jim's jump from the boat, Flora's suicidal appearance at the cliff's edge, Mrs. Schomberg's shawl)' makes 'each of its repetitions serve to mark an expanding realization, an advancing penetration, of the event.'[36]

But *leit-motifs* and the *progression d'effet*[37] rhythm – basically an unhelpful term and not specifically applicable to Conrad and Ford – are not in themselves indicative of the larger movements of fictional organisation. If he occasionally mentions the importance of the point of view, without using the actual term, Ford never seems to be aware of Lubbock's *Craft of Fiction*, which was published three years earlier and dealt with the ways in which a novel achieves its total effect. And yet, as Conrad once put it in a letter to Ford,

> Questions of phrasing and such like – *technique* – may be discussed upon a fragmentary examination. . . But phrasing, expression – *technique* in short – has importance only when the conception of the whole has a significance of its own apart from details that go to make it up – If it (the conception) is imaginative, distinct and has an independent life of its own – as apart from the life of the style.[38]

Conrad himself achieves such a conception of the whole through 'the thought for effects' which, as he says in a letter to Curle in 1923, can be detected in his 'unconventional grouping and perspective'.[39] To talk of one's own art as being 'fluid', as 'depending on grouping (sequence) which shifts, and on the changing light giving varied effects of perspective'[40] is to take the theory of the structuring of fictions onto a level of awareness which is beyond Ford's acutest observations. Conrad borrowed these critical notions from Garnett's study of Turgenev, where they indicate the interrelationships of characters and the relative significance of each in the context of others: 'In the difficult art of literary perspective, in the effective grouping of contrasts in characters and the criss-cross of the influence of the different individuals, lies the secret of Turgenev's supremacy.'[41] Conrad's own use of the word fluidity in the context of 'grouping' and 'perspective' seems to come from Garnett's phrase 'the fluidity of his nature' a few lines further on.

It is interesting that Conrad does not owe this notion of inner structure to the 'formalist' Ford, but to Garnett, a critic whose first interest was to relate art to history and society. And by using it, Conrad adumbrates a highly modern, relativistic, structural but open approach to art, which is closer to Umberto Eco[42] than to Ford Madox Ford. As he continues in his letter to Curle,

> It is in those matters gradually, but never completely, mastered that the history of my books really consists. Of course the plastic matter

of this grouping and of those lights has its importance, since without it the actuality of that grouping and that lighting could not be made evident, any more than Marconi's electric waves could be made evident without the sending-out and receiving instruments. In other words, without mankind my art, an infinitesimal thing, could not exist.[43]

Curiously enough, ten years earlier, in his book on Henry James, Ford implicitly suggested an awareness of these problems. Among extracts from James's prefaces he quotes James's reproduction of Turgenev's account of how he places his characters in mutual relationships.[44]

Another important difference between Conrad and Ford which transcends mere organisation is Conrad's art of achieving symbolic reverberations in the very texture of his stories. He speaks about this occasionally, as in his well-known letter to Barrett H. Clark[45] and in the author's notes to *Heart of Darkness* and 'The Shadow Line'.

In contrast perhaps, by toning down melodramatic effects and re-sounding phrases,[46] Ford somewhat reduced his vision. The implications of *The Good Soldier* and the Tietjens series are close to Conrad's own view of the world, and yet they are indirect: they do not seem to come out of the very language of the story, in the way 'a glow brings out a haze in the likeness of one of these misty halos that sometimes are made visible by the spectral illumination of moonshine.' It may not have been an accident that the writer who developed Conrad's use of thematic imagery saw life as a 'luminous halo'. However, very shortly after the publication of Virginia Woolf's essay in which this reference appeared, Ford recognised the main inheritor of Conrad's innovations. In *The English Review*, in 1920, we read that 'Joyce has carried Conrad's early researches after ramified Form almost as far as they can go.'[47]

NOTES

1. Ford Madox Ford: *Joseph Conrad, A Personal Remembrance* (Boston: Little, Brown and Company, 1924), p. vi. Will hence be referred to as to *Joseph Conrad*.
2. *Joseph Conrad*, pp. vi–vii.
3. *Ibid.*, p. vi.
4. This spelling may be due to Ford's customary carelessness, but it may also be an echo of Ford's frequently repeated notion of Conrad as an 'Eliza-bethan', presumably both because of Conrad's unusual life story and because of the vivid language and the colourful melodramatic plots of his works.

5. *Joseph Conrad*, ibid.
6. *Ibid*.
7. *Ibid*.
8. Ford Madox Hueffer: *Thus to Revisit* (London, 1921), p. 44.
9. c.f. note 3.
10. G. Jean-Aubry: *Joseph Conrad, Life and Letters* (New York, 1927), Vol. II, p. 93.
11. *Ibid.*, p. 92.
12. See note 10.
13. *Joseph Conrad*, p. 136.
14. *Ibid.*, p. 137.
15. *Ibid.*, p. 194.
16. Ford Madox Ford: *Mightier Than the Sword* (London, 1938), pp. 264–92 *passim*; esp. p. 268.
17. Stephen Crane: *Letters* edited by R. W. Stallman and Lillian Gilkes (New York, 1960), pp. 154, 155.
18. *Joseph Conrad's Letters to R. B. Cunninghame Graham*, ed. by C. T. Watts (Cambridge, 1969), p. 130.
19. R. W. Stallman: *Stephen Crane: An Omnibus* (London, 1954), p. 190.
20. Joseph Conrad: *Youth, Heart of Darkness, The End of the Tether* (Dent's Collected Edition; London, 1946), p. 165.
21. Helmut A. Hatzfeld: *Literature Through Art, A New Approach to French Literature* (Chapel Hill, 1969), p. 180.
22. W. F. Wright: 'Conrad's "Rescue" from Serial to Book', *Research Studies of the State College of Washington*, Vol. XIII, no. 4, p. 206. cf. Conrad's 'I don't want the word. I want the idea' even before he met Ford (*Letters from Joseph Conrad*, ed. E. Garnett, Indianapolis and New York, 1962, p. 55).
23. This appears also from his study 'On Impressionism', published ten years before the Conrad book in *Poetry and Drama*, Vol. II, no. 2, June 1914, and Vol. II, no. 4, December 1914.
24. Ford Madox Ford: *The English Novel From the Earliest Days to the Death of Joseph Conrad* (London, 1930), p. 26.
25. Roman Ingarden: *Das literarische Kunstwerk*, Halle, 1931.
26. *Joseph Conrad*, p. 199.
27. *Ibid.*, p. 126.
28. *Ibid.*, pp. 206, 225–6.
29. Ford Madox Hueffer: *Thus to Revisit* (London, 1921), p. 40.
30. *Joseph Conrad*, p. 179.
31. *Thus to Revisit*, p. 44.
32. *Joseph Conrad*, p. 221.
33. The rhythm of events in this part of a novel is defined as *progression d'effet*: every word must carry the story forward, and as the story progresses 'the story must be carried forward faster and faster and with more and more intensity.' (*Joseph Conrad*, p. 225.)
34. H. L. Mencken (*Prejudices*, 5th Series, p. 38) uses this word to denote the verbal-thematic density of 'Heart of Darkness'.
35. G. Jean-Aubry: *Joseph Conrad, Life and Letters*, Vol. II, p. 296.
36. *The Portable Conrad*, Edited and Introduction by Morton Dauwen Zabel, New York, 1947, p. 37.
37. c.f. note 33. According to Ford, 'there is no English equivalent' for '*progression d'effet*' (*Joseph Conrad*, p. 225). He probably borrowed the expression from Flaubert's letter to J.-K. Huysmans, written in February or March 1879: 'The dedication in which you praise me for *Sentimental*

Education has illuminated me on the plan and the fault of your novel, which I did not realize at my first reading. Both *The Vatard Sisters* and *Sentimental Education* lack *falseness of perspective*! There is no progression d'effet. At the end of the book the reader keeps the impression which he had from the beginning. Art is not reality. Whatever one does one is obliged to choose among the elements that it provides. In spite of the School only this is the ideal, which means that it is necessary to choose well.' (Translation mine. Cf. Gustave Flaubert, *Correspondance*, huitième série, Paris, 1930, pp. 223–4.) Flaubert seems to blame both himself and Huysmans for not having organised their respective novels so as to stimulate the reader's interest and capacity of absorption. This is exactly what Ford maintains to have been his own and Conrad's intention.

38. Douglas Goldring, *The Last Pre-Raphaelite* (London, 1948), p. 80.
39. G. Jean-Aubry, *op. cit.*, p. 317.
40. *Ibid.*
41. Garnett's *Turgenev* was published in 1917. The quoted passage, is on pp. 94–5, and comes from the section on *On the Eve* that appeared as a preface to the translation of that novel in 1895. Conrad, in his Foreword to Garnett's book in the form of a letter to the author remembers 'your wonderful Prefaces as they appeared . . . in the volumes of Turgenev's complete edition'. c.f. Conrad's *Notes on Life and Letters*, 1949, p. 45.
42. Umberto Eco: *Opera aperta*, Milano, 1962 (*L'Oeuvre ouverte*, Paris, 1965).
43. G. Jean-Aubry, *op. cit.*, p. 317.
44. Ford Madox Heuffer: *Henry James* (London, 1913), pp. 164–5.
45. G. Jean-Aubry, *op. cit.*, pp. 204–5.
46. *Joseph Conrad*, p. 43.
47. *The English Review*, Vol. XXXI, September 1920, p. 215. c.f. *Thus to Revisit* (London, 1921), p. 65.

15 The Problem of Language*

BARBARA KOCÓWNA

The letters of Tadeusz Bobrowski to his nephew are an excellent and recognised source of material for Conrad's biography. However, they contain items of great interest to which, so far, little attention has been paid. The items referred to are Conrad's glosses on the letters in his own hand. Sometimes they supply a commentary on dramatic conflicts arising from the exchange of ideas between two men who were closely related and yet lived so far from each other; at other times they point out the geographical situation of the sailing pedlar on the seas. They might appear as a symbol or, at any rate, a forecast of decisive changes in the life of this Pole from the Ukraine who entrusted his fates to favourable or unfavourable winds. Whatever else might be said about the glosses, the most striking thing about them is the fact that they were all written in French.

That they should have been written in French is quite characteristic. It seems highly probable that at that time it was the language in which Conrad most easily expressed his thoughts. He had 'forgotten nothing' of his native language, Bobrowski states in his letter to Buszczyński (1879), but five years had passed since Conrad's leaving his country. Living among the French, he became accustomed to using their language every day. He wrote to his uncle in Polish, but undoubtedly it was a language he seldom used at that time. He had to learn English since he intended passing his examinations to become an officer in the merchant navy. Did he exchange letters with anybody else in Poland besides his uncle? As a matter of fact, he probably did not.

The glosses prove that French was the most convenient language for Conrad to use and that he had spoken it with the greatest fluency for a long time. There are two large volumes of his letters collected from different periods which had been written in French, and among all those that have been preserved there are considerably more in French than in Polish. Still, we must take into account the fact that the letters

* An extract from *Polskość Conrada* (*Conrad as a Pole*) (Warsaw, 1967).

to his uncle written during Conrad's youth have been lost and that no trace of them remains. It is true that Bobrowski was pleased with Conrad's Polish, that he blessed him for not forgetting his native language and praised his skill in handling it, though in a letter of 26 May 1882 he did correct Conrad's Polish. Three years later Bobrowski was still praising him for the correctness of his Polish, but a year later, when a plan was being considered for establishing the trading company Barr, Moering and Korzeniowski, and it was suggested that the folders to be circulated among the gentry should be written in French and Polish, Bobrowski wrote that the text should be drawn up by Conrad but that the Polish part had better be sent back to him for correction 'so that they might be phrased in good Polish'. Bobrowski probably meant 'correct Polish', and Conrad's must have shown, by that time, a substantial admixture of both French and English. Nevertheless, Conrad's powers of expression in writing must have been striking since his uncle encouraged him several times to send in contributions about his voyages to the Polish journal *Wędrowiec* in Warsaw.

Polish was Conrad's native speech, the language of those closest and dearest to him; but how distant they were. He had no contacts whatever with day-to-day Polish as it was heard and spoken. A born philologist, he turned passionately to the study of English; and he won this new language for himself by his own effort just as he had won a sailor's life for himself. Yet how painful the experience of adapting to a new environment must have been for this over-sensitive, patriotic man who remained, in spite of his young age, very much of a *vieux Polonais*. He was a conservative, but in the noblest sense of the word. As a conservative nobleman from the Eastern borderland he retained a nineteenth-century way of thinking and, in particular, Polish ways of thought on political matters.

Conrad remained loyal to the generation which had brought him up. He went out into the world equipped with their outlook and their ideas firmly implanted in his mind, and these formed a kind of stereotype for him. Their influence can be clearly seen in his attitude to Russia. He never lost his air of being 'different', and nobody ever took him for an Englishman. Though his command of English was excellent, whenever his emotions were stirred he spoke English with great difficulty, often resorting to exclamations in Polish and French, with the result that nobody could understand him.

A further illustration can be found in 'Amy Foster', whose autobiographical character has never been questioned – particularly since this was confirmed in his wife's memoirs.

Conrad heard Polish voices in his soul; he dreamt of Poland, and – being emotionally a conservative – remained always a Pole even while everything in his everyday life was alien to him. His uncle's repeated admonitions to bear in mind the 'dignity of the nation and families' to which he belonged were for Conrad – engaged at that time in a struggle to be naturalised in an alien country – the proverbial drop that caused an ocean of bitterness to overflow. Konrad Korzeniowski could not see himself returning to his country: the years at sea had developed his inborn love of freedom, which he was unable to renounce. He appreciated the fact that as a Pole and a sailor he had access to anywhere in the world. However, naturalisation was an absolute necessity. Bobrowski enthusiastically welcomes his 'Britisher'; for Conrad it was a move which made life simpler in one sense but still more complicated in another. He was quite free, after that, to visit his uncle without any fear for his personal safety, even if it meant going as far as the Ukraine; but it represented a definite break with the past.

There remained the problem of language. The year 1886 was decisive for Conrad. It was the year in which he passed his examination and obtained his certificate of first mate as a master mariner, became a naturalised British subject and wrote a short story in English, 'Black Mate'. It was clearly a trial of his strength. But had he renounced the Polish language? To think so would be a misunderstanding. When he left his country twelve years earlier with a parcel of Polish books, what could Conrad have known of the familiar sufferings of wanderers in foreign lands, of the feeling of alienation, of the nostalgia? Certainly nothing at all. He still felt very much a stranger in 1886; how did he feel living in a society which was not only unable to understand him but seemed to be positively afraid of him? The episode from 'Amy Foster' is connected in a peculiar manner with the story in 'The Secret Sharer' in which the narrator presents his alter ego, a young man who is being hidden, whose presence is to be kept secret from the ship's crew. The reasons for the captain allowing him to stay on board would be beyond the understanding of a common sailor on duty. This alter ego is an emanation of the artist's inner self.

The same problems of alienation and of a still greater solitude in a new role are given wider scope in Conrad's *Chance*: for reasons known only to the skipper he is not satisfied by the favourable circumstances of his real life. He has achieved what he desired; but along with the feeling of having achieved everything, is one of having lost everything. The literal interpretation of this atmosphere seems impossible; and for Conrad himself it was a matter of feeling rather than of rational understanding. His own comment was that 'all his subconscious skill must have left him.'

What was it that Conrad had to hide? Obviously matters of great complexity, equal to those of the tangles of misunderstandings in *Chance* and 'The Secret Sharer'.

With his sensitive conscience, and his uncle's admonishments to keep up the 'dignity of his nation and his families' in mind, Conrad felt guilty in exactly the same way as that officer in 'The Secret Sharer'. The reader's sympathy is on the side of the guilty man; but he is guilty. He must hide his crime. Conrad's guilt cannot be explained here by straight analogy – and yet he calls the hidden man his ally. He had entered into an alliance with those whose paths through life cannot be simple any longer, but must remain confused until the very end.

One may ask whether putting such a great distance between oneself and one's own country could be considered an act of betrayal? No reader of Conrad would do him the injustice of condemning him on this ground; and yet the writer himself had done so in his conscience. At the same time he realised that it was up to him to make a decisive move: he had to give up being alien, to take roots in his environment, and he succeeded in doing so after a time. But he had come near to wrecking his ship and sinking all of his crew. The loyalty of those strangers, their obedience, discipline and good will made him feel one of them.

Probably the torment resulting from this mood was one of Conrad's long unrevealed secrets; probably it was difficult for him to share his impressions even with his uncle for, obviously, he could not object to what he had achieved. He had wanted a new life, and he simply had to accept it. His feeling of restlessness came to him at first as too great a surprise for him to realise exactly what it involved; the proof of which can be found in his persistence in a state of mind which bordered on madness. Moreover, his uncle belonged to an older generation well accustomed, in face of disappointments, to saying ironically to themselves and others '*Tu l'as voulu, Georges Dandin*'. In this case Conrad could not manage to be ironical. He felt cruelly cheated by fate. It was only the deepest sympathy with man in a general sense – which he had learnt in the Congo – and his meeting a real Almayer that released his understanding of life's complexities and the simplicity of its few truths, one of which was loyalty.

Repeating to himself his uncle's '*Tu l'as voulu, Georges Dandin*', pen in hand, Conrad spun out his visions of ships and people that he had come to know and care for, or which attracted his attention in any way; and he was writing in English. Conrad learned it as the only language which he could use to communicate as a sailor, and the language of common people – of sailors – allowed him to master it in all the wealth of its idiom.[1]

NOTE

1. For a deeper understanding of this problem it might be helpful to examine the correspondence of Wacław Sieroszewski: in his case the process involving the loss of his native language and the loss of contact with his own country is much more clear-cut and less complicated than in that of Conrad. Moreover, it can be documented with the correspondence which has been preserved. Sieroszewski lived in Siberia in 1878–91, after being deported for his participation in the workers' movement. Living in poverty and hardship in the severe Siberian climate, working as a farmer, hunter and poultry farmer, he was at the same time trying his hand at literature and study. A reflection of his experience can be found in his letters to his sister which have been preserved in the National Library in Warsaw and were published in 1964.

16 The True Birthplace of Joseph Conrad

UGO MURSIA

Fifty years after Joseph Conrad's death, we still don't know exactly where he was born. The early biographies published in Conrad's own lifetime – those of Richard Curle[1] and Hugh Walpole[2] – dealt vaguely with his birthplace, speaking of the 'Ukraine in the South of Poland' or of 'Russian Poland in the Kiev area of the Ukraine',[3] and so on.

Writing in 1927, G. Jean-Aubry was the first to settle on a definite place, the city of Berdičev.[4] 'The following year . . . Apollo Korzeniowski rented the Derebczynka property in the jurisdiction of Mohilov, and on 3 December 1857, at Berdiczew, their only child was born,'[5] quoting in a footnote two sentences from the Bobrowski Document.[6] Twenty years later, G. Jean-Aubry himself changed his mind, writing as follows:

> . . . Apollo Korzeniowski loua . . . la propriété Derebczynka, dans le district de Mohilov. Vers la fin de l'automne, Madame Korzeniowska alla passer quelque temps dans une propriété voisine qui appartenait à l'un de ses oncles maternels, et c'est là à Terechowa, près de Berditcheff que, le 21 novembre/3 décembre 1857, elle mettait au monde un fils. . .[7]

Several geographical errors in this passage are to be noted: Derebczynka is indeed in the district of Mogilëv, but by no means near Berdičev, which is two hundred kilometres away, nor Terechovaja, which is about another ten kilometres further than Berdičev. Despite its inaccuracies, this passage may well have prompted Jocelyn Baines, in 1960, to identify the Derebczynka estate as Conrad's birthplace: '. . . the Korzeniowskis . . . took the lease of Derebczynka Manor, near Berdichev in the Ukraine . . . and it was here that Conrad was born.'[8]

Earlier, in 1950, another illustrious biographer, Oliver Warner, had written that 'Conrad was born . . . at Berdiczew near Mohilov in Podolia',[9] which is a geographical error, too.[10]

Zdzisław Najder, the Polish critic and one of the sharpest researchers into Conrad's Polish background, is positive about the city of Berdičev itself being Conrad's birthplace.[11] This is also the position of Norman Sherry, in *Conrad and His World*;[12] but in the caption to a photograph in the book (page 7) he seems to accept instead Jocelyn Baines's version, and writes: 'J. Conrad's birthplace, Derebczynka Manor, near Berdiczov', thereby incurring the same geographical inaccuracy we have seen above.

Thus, the major biographers to date have named three different places: Berdičev, Terechovaja and Derebczynka.

On the whole, it would seem that the matter, perhaps, was not given as much critical investigation as it deserves. At first sight, the best way to do so would be to go back to the documentary sources, mainly the Bobrowski Document and the so-called birth certificate, which is kept in Cracow.

The city of Berdičev is mentioned twice in the Bobrowski Document (the same two passages quoted, as we have seen, by G. Jean-Aubry):

I forgot to mention that you came into this world on the 21st November 1857 at Berdyczów, where you were christened with water, and your christening was confirmed with oil in 1862 in Żytomierz, by the Rev. Szczeniowski.[13]

You were born on the 21st November 1857, at Berdiczów./Your baptism took place in Żytomierz in 1860./Your birth certificate can be found at Żytomierz in the Rom. Cath. Consistory.[14]

The inconsistencies are quite apparent (*1862* and *1860*, for instance).[15] Whether they are evidence of a general inaccuracy or a clue to some other cause of confusion in respect of the facts concerned, they are likely to make the Bobrowski Document less reliable as a documentary source.

Definite confirmation of Conrad's birthplace should be found, then, in the document, two copies of which are kept in the Jagellion Library of Cracow – an original copy in Russian, and a Polish translation dated 10 November 1872.[16]   .

This 'excerpt … from the above-mentioned Parish Register' (of Żitomie), declared 'valid as certificate of baptism' is to be identified with the 'birth certificate' mentioned by Bobrowski. Unfortunately, on closer examination, this document reveals some amazing and also rather disappointing things.

We note, first of all, that both the Russian original and the Polish translation give (in long hand) the year of birth as being 1856. Now, that an official document of this kind should mistake – of all things – the date of birth seems to me very strange indeed. Must we add to the many mysteries surrounding Conrad even the year of his birth? For the time being, at least, it is a matter that I would prefer to leave for further research.

The second and most disconcerting thing one notices, is that *no birthplace is mentioned* in either of the two versions of the document. It only states, in fact, that confirmation took place in the year 1862 in the Catholic parish church of Žitomir, and that the christening had been celebrated, in the same month and year of the birth (21 November 1856!), by Father Romanski, a Carmelite *from* the monastery of Berdičev: this does not mean necessarily that it was performed *in* the monastery of Berdičev, and even less that the birth took place at Berdičev.

The place of birth is consistently ignored throughout this document, which can hardly be considered a birth certificate. On the other hand, the great number of names of witnesses remembered as having attended the christening (the same month and year of the birth) tend to suggest a desire to leave no doubt whatsoever as for the legitimate birth of the child, even if the place of the christening is mentioned vaguely or not at all.

An old photograph of a house – traditionally taken as being the place where Conrad was born – was first published, as far as I know, at the beginning of volume XV (*Victory*) of the Medallion Edition in 1925.[17] The caption says: 'The house in the Ukraine, Poland, where Joseph Conrad was born, on December 6th (*sic*) 1857.' The same photograph was published again in 1935 by Conrad's wife opposite page 41 of her book, *Joseph Conrad and His Circle*.[18] The caption reads: 'Berdiczew – the house where Joseph Conrad was born.' Lately, as we have seen, the photograph has been published by Norman Sherry, identifying it as 'Derebczynka Manor'.

So there are different, even contrasting views in respect of this photograph, too; but, first of all, we must ask whether this really is the place of Conrad's birth.

It is unlikely that Jessie Conrad would have had any reason for picking out a house in a nondescript photograph as her husband's birthplace. The author's son, Borys Conrad, says in a letter he kindly wrote me on 18 February 1974:

. . . I think the best way in which I can help you is to . . . tell you quite simply what my father told me himself and showed me in the family album . . . My father disliked that album, which he referred as 'The Graveyard' and always discouraged us from looking at it. Nevertheless, he did go through it with me on one or two occasions and on these occasions he invariably pointed to the photograph to which you referred in your letter . . . and told me 'I was born in that house', so you have the answer direct from him.

And in a letter which I received on 19 May, the author's other son, John Conrad, writes: 'I can only tell you that my father used to say that that was where he was born. . .' Apart from the fact that no one has ever doubted this identification, it is clear that the photograph itself was among those kept by the writer and that he showed it to members of his family as representing his birthplace.

But where is, or was, that house? During a trip I made to Russia in the autumn of 1972, I was told that a Soviet travel journal had dealt with the subject of Conrad's birthplace, and later, in Italy, I received a copy. Under the title 'Conrad's Sentry' the article by Dmitri Urnov, reports, among other things:[19]

> . . . At the Berdičev station square I showed directly to the taxi-driver the photograph of the house [of J. Conrad], which was so unique, with its towers and clocks, that he would have to recognize it if it still existed. And indeed the taxi-driver replied at once: 'Yes, come along! It's at Ivankovcy.' . . .
>
> 'For many years,' Borys Conrad writes in a letter, 'my father carried this photograph with him.' The photograph is now alive before our eyes; the house with the towers, the rivulets of water and the pool in the back. 'And Terechovaja?' . . . 'Terechovaja', replied the taxi-driver, 'is about twenty kilometers on the other side of Berdičev. . .'

The drawing illustrating the article is apparently based on the famous photograph. Later, in answer to a direct question, Mr Urnov wrote to me:

> . . . The house called 'the house where Conrad was born' and its photograph as found in Jessie Conrad's _Conrad and His Circle_ is situated in Ivankovcy, a village a few kilometers from Berdičev. Near it is the landowner's estate built later, where the school now stands. The owner had Conrad's house rebuilt as a riding-school. Today the building is used as a warehouse. . .[20]

Professor Z. Najder, whom I informed of this in view of his current work on Conrad's biography, replied as follows:

. . . Conrad's birthplace. In *all* documentary sources it is given simply as Berdiczów. Derebczynka, which his father at that time administered, is in another 'gubernia', over 200 kilometres south: there was no other place of that name. (*Słownik Geograficzny Królestwa Polskiego i innich ziem słowiańskich*, vol. I, Warsaw 1880.) Iwankowce, mentioned by Urnov – some eight kilometres from Berdiczów – was called by the same name at the time of C.'s birth (*Słownik* . . . vol. III, Warsaw, 1882.) Of course we cannot exclude the possibility that Conrad was born there but this leaves unanswered the questions: (a) Why was he baptized in Berdiczów, and not in the parish of Murachwa, where Iwankowce belonged? (b) Why is the name of the place, and that of its owner (Żurowski) never mentioned in documents, letters, memoirs, nor in the poem which Apollo wrote upon the birth of his son (dated 4 December 1857, at Berdiczów?). I suspect some misunderstanding. . .

To the first question one can reply that, as we have seen, it is not at all certain that the christening took place in Berdičev.

To the second question one could reply with a further query: why, throughout his lifetime, did Conrad never let his biographers know that he had been born at Berdičev, a town of some importance, leaving instead the matter of his birthplace rather vague? My answer is because Berdičev was not his real birthplace.

A bit of guesswork could provide several explanations in answer to this second question, relating to the circumstances accompanying the birth or eventually to some stratagem adopted so that in the future it would be possible for the newborn child to claim some other nationality than Russian.

In a second letter, Professor Z. Najder insists: '. . . what, I believe, settles the problem of Conrad's birthplace are: 1. birth certificate (in Cracow), 2. a baptismal poem written by his father. . .' It is interesting to note, in passing, that if the poem was 'baptismal', for the christening and not for the birth of the child, its date (4 December 1857 – the very day after the birth?) is worth considering. The suggestion that it was dated from Berdičev is by no means conclusive, for the reasons given above. The tone of the poem itself would rather seem to support the possibility that there may have been a desire to conceal, or at least not to mention for sure, a birthplace which was not part of the mother country: '. . . My child, my son . . . tell yourself that you are without land, without love, without Fatherland, without humanity – as long as Poland, our Mother, is enslaved.'[21]

Finally, as we have repeatedly seen, the least conclusive and even the most ambiguous of all the documents is actually the famous certificate, not of birth, nor of baptism, but, in fact of *confirmation* (to which the word 'baptism' seems also to apply in Russian), which is kept in Cracow.

Therefore, if the photograph referred above portrays the house where the writer was born; if, as it seems from the statements made by D. Urnov, this house is still standing in a locality not far from Berdičev called Ivankovcy, which had the same name at the time of Conrad's birth, as appears from the information from *Słownik* etc. supplied by Z. Najder; then it follows that Conrad's real birthplace should be Ivankovcy, and not Berdičev as uncle Tadeusz Bobrowski wrote and various biographers continue to claim; and even less should it be Derebczynka or Terechovaja.[22]

NOTES

1. R. Curle, *Joseph Conrad: a Study* (London: Kegan Paul, Trench, Trübner & Co., 1914), p. 15. The author, among other things, indicates the date of birth as 6 instead of 3 December (21 November, according to the Julian calendar).
2. H. Walpole, *Joseph Conrad* (London: Nisbet & Co., 1916), p. 8. This author repeats the same error as R. Curle concerning the date of birth.
3. See, for instance, the anonymous pamphlet *Joseph Conrad – A Sketch with a Bibliography* (Garden City, New York: Doubleday Page & Co., 1924), p. 8.
4. For the spelling of geographical names I follow the diacritical transcription from the Russian except in quotations from other authors, where I maintain the spelling used by them. Thus, it is clear that Berdičev is the Russian spelling, Berdyczów the Polish spelling, Berdichev or Berdiczew the English spelling, and Berditcheff the French spelling.
5. G. Jean-Aubry, *Joseph Conrad – Life and Letters* (London: Heinemann, 1927), vol. I, p. 4.
6. The English translation of the complete text appears in Z. Najder, *Conrad's Polish Background* (London: Oxford University Press, 1964), pp. 183–202.
7. G. Jean-Aubry, *Vie de Conrad* (Paris: Gallimard, 1947), p. 18.
8. J. Baines, *Joseph Conrad – A Critical Biography* (London: Weidenfeld and Nicolson, 1960), p. 7.
9. O. Warner, *Joseph Conrad*, 'Writers and Their Work Series', (London: Longmans, Green & Co., 1950). In the subsequent book which appeared in 1951 in the series 'Men and Books' from the same publisher, there is only an indication of Berdičev (p. 2).
10. Mogilëv on the Dniester is situated in Podolia on the border with Moldavia. It should not be confused with Mogilëv on the Dnieper, which is east of Minsk in Belorussia (White Russia).
11. *Op. cit.*, p. 2, and in various direct communications, as further specified.
12. London, Thames & Hudson, 1972.

13. See Z. Najder, *op. cit.*, p. 184.
14. Najder, pp. 201–2.
15. The 'Document' contains a number of chronological errors; for instance, it states that Conrad's father moved to Warsaw in the spring of 1862 and that he was arrested in the autumn of the same year, when it is generally known that all this happened the year before.
16. Through the courtesy of Professor Mroczkowski of the University of Cracow, I obtained a photographic copy of both documents as well as the English translation of the same. Owing to the capital importance of the interpretation of these documents for Conrad's biography, in due time I shall reproduce them, so that scholars can collate them more carefully than I have found it possible to do, despite the help provided by Russian and Polish friends.
17. *The Works of Joseph Conrad* (London: Gresham Publishing Co., 1925–27), 22 volumes.
18. Jessie Conrad, *Joseph Conrad and His Circle* (London: Jarrolds, 1935; second edition, Port Washington, New York: Kennikat Press, 1964).
19. *Vokrug Sveta* (Round the World), Moscow, No. 2, February 1972, pp. 45–9.
20. A further letter from Mr Urnov, dated 25 February 1975 (after this paper was first written), confirms: 'I was to Berdicev some years ago but I refer to my notebook. The building with a tower which is shown as the house of his birth in Jessie Conrad book is standing on the outskirts of the town in a small village named to-day Ivankovcy. It is fifteen minutes by car along the railway to Moscow on the right side of it. The house is now in possession of a secondary local school and used as a store. According to the local people it was used as such for a long time so far as . . . the last owner of the estate built up near it another house of quite different type and converted the former one into a stable or a riding ménage. I talked to one old man who remembered the clock on the tower working and he himself as a boy used to climb the tower to shift the hands . . . (signed) D. M. Urnov, Member of A. M. Gorky Institute. P.S. I am still working over Joseph Conrad's places in Russia description and if I make the photo of the house with the tower (that I failed to do then being lack of a camera) I shall gladly send you a copy.'
21. Najder, *op. cit.*, p. 5.
22. Terechovaja, about ten kilometres from Berdičev, was the property of the writer's maternal uncle Adolf Pilchowski, mentioned in the Cracow excerpt as having been the godfather at little Conrad's baptism.

17 Conrad's Reception in Poland for the Last Sixty Years*

ADAM GILLON

On 14 October 1874, Conrad left Poland as a youth of not yet seventeen. When he returned for a visit forty years later, in 1914, he was an established English novelist, with his major artistic achievement behind him. As early as 1896, the year in which his first novel was published, two articles about his work had appeared in *Kraj* (*Homeland*, No. 41, St Petersburg) and in *Przegląd Literacki* (*Literary Review*, No. 11, Cracow). Other articles that followed bore ample testimony to the fact that Conrad was not a stranger to the Polish public. If anything, a few of the early critical pieces had turned him into a rather controversial figure in his native land, for example Wincenty Lutosławski's '*Emigracja Zdolności*' ('The Emigration of Talent', *Kraj*, No. 12, 14, Petersburg, 1899), Kazimierz Waliszewski's '*Polski powieściopisarz w angielskiej literaturze*' ('A Polish Novelist in English Literature', *Ibid*, 1904), and T. Ż. Skarszewski's and Eliza Orzeszkowa's denunciatory articles in *Kraj* (1899).

1914 was a memorable year for Conrad. During his stay in Zakopane he established a more intimate contact with the Polish language and literature. But, more importantly, the year marks a turning point in his Polish 'career'. From the first, Polish critics were preoccupied with Conrad's personality, regarding the novelist as *Polish*. In 1914 Marian Dąbrowski published his 'Conversation with J. Conrad' in *Tygodnik Ilustrowany* (*Illustrated Weekly*, No. 16), in which Conrad confessed to the Polishness in his work but also stressed the fact that, after all, he was an *English* writer. To some extent, the biographical emphasis (which at times lapsed into pure chauvinism and which has still not been eradicated from Polish Conradiana), represented an aspect of Young Poland – a literary movement which coincided with Conrad's

* Parts of this chapter are included in my article 'Conrad in Poland', *The Polish Review*, New York, XIX, Nos. 3–4 (1974), pp. 3–28.

early creative years. As in Polish and European romanticism, the personal life of the author was considered to be an integral part of critical evaluation; and since Conrad was initially viewed as a Polish novelist, his work was discussed by such luminaries of Polish literary criticism as Wacław Borowy, Julian Krzyżanowski, Juliusz Kleiner and Joseph Ujejski, to mention a few. Some of the leading Polish novelists, such as Stefan Żeromski, Maria Dąbrowska, Juliusz Kaden-Bandrowski and Jan Parandowski, also wrote about Conrad. The Polish critics examined and re-examined the key elements of the novelist's life: Conrad's decision to leave Poland, his writing in a foreign language, and his attempts to return to Poland. They also stressed Conrad's loneliness and his inner conflicts, and found evidence of two major Polish literary traditions in his work: romanticism and positivism.

Polish critics abroad also stressed the element of tradition in their approach to Conrad whom they regarded as *their* precursor. Thus, for example, on the title page of *Conrad Żywy* (*The Living Conrad*, London, 1957), a collective work of Polish authors (published under the sponsorship of the Union of Polish Writers Abroad to celebrate the centenary of Conrad's birth), there appears a motto from *Lord Jim*: 'He was one of us.' This personal identification with Conrad affected the nature of Conradian studies among the *émigré* writers, some of whom had begun their Conradian criticism before 1939 (e.g. Tymon Terlecki, Joseph H. Retinger, Maria Kuncewicz, Wit Tarnawski, Alexander Janta).

While pre-war Conradian studies were conducted chiefly by specialists in Polish literature and by Polish novelists and poets, the post-war period of Conradian scholarship has been marked by the emergence of Polish specialists in English literature, notably Stanisław Helsztyński and Róża Jabłkowska. Both sought to present the personality of Joseph Conrad in terms of the Polish positivist movement, rejecting the romantic–modernist approaches. Stefan Zabierowski, whose *Conrad w Polsce* (*Conrad in Poland*)[1] provides a much needed systematic analysis of Conrad's reception in Poland during the past seven decades, believes that the 'new' critics are only partly successful because they are still operating within the vicious circle of the largely biographical study of Conrad; furthermore, Conrad's cultural ties with the romantics and the Young Poland movement cannot be challenged by a mere literary hypothesis; they can easily be ascertained as objective facts, corroborated by Conrad's correspondence no less than by the textual affinities, and also by the favourable reception of Conrad's work during the period of Young Poland.

Polish critics endlessly mull over Conrad's motives for emigrating. Only a few instances of this obsessive topic can be cited here. Thus, Rafał Blüth blamed Polish society itself, both the superpatriots and the opportunistic Stańczyk group. He suggested later (in 1936) that Conrad's departure from Cracow was an act of psychic self-defence, a conscious break with the whole gnawing heritage of his father and with the oppressive atmosphere of the national struggle, if not with the world of European culture. The flight to the sea was an attempt to solve his feelings of loneliness. Conrad's writing career was both testimony of his new-found adaptation to society, and a release from his early psychic complexes. His remaining in Poland would have been detrimental not only to Conrad the writer but also Conrad the man. To upbraid Conrad for leaving Poland and for concealing his Polish origin for a time is simplistic, uncharitable and absurd.

A similar view was advanced a few years earlier in *The Polish Heritage of Joseph Conrad* (1930) by Gustav Morf who, however, did not have access to Blüth's source materials. Other critics such as Wit Tarnawski, Stefan Zabłocki, Jerzy Andrzejewski and Mieczysław Lisiewicz, also expounded the theory that the defeatist atmosphere in Galicia after the uprising caused Conrad's departure.

According to Zabierowski, all these interpretations fit into the romantic stereotype of Conrad's biography. He suggests that the critics were trying to link Conrad's emigration with that of the leading representatives of the cultural elite. There was the romantic tradition of 'great' emigrants who were motivated by patriotic impulses: Mickiewicz, Słowacki and, to some extent, Krasiński. Thus it was possible to interpret Conrad's departure as having been motivated by patriotism. In 1927, for example, Karol Wiktor Zawodziński[2] stated that Conrad's emigration was proof of his 'excessive' love of fatherland and not, as Eliza Orzeszkowa claimed, the absence of it. Conrad allegedly left for England because it counter-balanced the hated Czarist Russia. The anti-Russian stance of England during the Russo–Japanese War proved that this was no fiction. Artur Prędsk showed the 'mythological' character of Zawodziński's hypothesis. He pointed out that what should be discussed was why Conrad began writing in English rather than what motives prompted him to leave Poland. Zawodziński had the old-fashioned 'romantic' notion that literature could evolve only from patriotic impulses. This discussion deteriorated into personal polemics. It is interesting that Zawodziński himself retracted his views ten years later, when he argued that Conrad's emigration was caused by his refusal to reconcile himself with the surrounding world, and that therefore it had all the characteristics of the romantic rebellion against reality. Z. Najder rejected the view that the Galician atmosphere or political motivations had much if anything to do with the actions of a seventeen-year-old boy. 'There is no single communication which testified that either Korzeniowski himself, or anybody from his environment, considered the departure to France from the "national" point of view.'[3] Zabierowski contradicts Najder vehemently, quoting Conrad's references to patriotism in the Author's Note to *Nostromo*, and a letter to his father's friend, Stefan Buszczyński: '. . . I always remember your charge to me as I was leaving Cracow. "Remember", you said, "wherever you are that you are sailing toward Poland!" This I did not forget – and will not forget!'[4]

Polish critics vied with one another in an undeclared contest as to who could offer the most ingenious reason for Conrad's departure from Poland. Fascinating though the numerous theories are, the scope of this essay does not permit the author to present the views of eminent writers like Roman Dyboski, Witold Chwalewik, Witold Ostrowski, Boy-Żeleński, Joseph Ujejski, Zbigniew Grabowski, Wit Tarnawski, Stanisław Sierosławski, Joseph Retinger and others.[5]

During the two decades between the wars, Polish critics argued with their foreign counterparts over whether Conrad could have written in French, a hypothesis advanced by, among others, John Galsworthy and J. H. Retinger.[6] The Poles refuted the idea. The notion of a conscious choice by Conrad was unpalatable, since it would have implied a deliberate severance of his ties with Poland. Yet it was a Polish critic, Róża Jabłkowska, who showed that the idea of writing in French was indeed conceived by Conrad himself.[7]

Polish critics emphasised Conrad's loneliness, which they saw as a typical romantic trait; some indicated that Conrad was a loner on land as well as on the sea and, moreover, had been alone in Poland. Only Zdzisław Najder differed: to him the disastrous Congo expedition was Conrad's first and last attempt to become a social animal, a cog in the social machine. The failure of this attempt deepened Conrad's essential asocial stance, and thenceforth he avoided any intimate contact with any class, or professional or institutional group. The novelist brought this sense of alienation into his work, which partly accounts for the difficulty he experienced in becoming a popular writer.

Hanna Peretiakowicz tried to attribute Conrad's apartness in the English literary environment to the Korzeniowski tradition of landed gentry – a rather simplistic position, in Zabierowski's view. Conrad did not regard his writing as an expensive hobby, but always stressed the dignity of his profession, aiming for the highest standards of art. The Poles thus connect Conrad's psychic apartness with the ideals he had carried out of Poland.

Zabierowski refers to the significant title of Adam Gillon's book, *The Eternal Solitary: A Study of Joseph Conrad*, which explores the theme of isolation in Conrad's life and works. He regards critics like Gillon as *émigré* writers, suggesting that they are preoccupied with this particular trait of the novelist's personality.[8] While Zabierowski does not support this argument with specific illustrations, his statement does apply, to some extent, to most Polish critics who agree that the tragedy of loneliness was a prime motive in Conrad's becoming a writer. Wit Tarnawski summed up the view (shared also by H. G. Wells and Bertrand Russell) by stating that literary fame, family, and friendships notwithstanding, Conrad remained to the end a stranger in his adopted fatherland, seeking a safe haven in his creative work.

The Polish personality of Conrad, naturally, captivated critics and readers in Poland. Conrad was born in Eastern Poland, or the Ukraine, where the sense of national consciousness among the Poles was rather strong. Moreover, as Joseph Ujejski noted, Conrad's birthplace was in the general area where Polish Romanticism was born, and the future novelist was of 'splendidly romantic parents – in thought, action and martyrdom'. From those parts came other great writers: Mickiewicz, Słowacki, Zaleski, Goszczyński, Czajkowski, Witnicki, Syrokomla, and 'the last Romantic playwright', Apollo Korzeniowski, Conrad's father. Thus, Conrad grew up in the lands celebrated by the Romantic poets in *Maria* and *Beniowski*.

Some Polish critics suggested that Conrad liked the sea because it reminded him of the Ukrainian steppes. Witold Chwalewik believes that in Polish Romantic literature, which Conrad knew well, the sea and the steppes are interchangeable symbols of infinity. Stefan Żeromski saw Conrad's crib surrounded by a group of Poland's faithful knights, by exiles and deportees – all men devoted to the Cause. Among those who gazed at young Conrad was that 'arch-knight of the 1863 uprising, Stefan Bobrowski', Conrad's uncle. Adolf Nowaczyński claims that Mickiewicz's son, Władysław (who was an emissary in Żytomir), must have rocked young Conrad on his knees. Rafał Blüth stresses that for the Poles, such names and concepts as Konrad, Konradian, Konradianism are the quintessence of their Romanticism. He holds that Conrad's dropping of his family name was a conscious act, stressing the Romantic association of Mickiewicz's KONRAD. And Conrad's own father, Apollo Korzeniowski, wrote to his son:

Baby, son, tell yourself,
You're without land, without love,
Without fatherland, without mankind
As long as Poland-Mother is entombed.
For your sole family
Is that of mourning – that of faith;
It is complete, though a victim.[9]

In her letters to her husband, Ewelina Korzeniowska, Conrad's mother, recalls how the patriotic population of the Ukraine began to dress in black in a demonstrative manner before the January uprising. Little Conrad, too, donned the mourning garb, at his own request. From the first, therefore, Conrad appears to the Poles as the spitting image of his self-sacrificing, patriotic parents.

Stefan Żeromski and Stefan Pomarański uncritically accepted the somewhat biased fiction of Tadeusz Bobrowski's *Memoirs* that Ewelina Korzeniowska went into exile of her free will, taking her little son along. Rafał Blüth proved that this martyrological legend was false; Zdzisław Najder confirmed after the war that Ewelina, like her husband, was sentenced to exile by a Russian court. The biographical error is found even in the fairly recent work of Róża Jabłkowska.[10] But Zabierowski cannot disagree with Wit Tarnawski's conclusion that Conrad had the most Polish childhood and youth one could imagine.

The early biographers, scholars and pseudo-scholars took a rather simplistic view of Conrad's youth. He was an adventurous young lad who joined first the French, then the British Merchant Marine out of boredom, or because of his romantic *Wanderlust*. Like all great romantics, the future novelist had to embark on an exciting tour of the East, which eventually provided a source of inspiration for his creative efforts.

The positivist school showed up another aspect of Conrad's maritime period revealing, among other things, the role of money in his life. Thus, for example, by the time Conrad reached the age of thirty the sum of over fifty thousand francs had been spent out of the estate of Uncle Tadeusz Bobrowski, who had provided a solid financial base for Conrad's career. Róża Jabłkowska's monograph stresses the social and economic factors of Conrad's environment. But she also contends that the influence of Bobrowski went beyond financial assistance to his nephew. He profoundly affected Conrad's moral views. Not only did Conrad paraphrase whole passages of his uncle's *Memoirs*, but he was also planning to write a history of the Ukrainian peasants' enfranchisement, based on his uncle's writings and his activities on behalf of the peasants. Moreover, he learned from Bobrowski's writings the ironic method of presenting reality. Uncle Tadeusz also taught the young man respect for work and hard-earned money. He tried to persuade Conrad that armed resistance to the conqueror made no sense, but that the Poles had to cultivate their national cultural traditions, and suggested that Conrad write travel pieces for Polish newspapers.

It is clear, therefore, that the posthumous edition of the *Memoirs* constituted another literary source, and that the young officer of the British Merchant Marine learned his early lessons in devotion to duty, scepticism towards life, and respect for reason from his Polish uncle, who was considered a somewhat anachronistic rationalist in the eighteenth century style. The clash between the romantic and the positivist appraisals re-emphasises the basic conflicts in Conrad himself: he wanted to be faithful to his father's injunctions yet also heeded the advice of Bobrowski, who caricatured Apollo's ideas. Only when Conrad found his independent way was he able to continue on the path set for him by his father, with some deviations induced by Uncle Tadeusz. The positivist criticism, then, without denying Apollo's role in Conrad's life, attributes much greater achievements to Tadeusz Bobrowski, who was regarded as a positivist in the Polish sense of the word.

Conrad's complex, contradictory nature baffles Polish critics who cannot separate Conrad the Pole from Conrad the English novelist. Zabierowski's account of the continuing debate on the subject is fairly thorough and balanced. If it appears redundant, it is mainly because the same 'Polish' problems tend to be magnified, at times out of all proportion, by the critics in Poland. Thus, for example, *Prince Roman*, a minor piece in Conrad's novelistic canon, receives a great deal of attention primarily because of its theme rather than its intrinsic artistic merit. Polish critics harp on the duality of Conrad's nature, occasionally drawing sweeping conclusions about his philosophical outlook. To some of them, Conrad is no less than a romantic *wieszcz*, a poet-prophet. Indeed, it is not too difficult to find some prophetic statements in Conrad's fiction, essays and correspondence. But again, in their ardent desire to depict Conrad as a modern Mickiewicz or Krasiński, Polish critics tend to exaggerate Conrad's art of presaging the future.

Yet others, like Róża Jabłkowska, Witold Chwalewik, Wit Tarnawski, Adam Gillon, Przemysław Mroczkowski, Maria Dąbrowska, and Stanisław Helsztyński, have related Conrad's work to some of the traditions of nineteenth and twentieth century English and European literature. Some Polish critics agreed that Conrad was basically a cosmopolitan writer who could not fit into any narrow national pigeon-hole of classification – for example, Zygmunt Nowakowski, Adam Gillon, Roman Dyboski. It appears then that Polish critics of Conrad have gone a long way from the early parochial views to a broad consideration of Conrad as a world writer. Thus, contemporary Polish students of the novelist can now examine not only Conrad's affinities with Polish romantic poets, but also with English, French and German romanticism.

Polish scholars have also touched upon Conrad's connections with Victorian literature, mentioning Charles Darwin and Thomas Carlyle as prime philosophical influences. Aniela Kowalska considered Conrad's cult of heroism to be similar to the philosophical views of Thomas Carlyle, citing his *Sartor Resartus* rather than *On Heroes, Hero-Worship and the Heroic in History*, a volume more likely to have suggested to Conrad a notion of heroism. Maurycy Staniewski, Róża Jabłkowska and Witold Chwalewik dwell on the Dickensian elements in Conrad. Gillon mentions the resemblance between Conrad and Matthew Arnold; Dyboski, the resemblance with George Eliot, Thomas Hardy and Rudyard Kipling; Chwalewik, the connections with Henry Fielding; and Jabłkowska says that Conrad dreamt of becoming 'a minor Thackeray'. All these analogies are more important as testimony to the continuing expansion of critical vistas by Polish Conradians than as solid comparativist textual studies of Conrad and other writers.

The initial impact of Conrad's work was that of a Polish Jack London. His 'maritime' aspects was stressed and only a few scattered attempts were made to relate his fiction to Polish literary tradition. He was viewed as a romantic or as a realist, with most critics ignoring his contribution to the narrative art of the twentieth century. During the twenties Polish critics were primarily interested in Conrad the thinker, the moralist. The thirties saw some decline of interest in Conrad, mainly because of the direction Polish literature had taken. Conrad now appeared to some leading critics like Joseph Ujejski as an incorrigible conservative, a term which did not endear him to the average member of the hard-pressed Polish intelligentsia. This was an ironic reversal of the earlier view of Conrad as being somewhat too *avant-garde*. The thirties regarded him as rather anachronistic. He was charged with decadence, with smacking too much of the Young Poland style, with being a mere 'visionary' – in those days of practical preoccupations a term less than complimentary.

A few Polish periodicals reprinted Upton Sinclair's derogatory statements about Conrad as a writer who had sold out to capitalist interests, notably to shipping companies. This was a classic example, according to Zabierowski, of 'vulgar sociologism' which, however, did not have a lasting negative effect.[11]

One can only wonder whether the reasons for the Conradian renaissance during the past two decades are similar to those which made Conrad's work and life an existential or a romantic phenomenon in Poland in the years of World War II. Conrad's writings appealed to the Poles under Nazi occupation because the daily existence of the population was often no less dramatic and fraught with moral choices than that of many Conradian protagonists. Men and women had to make the either-or kind of decision, and even when decisions were made in terms of a profound moral conviction, they did not prevent the conditions of isolation nor the feelings of guilt. Like Lord Jim, Razumov, Heyst and other Conradian heroes, ordinary Poles often had to choose defeat which, nonetheless, constituted moral victory; or they could save themselves from their German oppressors at the price of moral defeat. Moreover, Conrad's fiction appeared to the reader of those war-torn years as more than literature; it was read with a special kind of reverence, reserved for works revealing the true nature of surrounding reality. Conrad's portraits of isolated heroes, who know darkness and despair and whose tragic fate is an affirmation of man's ideal values, had a familiar ring; they were recognisable depictions of men and women whose daily actions spelled self-destruction and an ironic triumph. 'For us,' wrote Jan Joseph Szczepański, 'Conrad was as topical as never before. His books turned into collections of practical maxims for men fighting alone and in darkness.'[12] Little wonder, then, that nobody during the war questioned Conrad's biography, nor were any charges of treason levelled at the novelist. The word 'treason' has assumed a tragic resonance.

Ironically, it was the very nature of Conrad's ethical view of the universe that provoked a new quarrel about his position in the period after the war had ended. The memory of the Warsaw Uprising, ruthlessly crushed by the Germans, was still fresh, and people were looking for scapegoats who could be blamed for the tragic blood-bath. Critical voices were raised against the Polish Underground Army (*Armja Krajowa*, often referred to as A.K.) and the attitudes which were responsible for the hopeless struggle in Warsaw.

The new intellectuals of the Left, connected with the weekly *Kuźnica* (Ironworks), launched a campaign for the minds of the young by way of attacking Conrad as a moralist of the middle classes. Their chief spokesman was Jan Kott whose essay 'On the Lay Tragedy' struck a severe critical blow at Conrad's ethos, without, however, negating Conrad's artistic achievement. Conrad's philosophy which, Kott contends, defies history,

> is in reality, the concrete social reality, obedience to the laws of a world which one innerly despises; it is a rejection of one's right to rebel. Conradian fidelity to oneself is the fidelity of slaves, for a slave is he who obeys the lord whom he despises, and cares only about his inner rectitude.[13]

Najder views Kott's position as being primarily a political settling of accounts with the ideologists of A.K., which opposed the Communist regime in Poland, rather than as a literary condemnation of Conrad's work. Writers like Maria Dąbrowska, Joseph Chałasiński and Antoni Gołubiew attempted to counteract the attempt to compromise Conrad's stature, mainly by encouraging the preservation of past appraisals which dated from the pre-war period. Najder himself took an enlightened, balanced stance toward Conrad, which he has since maintained, emerging as one of the leading Conradian critics in the country who can draw the line between the early emphasis on Conrad as a romantic and the perfunctory dismissal of the artist on ideological grounds. Thus he now refers to Kott's view of Conrad as 'a primitive interpretation'.[14] Primitive or not, the official policy of the government obviously favoured Kott's narrow evaluation of Conrad and, to all intents and purposes Conrad became a non-person for the ten years following the publication of Kott's famous (or infamous, depending on one's point of vantage) essay. Publication of his works ceased.

The lean years of Conrad's popularity in Poland during the decade of 1945–55 have since been superseded by the fat years of publication and its attendant outpouring of critical writings. According to Zdzisław Najder, the editor of Conrad's selected stories in Polish, Conrad's popularity in the land of his birth is now at its highest, if one considers the number of recent editions of the novelist's work, the size of the printings, and their ratio to the population of the country.

Najder divides Conrad's reception in Poland into five periods:[15] 1896–1918; 1918–39; 1939–45; 1945–55; 1955 to the present. The first is marked by the controversy concerning the 'emigration of talent' – the charges levelled against Conrad by W. Lutosławski and Eliza Orzeszkowa, and a relative dearth of critical writings. Najder mentions three names only: Maria Komornicka,[16] Wiktor Gomulicki[17] and Stanisław Brzozowski,[18] whose critiques he finds 'very interesting'.

The second phase is characterised by the proliferation of Conrad's work in Polish translations, including two editions of collected works. The first, *Pisma Wybrane* (Selected Writings), begun in 1922 with *Almayer's Folly*, translated by Aniela Zagórska and with an enthusiastic preface by Stefan Żeromski, was never completed. Only four of the announced eighteen volumes appeared. The other project, *Pisma zbiorowe* (Collected Writings), was published during the years 1928–1939 in Warsaw; this edition, also unfinished, included all the novels except *Chance*, *The Arrow of Gold*, *Suspense*, and *The Sisters*. Although there were endless discussions of the 'Conrad and Poland' variety, few basic studies of the novelist's work appeared during that period. Najder singles out the contributions of the following (somewhat echoing Zabierowski's account): Joseph Ujejski, Rafał Blüth, Wacław Borowy, Maria Dąbrowska, Roman Dyboski, Ludwik Fryde, Konrad Górski, Stefan Kołaczkowski and Manfred Kridl. Najder implies that these critics generally suffered from a parochial omission of the historical-literary background, and he is chagrined that, with the exception of Maria Dąbrowska, they failed to relate Conrad to Polish literature.

The third period saw an enormous rise in Conrad's popularity, which Najder ascribes to the affinity of the moral climate of Conrad's works with that of Poland at war.

The fourth period started with new approaches and many critical essays which eschewed the earlier preoccupation with biographical and national themes. Midway, however, came Kott's essay, some refutations and the subsequent silence.

The fifth era is that of a consistent 'rehabilitation' of Conrad's fame, its keynote being the celebration of the centenary of his birth in Warsaw, and a dramatic increase in the publication of Conrad's works. Najder notes that new source materials have been provided by Róża Jabłkowska, Barbara Kocówna and himself.

Some of the other new voices in Polish Conradiana are those of Captain Joseph Miłobędzki and Andrzej Braun; the former investigates Conrad's maritime career and his use of language from the professional point of view;[19] the latter's massive (627 pages) *Sladami Conrada* (*In Conrad's Footsteps*),[20] an illustrated study of Conrad's Malayan backgrounds, is a worthy companion to Norman Sherry's books[21] or to the work done by the Dutch critics, G. J. Resink and A. van Marle. Braun's well-documented volume, though not as aesthetic in appearance as Sherry's books, is nevertheless an exciting account of Conrad's East. Since the author is a novelist rather than a literary critic, we see the East through the prism of Conrad's text yet, essentially, it is a novelist's point of vantage, almost a kind of fictional travel guide, with Mr Braun playing Marlow to Conrad's fiction of the East.

The fiftieth anniversary of Conrad's death (in 1974) encouraged a great deal of critical writing on Conrad in Poland, apart from sundry events planned to commemorate the occasion. Two main problems are still plaguing Polish Conradiana. One is the frequent weakness of the comparative approach, the reluctance to become involved in a methodical *explication de texte*. Polish critics whet the reader's appetite, suggesting perfectly sound correspondences between Conrad and some masters of Polish literature, without pursuing the matter analytically and textually.[22] The other problem is redundancy. Perhaps some of the Polish critics find it difficult to keep up with Conradian criticism abroad (no mean task, to be true), and even with their own fellow commentators on the Conradian scene.

It would be more proper to allow Zdzisław Najder, whom I regard as the dean of Polish Conradiana, to express some final reservations on the subject:

> One must state, however, that Polish Conradiana has kept up neither with the popularity of the author of *Lord Jim* in Poland, nor with the excellent progress of American and English Conradists. We publish only a few critical literary studies of Conrad, which only rarely attain a standard which could be defined as international.[23]

Najder the editor is no less conscientious than Najder the critic, judging from his 'Remarks on the Texts' in *Wybór Opowiadań* (Selected Stories), in which he explains the necessity of correcting Aniela Zagórska's translations of Conrad, citing some of her inaccuracies and distortions. Acknowledging the well-deserved reputation of this renowned Conrad translator – who is no longer alive – Najder notes apologetically: 'Correcting her errors is continuing her efforts – and that is why they ought to agree with her intentions. We owe her our grateful memory – to Conrad we owe fidelity'.[24]

Conrad's reputation in Poland today is indeed a fittingly ironic reversal from that of an earlier period, a peculiarly Conradian 'smile of fortune'. No longer is Conrad accused of unfaithfulness to his Polish heritage. It is now Poland's turn to manifest one of Conrad's central ideals – that of fidelity toward her illustrious son. Conrad would have appreciated Najder's editorial conviction, his quest for *le mot juste* of a faithful Polish rendering of his artistic intent, as a supreme compliment to his own love of letters. For he was, by his own admission, '. . . jealous of their honour and concerned for the dignity and comeliness of their service'.[25]

NOTES

1. Stefan Zabierowski, *Conrad w Polsce: Wybrane problemy recepcji krytycznej w latach 1896–1969* (Conrad in Poland: Selected Problems of Critical Reception in the Years 1896–1969), (Gdańsk: Wydawnictwo Morskie, 1971).
2. Karol Wiktor Zawodziński, *Nieuwzględnione motywy decyzji życiowej Conrada* ('Unfounded Motives of Conrad's Life Decision') *Wiadomości Literackie*, 1927, No. 39.
3. Zdzisław Najder, 'Polskie Lata Conrada' ('Conrad's Polish Years'), *Twórczość*, 1956, No. 11.
4. Zabierowski, *op. cit.*, p. 47, my translation.
5. For fuller treatment of this aspect of Polish Conradists, see my 'Conrad in Poland' (*The Polish Review*, New York, Vol. XIX, Nos. 3–4, pp. 3–28).
6. Zabierowski, *op. cit.*, p. 27.
7. *Ibid.*, p. 66.
8. *Ibid.*, p. 67.
9. *Ibid.*, p. 22. My translation.
10. Róża Jabłkowska, *Joseph Conrad: 1857–1924* (Wrocław, Warsaw, Cracow, Zakład Narodowy imienia Osolińskich, Wydawnictwo Polskiej Akademii Nauk, 1961).
11. Zabierowski, *op. cit.*, p. 215.
12. Joseph Szczepański, *'Conrad mojego pokolenia'* ('The Conrad of My Generation', *Życie Literackie*, Literary Life, No. 49, 1957). My translation.
13. Jan Kott, 'O laickim tragizmie' ('On the Lay Tragedy'), *Twórczość* (Creative Work), No. 2, 1945. My translation.
14. Najder, *op. cit.*
15. Najder, *op cit.*, p. lxxi.
16. Maria Komornicka (under the pseudonym of Włast), *'Lord Jim przez Conrada'* (Conrad's *Lord Jim*), *Chimera*, 1905, pp. 333–4.
17. Wiktor Gomulicki, 'Polak czy Anglik? ('Pole or Englishman?'). *Życie i Sztuka* (Life and Art), 1905, No. 1.
18. Stanisław Brzozowski, *'Głosy wśród nocy'* ('Voices in the Night') (Lwów), 1912.
19. Joseph Miłobedzki, 'Rekwizycja pisarska Conrada' ('The Requisites of Conrad's Writing'), *Morze* (The Sea), 1968, No. 4. Also: *Conrad w żeglarskiej kurcie* (Conrad in a Peajacket), *Morze*, 1968, No. 11–12. Also: *Morze*, 1969, No. 1–2.
20. Andrzej Braun, *Śladami Conrada* ('In Conrad's Footsteps') (Warsaw: *Czytelnik*, 1972).
21. Norman Sherry, *Conrad's Eastern World* (Cambridge: Cambridge University Press, 1966). Also Norman Sherry, *Conrad's Western World* (Cambridge: Cambridge University Press, 1971).
22. This subject is treated more fully in my 'Conrad in Poland'; see note No. 5.
23. Najder, ed. *Wybor opowiadan, op. cit.*, p. lxxxiv, my translation.
24. *Ibid.*, p. lxxviii, my translation.
25. Joseph Conrad, *A Personal Record* (Garden City, New York: Doubleday, Page & Co., 1924), p. 101.

Index